Zaha Hadid Architects

Zaha Hadid Architects

REDEFINING ARCHITECTURE & DESIGN

images
Publishing

"I believe there should be no end to experimentation."

Published in Australia in 2017 by
The Images Publishing Group Pty Ltd
ABN 89 059 734 431
6 Bastow Place, Mulgrave, Victoria 3170, Australia
Tel: +61 3 9561 5544 Fax: +61 3 9561 4860
books@imagespublishing.com
www.imagespublishing.com

The Images Publishing Group Reference Number: 1240

National Library of Australia Cataloguing-in-Publication entry:

Title: Zaha Hadid Architects: Redefining Architecture & Design/Zaha Hadid Architects
ISBN: 9781864706994 (hardback)
Subjects: Zaha Hadid Architects/monograph
Architecture, Modern—20th century.
Architecture, Modern—21st century.
Architecture, Domestic.
Public architecture.
Design, Architectural.

Dewey Number: 724.7

Production manager: Rod Gilbert
Senior editor: Gina Tsarouhas
Assisting editor: Helen Koehne
Graphic designer: Nicole Boehringer

IMAGES acknowledges the wonderful assistance of the Zaha Hadid Architects Press Department throughout the production of this book.

Printed on 157gsm GoldEast Matt Art paper by Everbest Printing Investment Limited, in Hong Kong/China

IMAGES has included on its website a page for special notices in relation to this and our other publications. Please visit www.imagespublishing.com

CONTENTS

FORMALISM AND FORMAL RESEARCH

'Formalism' and its derivative 'formalist' (as noun or adjective) remain potent derogatory terms within architectural discourse. It is taken for granted that the creative investment into the elaboration of forms detracts from the concern for function. A moment's reflection reveals that all concern for a design's function must be achieved by working on its form. My formula for this truism is *Form delivers function*. My comprehensive theory of architecture—the theory of architectural autopoiesis[1]—identifies the distinction of form and function as the lead distinction of architecture, whereby form is the discipline's *internal reference* (that is, our immediate responsibility), and function is the discipline's *external reference* (that is, our ultimate responsibility to society mediated via our production of forms). My theory further emphasises that the functionality designers (in contrast to engineers) should be concerned with social (rather than technical) functionality. In general terms, the societal function of architecture and the design disciplines are the spatio-morphological ordering and framing of all social interaction processes.

Aggressive formalism: A productive provocation

Since the designers' immediate work is inevitably always concerned with forms, the charge of formalism must be elaborated as follows: The 'formalist' works on the form *for the form's sake, without regard to its function*, concerned *only* with formal characteristics and matters of visual appearance. If this concern with formal characteristics is exclusive and entails the rejection of functional concerns, then this formalist stance might be hard to defend. According to my theoretical reconstruction of our discipline's rationality (AoA, vol. 1), architecture is operationally encoded by the double code of utility (functionality) and beauty (formal resolution) and a one-sided insistence on only formal aspects is indeed an anomaly. However, there have been protagonists within architecture who have explicitly taken this stance, most notably Peter Eisenman and Jeff Kipnis. Peter Eisenman's notorious 1976 article 'Post-functionalism' argues that architecture lags behind abstract art and absolute music, and must cast aside its concern with function to emancipate itself and become truly modern. In the early 1990s, Jeff Kipnis turned the maledictum 'Formalism' into his primary positive headline slogan for his AA Graduate Design Group. His investment into formal research and innovation was also posited as exclusive, claiming to represent the discipline's true essence. However, we should not allow ourselves to get distracted by the (ultimately questionable) exclusiveness of this protagonist's investments, but ask if the attention to formal-compositional properties, such as symmetry, proportion, repetition, rhythm, syncopation, and dynamic equilibrium, makes sense and can be defended at all, and on what grounds.

Although we must certainly reject the proposition that the exclusive concern with formal characteristics is or should become the discipline's true stance and calling, I will argue for the necessity of investing in formal research and innovation. This also entails the necessity of the elaboration of formal concepts and an attendant terminology for formal analysis. Jeff Kipnis together with Greg Lynn—building on prior protagonists such as Robert Venturi, Colin Rowe, Peter Eisenman, and Bernard Tschumi—have made a crucial contribution to both the innovation of our formal repertoires and to the elaboration of an attendant conceptual repertoire and terminology for tracking and guiding these formal innovations. Key concepts proposed by Kipnis and Lynn include 'intensive coherence' (Kipnis) and 'multiple affiliation' (Lynn). We might also add here Stan Allen's concept of 'field'. Key concepts from the earlier protagonists mentioned include 'difficult whole' (Venturi), 'phenomenal transparency' (Rowe), 'space of becoming' (Eisenman), and 'super-imposition' (Tschumi). All these protagonists and concepts have had their precursors: Giedion, Moholy, Kepes and so on.

A productive division of labour

My defense of this (largely American) formalist tradition rests on the recognition that formal repertoires are ultimately functional problem-solving repertoires, and that design choices benefit from the explicit reflection on formal possibilities. Therefore, formal research and innovation can be looked at as partial contributions to the discipline's problem-solving capacity and we can posit a division of labour between formal analysis and repertoire expansion on the one hand, and the analysis of contemporary programmatic/functional requirements (with program innovations) on the other side, together enhancing the innovative, ultimately functionally oriented instrumentalisation of forms. My defense of formalism even goes so far as to

Patrik Schumacher, London 2016

concede the rationality of exclusive concentration on formal and formal-conceptual innovation as a rather useful (and probably necessary) aspect of an effective division of labour. The overall research effort aimed at innovative forms delivering innovative functional capacities must be divided and phased. Formal research should not always already be burdened with immediate functional concerns. Research should be modelled on the evolutionary dialectic of variation (mutation, recombination) and selection (testing). Variation must come first and should not be too tightly constrained by preconceived functionality criteria. Here resides the implicit rationality of the exclusiveness of the formalists' pursuit. Their rejection of function is ultimately false—and suicidal if generalised across the discipline—but it is an important protective stance that protects the crucial zone of formal research against overly impatient functionalists. I have therefore theorised Eisenman's and Kipnis' aggressively formalist polemical position as a 'necessary false consciousness'. There is another aspect that feeds into the tendency of the disciplinary division of labour to become exclusive and overly myopic. Not everybody has a comprehensive set of talents or commands the fully comprehensive range of intellectual resources to encompass the overall scope of the discipline's task. Exclusive focus is therefore not only often a virtue, but an inevitable limitation. This is viable, if the distributed collective effort covers the full scope of the task and some generalists step up and offer synthesis within a unified theory.

Two analogies: Mathematics and syntax

The following analogies might help to clarify the role of formal research with its often formalist outlook. We should learn to respect our purely formalist protagonists in the same way we respect protagonists of pure mathematics, some of whom might conceive of their field's essence as indeed untethered from the mundane concerns of mathematics' pragmatic application. This myopic and ultimately indefensible self-conception might nevertheless be conducive towards mathematical creativity, which might eventually, via more pragmatically grounded colleagues, find its way into unexpected applications. Once more, formal repertoires are problem-solving repertoires.

Another analogy that might be helpful here is the division of labour in linguistics between the subfields of syntax, semantics, and pragmatics. There is no doubt that language evolution is ultimately pragmatically driven. It is equally beyond doubt that its communicative potency depends on the systemic intricacy of its formal structures, which are being investigated in the theory of syntax without taking into account the semantic and pragmatic aspects. Investment into formal research and architectural formalism might thus be seen as analogous to the linguists' research investment into syntactic structures.

Synthesis: Confronting the formal apparatus with a catalogue of functional tasks

What is lacking in the formalist tradition is the explicit attempt to confront the well-elaborated formal repertoire (together with its conceptual-terminological apparatus) with a relevantly abstracted descriptive apparatus elaborating the functional task domain. There have been no systematic attempts to map formal repertoires (solutions) onto functional problem registers. Within individual professional design projects, functional problems search for formal solutions, and in academic design research projects the inverse procedure is often attempted: formalistically generated formal structures and possibilities are searching problem domains and tasks where they might be productively put to work. This is important and necessary. Both routes will lead to the sought-after new, productive form-function correlations that constitute the endgame of design and design research. However, this is intuitive design work without systematic reflection. A systematic theoretical confrontation and mapping would provide a useful guide to the search efforts in either direction. So far, however, the teaching of composition has remained isolated from any functional concerns. The division of labour has been too perfect, leading to hermetic specialist discourses and even subdisciplines, taught in separate classes by separate professors, such as the teaching of architectural composition as a purely formal discipline. However, if we go back to the beginning of our discipline in the Renaissance, we find clues about how compositional issues are tied instrumentally to functional issues. From Alberti, we learn how the composition of the city-form relates to the order of the polis, and how the composition of the house relates to the social order of the household. From Palladio, we learn how the rules of symmetry and proportion codify structural and environmental logics.

The only attempt at systematically mapping a formal register onto a catalogue of functional effects I have come across so far is Alejandro Zaera-Polo's attempt to systematically correlate a formal classification of basic building forms with a set of functional, micro-political effects in his article 'The Politics of the Envelope'.[2] My own account of a similar system of form-function correlations with respect to building forms, and another attempt at correlating a typology of distinct city geometries with distinctive social ordering capacities or biases, can be found in volume 2 of my treatise, *The Autopoiesis of Architecture*.[3] However, these attempts only deliver a tentative beginning and signal the possibility and importance of a task yet to be accomplished. However, with respect to the groundbreaking formal innovations of the 1980s and 1990s alluded to above, I have been emphasising their functional rationality and historical pertinence for more than 20 years. 'Superimposition' (spatial overlap or interpenetration) lines up with the interpenetration of social domains like overlapping departmental responsibilities or interpenetrating domains of competency and interdisciplinary teams in contemporary corporate organisations. Continuously differentiated 'field conditions' with 'gradients' or 'morphing trajectories' align with increasing economies of scope and the proliferation of hybrid in-between conditions, as well as with the blurring of a corporation's boundaries within collaborative networks, and with the blurring of departmental boundaries within corporations, as occurs in open, differentiated office landscapes. The concept of a 'space of becoming' relates to the condition of field transformations but also to the related concept of 'phenomenal transparency', which aligns with the condition of multiple audiences with multiple perspectives and respectively divergent readings of the same space. The concept of 'multiple affiliation' aligns with the complexity of urban synergetic social and programmatic networks, where a particular functional offering relates to and ties in with multiple complementary urban offerings and their users. These alignments of the new innovative set of formal tropes and compositional registers with new social-functional tendencies and requirements are crucial for the effective utilisation and thus validation of the formal research and innovations in question. The founding of the Design Research Laboratory at the Architectural Association School of Architecture (AAADRL) in 1996 was explicitly geared toward this task of socio-functional validation of the recent formal innovations that had captured the imagination of the field at that time, while also continuing the formal research via new computational tools, albeit always guided by this sense of productive historical pertinence with respect to the socio-functional requirements and opportunities of the new era of post-fordism.[4]

The functional rationality of Zaha Hadid's radical formal innovations

The formal innovations from the 1980s and 1990s owe much to the radical formal iconoclast innovations delivered by the early work of Zaha Hadid. What were the major expansionary moves that Hadid gifted to our discipline? We can identify and distinguish four wholly original and empowering 'discoveries': explosion, calligraphy, distortion, and landscape. The design moves indicated by these concepts were so radical that they seemed utterly surreal or absurd at first. (I guess that's why nobody else had ever hit upon them before.) They are formal repertoire expansions, and thus might initially be viewed as artistic moves, and indeed they first showed up in Hadid's often conceptual, rather obscure, seemingly utterly abstract drawings and paintings. However, in the hands of a designing architect, a formal repertoire is always also a problem-solving repertoire, addressing the problems of spatial organisation and morphological articulation in the service of the prospective building's social and technical functioning. An expanded formal repertoire thus delivers an enriched problem-solving toolbox. So we need to grasp and discuss the new moves together with their empowering affordances, affordances that are indeed congenial to the requirements and desires of our time, and are thus potentially able to deliver momentous advantages. Of course, we should not expect these advantages to become fully manifest in the early explorations, but they have started to become manifest in our major mature works of recent years (and I argue they promise further compelling manifestations):

Explosion: The surreal move to treat explosion as a compositional move soon reveals its power when a plan is no longer a closed and rigid array of nested boxes but a centrifugal force-field that is eminently permeable, varied, yet ordered through the directed and progressive expansion of all fragments in relation to the implied point of origin. This dynamic and lawful fragmentation of the plan was a decisive step forward from the random, disordered fragmentation proposed by deconstructivism. However, the explosion delivers more order than just random fragmentation. It delivers a lawfully differentiated field where the fragments' directionality points back to the shared origin and where the increasing spacing of fragments also indicates the relative position in the field.

Calligraphy: The surreal move of translating the dynamism of rapid calligraphic sketching literally (by hard-lining them with the use of an expansive range of 'French curves' or 'ship curves') into an architectural drawing that is then read as an intended geometry to be built, rather than treating the pulsing curvature of a rapid sketch as a rough accidental indication of an ideal geometric form meant to be rationalised into straight lines and arcs. Hadid's intricately variegated curves offer more adaptive versatility to push into irregular sites or bulge to give room to internal requirements where needed. Further, as a function of the changing centrifugal force of the rapid acceleration and deceleration of the hand/pen, the curves and curvilinear compositions display lawful and coherent trajectories that we can recognise as coherent and legible figures, each with its own poise, dynamism, or degree of fluidity. This increases legibility and navigability in the face of unavoidable programmatic diversity and complexity.

Distortion: This is the surreal move of using perspectival projection not to depict regular forms but to create and posit distorted forms. Hadid built up pictorial spaces within which multiple perspective constructions were fused into a seamless dynamic texture. One way to understand these images is as attempts to emulate the experience of moving through an architectural composition, revealing a succession of rather different points of view. Another, more radical, way of reading these canvases is to ignore the implied views and to read the distorted forms as creating a peculiar architectural world in its own right with its own characteristic forms, compositional laws, and spatial effects. Usually these compositions are polycentral and multi-directional. All these features are the result of the use of multiple, interpenetrating perspective projections. Often the dynamic intensity of the overall field is increased by using curved instead of straight projection lines. The projective geometry allows us to bring an arbitrarily large and diverse set of elements under its cohering law of diminution and distortion. The resultant graphic space very much anticipates the later (and still very much current) concepts of *field* and *swarm*. The effect achieved is very much like the effects later pursued with digitally simulated 'gravitational fields' that distort a mesh or grip, align, orient, and thus integrate a set of elements or particles within the digital model.

Landscape: Instead of dissecting and ordering space by walls, the landscape analogy suggests a continuously flowing space where transitions are soft, where zones are gradually differentiated and bleed into each other, where a smooth topographic ground relief rather than hard edges structure spatial relations. This opens up a whole new ontology of spatial and territorial definition, no longer premised on outline but on a modulated internal texture. We are talking of fields rather than spaces. In contrast to (empty) spaces, fields (like a forest) are full, filled with a modulated medium, that is, they are structured via continuously differentiated field conditions and thus navigation can follow various vectors of gradual field transformation like density or directionality, rather than only orienting by tracking boundary crossings. Hadid's painterly techniques, including color modulations, fading effects, and pointillism techniques, also reinforce this new ontology of blurred boundaries and soft transitions, which is congenial to the contemporary social life and institutions where the formerly strict distinction of social classes and arenas are blurred, and where domains of competency penetrate and bleed into each other.

Through these congenial and empowering repertoire expansions, a new language of architecture with a much increased versatility (and thus problem-solving capacity), and with a much richer, more expressive, and more communicative repertoire of organisation and articulation (and thus ordering capacity) was born. The writings of the American formalists (Kipnis, Lynn and others) delivered a congenial terminology for the verbal articulation of our work. This explicit conceptual articulation is important as it focuses attention and directs the continuing innovative thrust. The relationship between theory and creative practice is a progressive dialectical exchange, rather than a hierarchical sequence.

From composition to communication: Organisation, articulation, signification

The general insight that formal repertoires are problem-solving repertoires is valid with respect to the problem domains of both technical and social functionality. The dimension of social functionality poses three distinct task dimensions: organisation, articulation, and signification, as elaborated in my theory of architectural autopoiesis.[5] Organisation is concerned with functional layout: the spatial distribution of program domains concerned with physical distances, adjacencies, and connections. The traditional term 'composition' entails this organisational effort. However, composition has always implied more than mere adjacency arrangements. It was and is understood as an 'artistic' effort regulated by aesthetic criteria, that is, it is concerned with the visual appearance of a spatial arrangement. I am putting the word 'artistic' in quotation marks here because I am distinguishing design sharply from art and insist—also with respect to composition—that the design effort (as distinct from contemporary art) is ultimately always instrumental according to pragmatic criteria. We must grasp the instrumentality of visual appearance. Mere organisation is not enough to secure the ordering of social processes (social functionality). A building functions only if its organisation is legible and navigable to its users. Adjacencies, connections, and programmatic designations work only if they are recognised. In complex urban scenes and arrangements, this is not trivial. Users must be able to perceptually break down the scene into units of interaction. They need to recognise what belongs and works together. This is facilitated by composition in the second 'artistic' sense. It is the attempt to articulate the spatial organisation into a perceptually tractable scene, to ascertain that the massing emphasises the functional hierarchy of elements and their relation, that it remains legible from different perspectives, that important features such as primary entrances become conspicuous, and so on. For instance, the concern that a composition be balanced, positing dynamic equilibrium as formal-compositional value, entails the effort to unify an asymmetric arrangement (like the Dessau Bauhaus) by allowing us to locate a 'centre of gravity' around which an asymmetric ensemble can unify into a figure rather than falling apart or disappearing into an amorphous background context. Composition in this sense is about the visual clarification of significant functional relations. This task demands that the forms we choose are not only selected according to their physical functioning but also with respect to their visual functioning; we must orchestrate the formal problem-solving choices according to the criteria of overall articulation. This implies that we must bring all functional features under a ruthless project-specific, formal-compositional system or formal regime. We must try to turn structurally necessary features into characterising features or else suppress them (lest they distract), while we must accentuate features that must be easily recognisable for the smooth social functioning of the building. The imposition of a formal regime for the sake of the design's communicative capacity does not have to interfere with the physical functioning of the design. The technical and formal choices available today are rich enough to allow for two sets of criteria to be at play in constraining the selection of functioning forms. An expanded repertoire makes this easier. In my theory, this visual aspect of the task of composition is termed 'phenomenological articulation', and in order to clarify this dimension I am distinguishing the 'phenomenological project' from the 'organisational project'. The architectural project also comprises the semiological project, which further articulates the design with respect to social communications beyond the mere identification of figures and their relations. The task of semiological articulation (signification) leads us beyond the scope of the compositional stance and demands that the design of a building (or complex of buildings) is conceived as the design of a system of signification positing information-rich visual communication. Once more this semiological project, just like the organisational and the phenomenological project, must resort to forms. To what else could it resort? And once more we must construct and impose a rich formal system or formal regime to deliver this project. And again, with a third set of constraining criteria at play, the expanse and richness of the underlying formal repertoire is a crucial factor for the chances of success of the project. In this context, it is important to remind ourselves of the evident fact that parametricism offers a much richer and versatile formal repertoire than all the prior styles put together.

The built environment's social functionality resides in its communicative capacity. The elaboration of spatial complexes as systems of signification is the key to upgrading architecture's core competency. The semiological project implies that the design project systematises all form-function correlations into a coherent system of signification, designed as a network of similitudes and contrasts, organised via a spatio-visual grammar. On the basis of the formal research and repertoire of parametricism, the design of semiological systems of significations with a much enhanced information-richness and communicative capacity becomes possible.[6]

Notes

1 Patrik Schumacher, *The Autopoiesis of Architecture, Volume 1, A New Framework for Architecture*, John Wiley & Sons, New York, 2010.

2 Alejandro Zaera-Polo, 'The Politics of the Envelope—A Political Critique of Materialism', *Volume, Archis,* 2008, no. 17, 77–105.

3 Patrik Schumacher, *The Autopoiesis of Architecture, Volume 2, A New Agenda for Architecture*, John Wiley & Sons, 2012, 6.1.5 Problem-types vs Solution-types

4 See the author's publications from this time:
Patrik Schumacher, 'Productive Patterns', *architect's bulletin, Operativity*, vol. 135–6, Slovenia; also published in *architect's bulletin*, vol. 137–8, Slovenia; 'Produktive Ordnungen', *ARCH+ 136, Your Office Is Where You Are*, Berlin, 1997.

Patrik Schumacher, 'Business-Research—Architecture', *Daidalos*, no. 69/70, 'Wirtschaft Forschung Architektur', Deutsche Ausgabe, 1999.

Patrik Schumacher, *The AA Design Research Lab—Premises, Agenda*, Methods, paper delivered at Conference: Research and Practise in Architecture, at Alvar Aalto Academy, Published in E. Laksonen, T. Simons, A. Vartola (eds), *Research and Practise in Architecture*, Building Informati. Ltd, 2000.

5 Schumacher, *The Autopoiesis of Architecture, Volume 2*, 6.2 Order via Organisation and Articulation.

6 See Patrik Schumacher, 'Advancing Social Functionality via Agent Based Parametric Semiology', Patrik Schumacher (guest ed.), *AD Parametricism 2.0—Rethinking Architecture's Agenda for the 21st Century*, no. 240, March/April 2016; Patrik Schumacher, 'Parametric Semiology—The Design of Information Rich Environments', Pablo Lorenzo-Eiroa and Aaron Sprecher (eds), *Architecture in Formation—On the Nature of Information in Digital Architecture*, Routledge, Taylor and Francis, New York, 2013.

BUILT PROJECTS

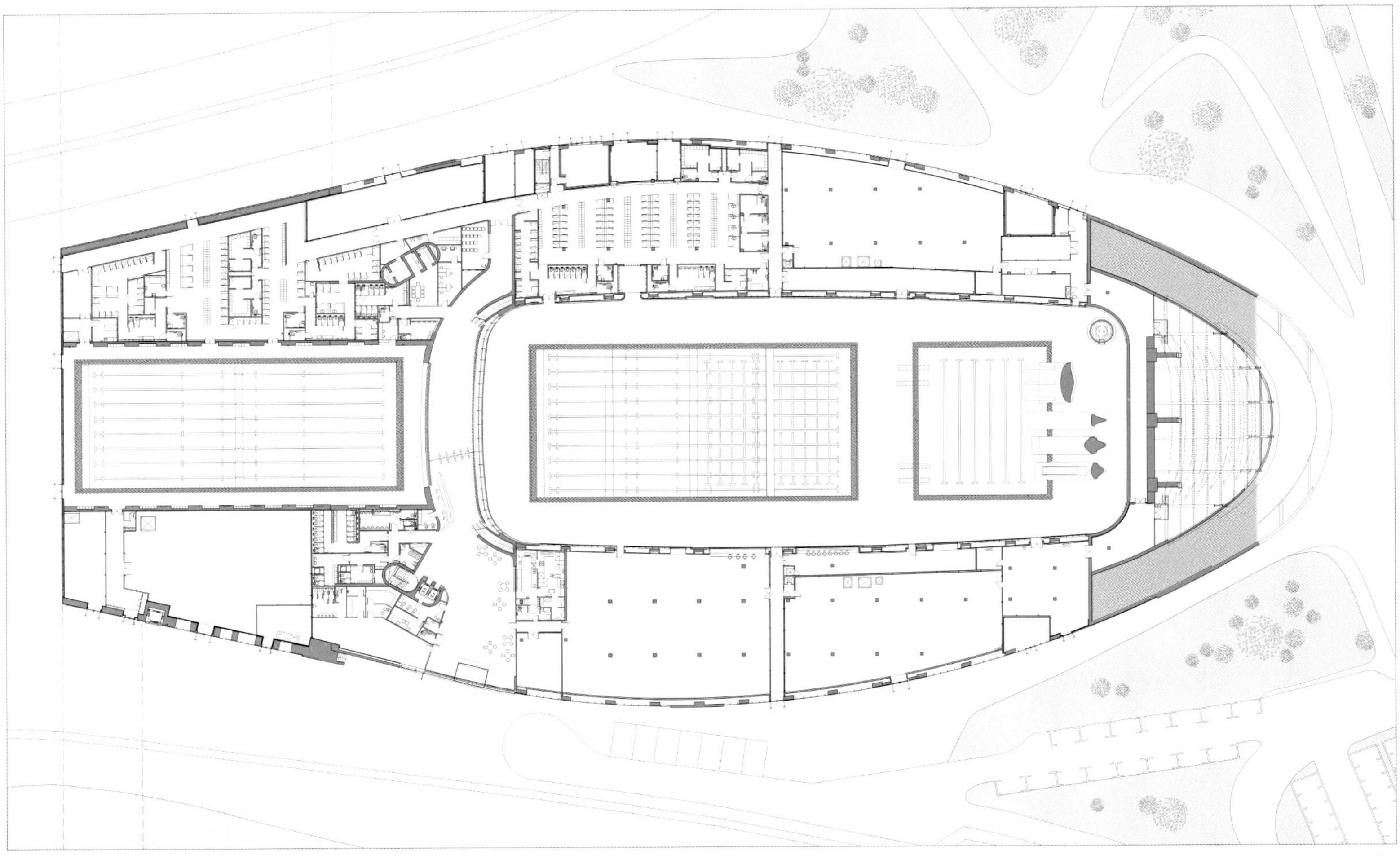

Ground-floor plan

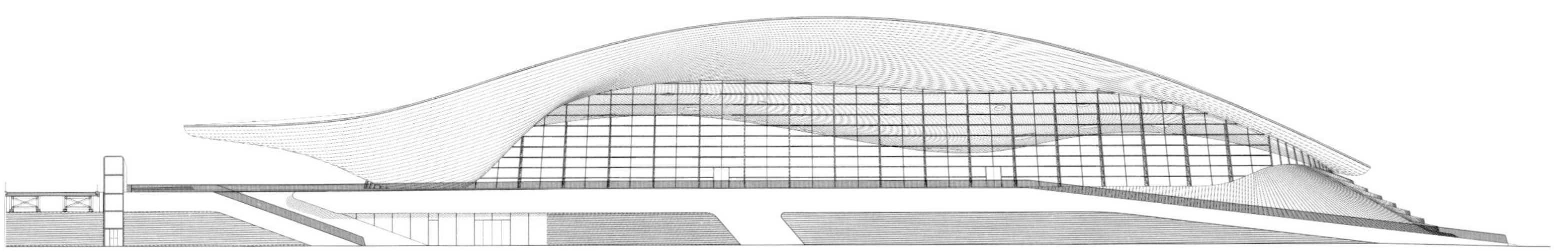

West elevation

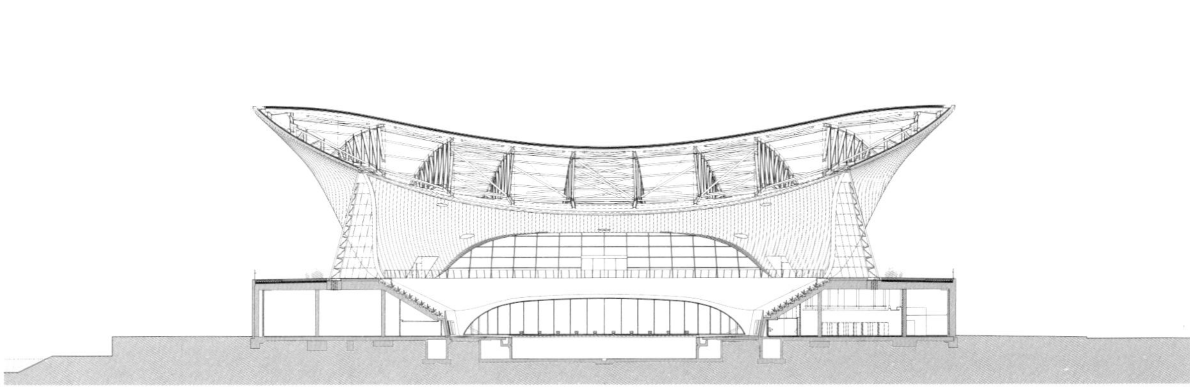

Cross-section

LONDON AQUATICS CENTRE

The architectural concept of the centre is inspired by the fluid geometry of water in motion, creating an environment in sympathy with the river landscape of the Olympic Park. An undulating roof sweeps up from the ground as a wave, enclosing the pools with its unifying gesture of fluidity.

The centre is planned on an orthogonal axis, perpendicular to the Stratford City Bridge, along which the three pools are laid out. The training pool is located under the bridge, while the competition and diving pools are in a large pool hall. The overall strategy was to frame the base of the pool hall as a podium by surrounding it and connecting it into the bridge.

Double-curvature geometry has been used to create a structure of parabolic arches that define its form. The roof undulates to differentiate the volumes of the competition and diving pools, and extends beyond the pool hall to cover the external areas of the podium and entrance on the bridge. The roof structure is grounded at three points of the centre (two points at the northwest end on the bridge, and one single point to the southeast end).

The London Aquatics Centre was designed with long-term community use in mind and, thus, both sustainability and cost-effective operation were design priorities. Crucially, the design team focused on designing sustainability into the building rather than adding it on at the end.

The venue requirements and site constraints led to a heavy-weight design, which meant that reducing the embodied carbon and impact of materials used within the structure was a priority.

High levels of insulation and envelope air tightness, low-velocity ventilation systems with high-efficiency heat recovery, and water-based heating systems with variable speed pumps maximise energy efficiency.

Location London, England
Client Olympic Delivery Authority
Area 15,950 m^2 (171,684 ft^2)
Date 2005–2011/2014

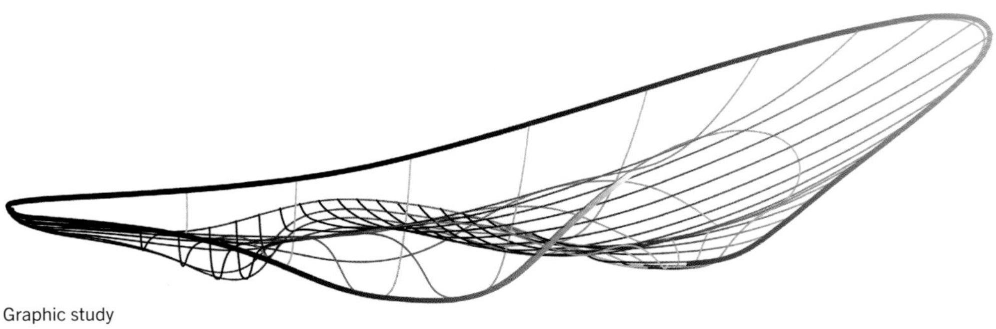

Graphic study

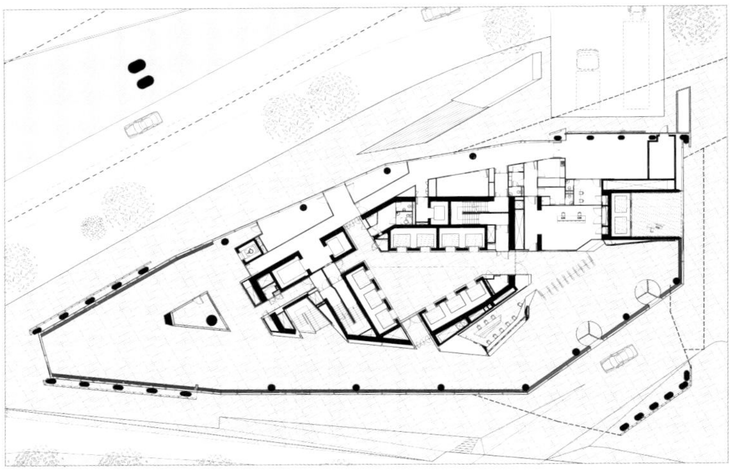

Ground-floor plan

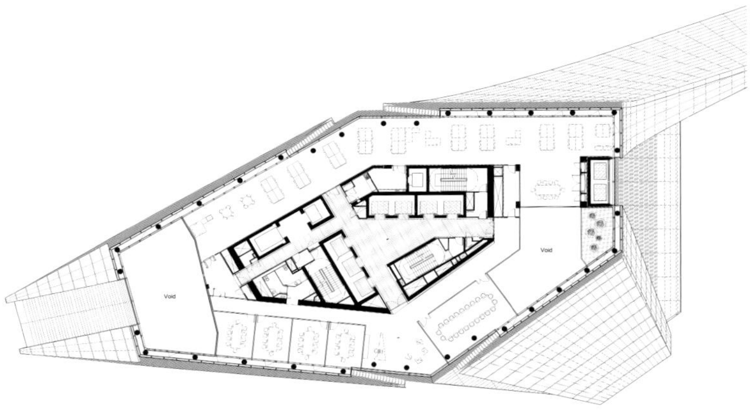

30th-floor plan

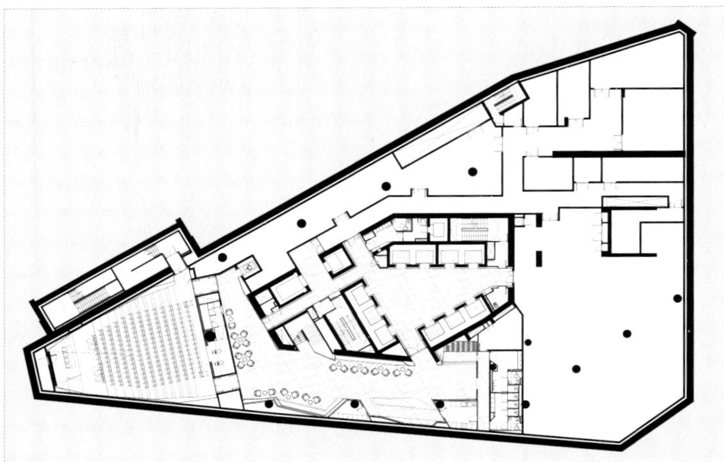

Basement floor plan

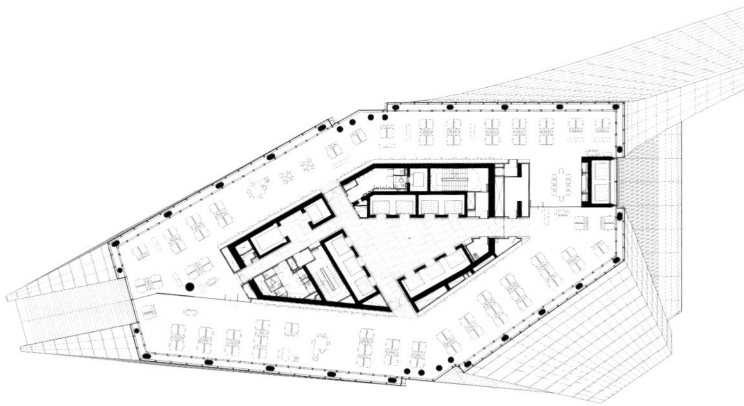

10th-floor plan

0 10m

West elevation

0 25m

CMA CGM TOWER

The tower stands at the centre of the city's ambitious regeneration project, Euroméditerranée, located north of the historic centre, adjacent to the commercial port. The site lies 100 metres (328 feet) back from the sea edge where the elevated motorway viaduct separates as it arrives at the north of the city. At ground level, the site is dominated by the sweeping concrete viaducts overhead and the rhythmic colonnades of their supporting columns. There are spectacular views over the bay of Marseille, the city and the docks.

The building is in two parts: the tower and the annexe. The new building accommodates up to 2700 employees, 700 cars and 200 motorcycles in a covered car park, an 800-seat company restaurant, gym, auditorium, and all the associated technical equipment areas. The design strategy to deal with an awkward, elongated site was to break down the volume of the façade into vertical segments and differentiate them using light and dark glazing. These are then offset from one another with the clear glazing set forward as a separate skin.

Architecturally, the external skin has a dual purpose. Firstly, it is to act as a solar screen enabling the use of light and non-reflective glazing, and secondly, it frees the façade from the constraints of a modular office interior. Movement and fluidity are introduced into the volumes and façades by generating vectors from the ground up, which gradually and gently converge toward each other and then bend apart towards the top of the tower. The peripheral structural columns and the nomenclature of the external façade panels follow these vectors to create an elegant and coherent tower.

Location Marseille, France
Client CMA CGM
Area 94,000 m^2 (1,011,808 ft^2)
Date 2006–2011

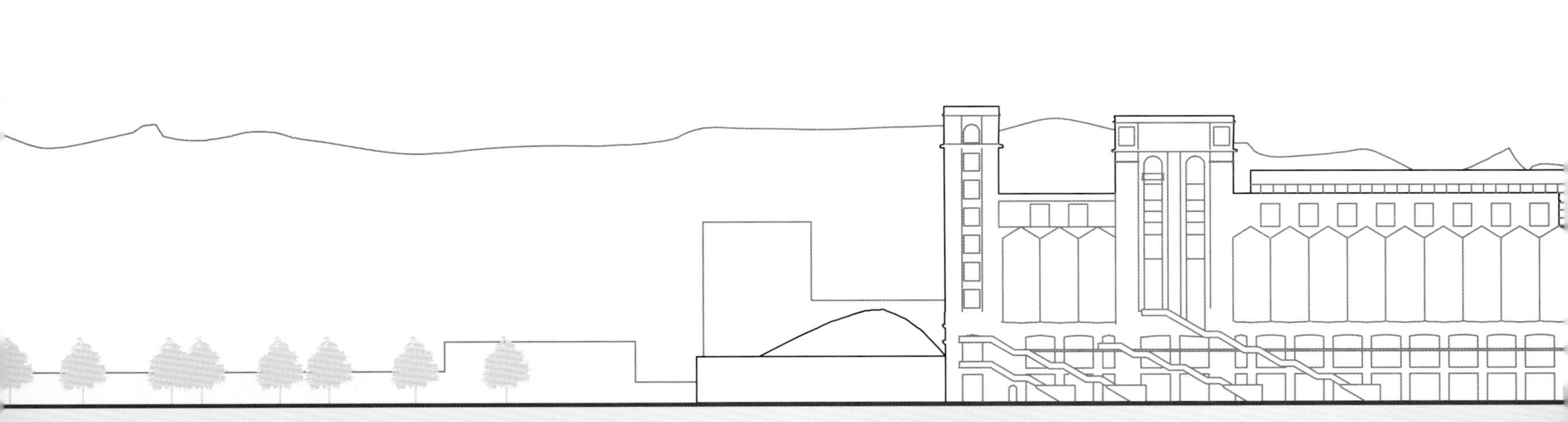

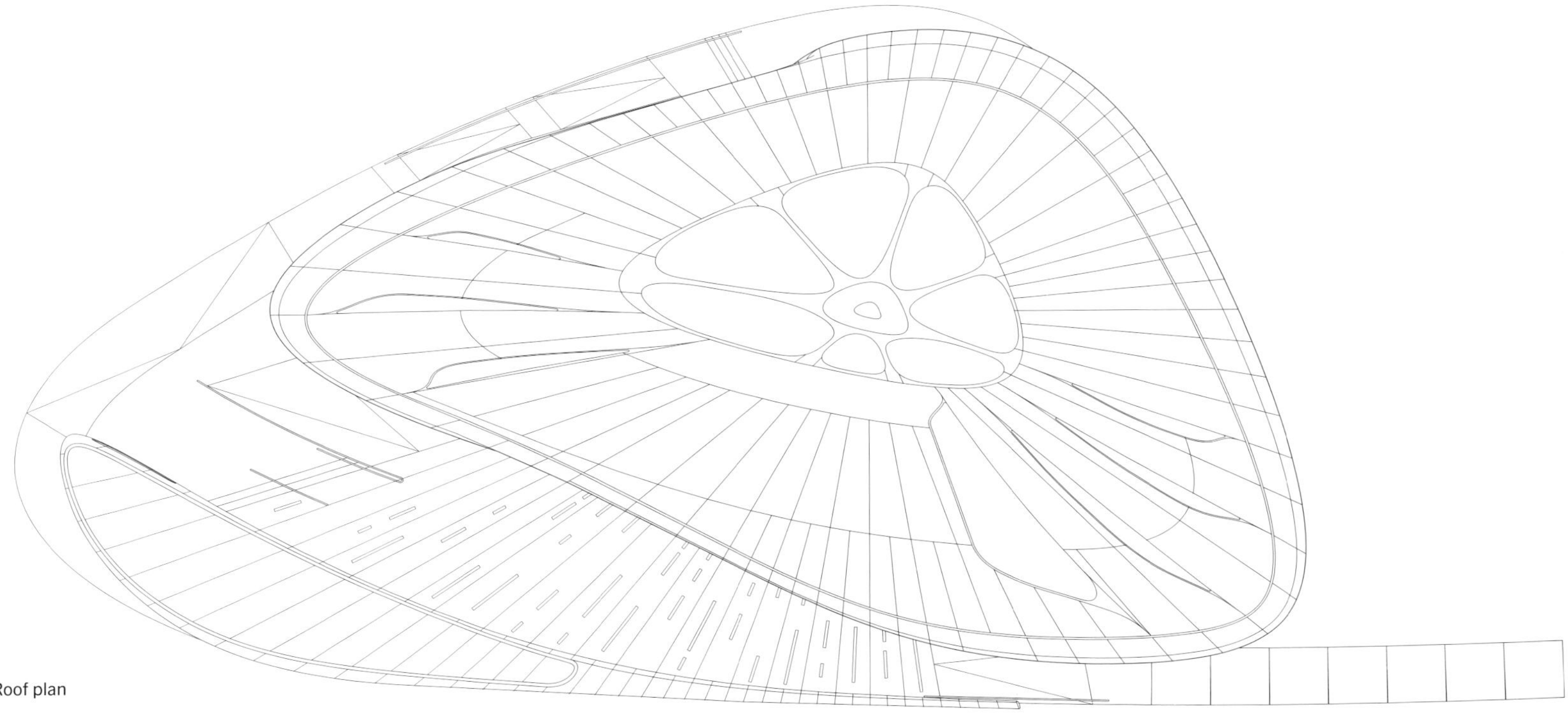

Roof plan

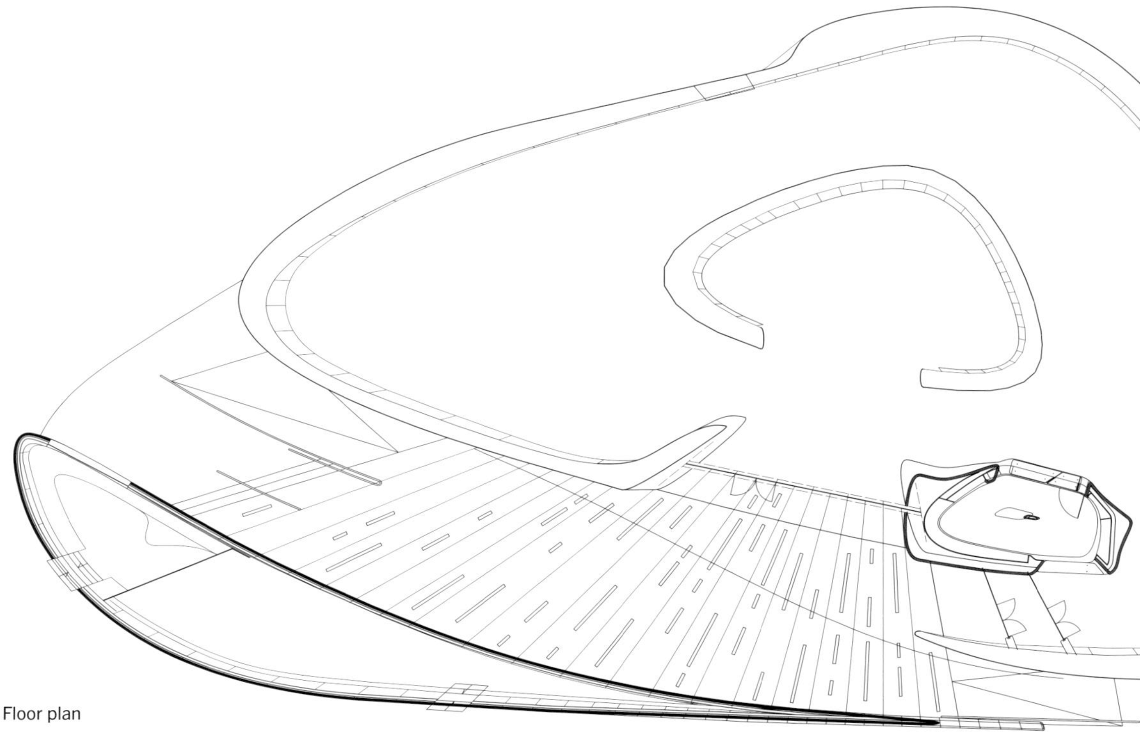

Floor plan

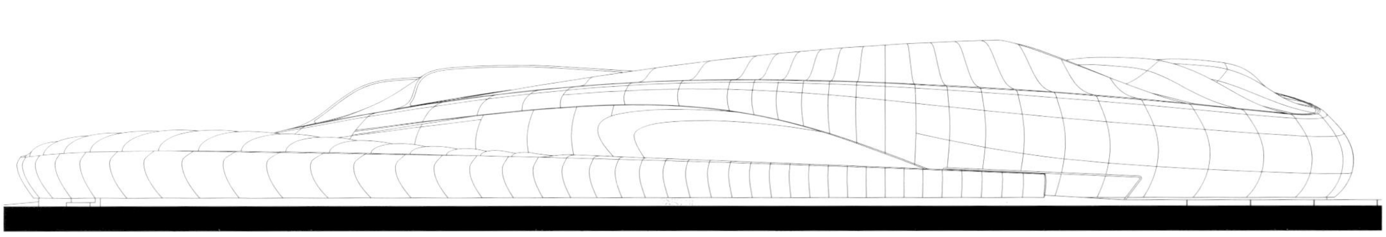

Elevation

MOBILE ART CHANEL CONTEMPORARY ART CONTAINER

The Mobile Art Pavilion by Zaha Hadid Architects has been inspired by one of Chanel's signature creations: the quilted bag. In creating the Pavilion, Zaha Hadid has developed the fluid geometries of natural systems into a continuum of fluent and dynamic space, where oppositions between exterior and interior, light and dark, natural and artificial landscapes are synthesised.

The form is a celebration of the iconic work of Chanel, unmistakeable for its smooth layering of exquisite details that create an elegant, cohesive whole. The resulting functional and versatile architectural structure of the Pavilion is a series of continuous arch-shaped elements, with a courtyard in its central space. Artificial light behind the translucent ceiling washes the walls to emphasise the 'arched' structure, and assists in the creation of a new artificial landscape for art installations. A large skylight opening dramatically floods the entrance in daylight to blur the relationship between interior and exterior.

The central courtyard has large transparent openings to the sky and is designed to host events as well as provide an area for reflection after visiting the exhibition. The courtyard serves as an intermediate space between the exhibition and public area of the Pavilion. With a direct visual connection to the courtyard, the terrace continues the dialogue between the Pavilion's exterior and interior. During an event, the two spaces can be linked to become one large zone.

Reflective materials allow the exterior skin to be illuminated with varying colors, which can be tailored to special events in each city. The dichotomy between the powerful mass of the Pavilion's structure and the lightness of its envelope creates a bold and enigmatic element. The Pavilion's exterior develops into a rich variety of interior spaces that maximise the potential to reuse and rethink space due to the innate flexibility of its plan.

Location Hong Kong, Tokyo, New York, Paris
Client Chanel
Area 700 m^2 (7,535 ft^2)
Date 2008–2010

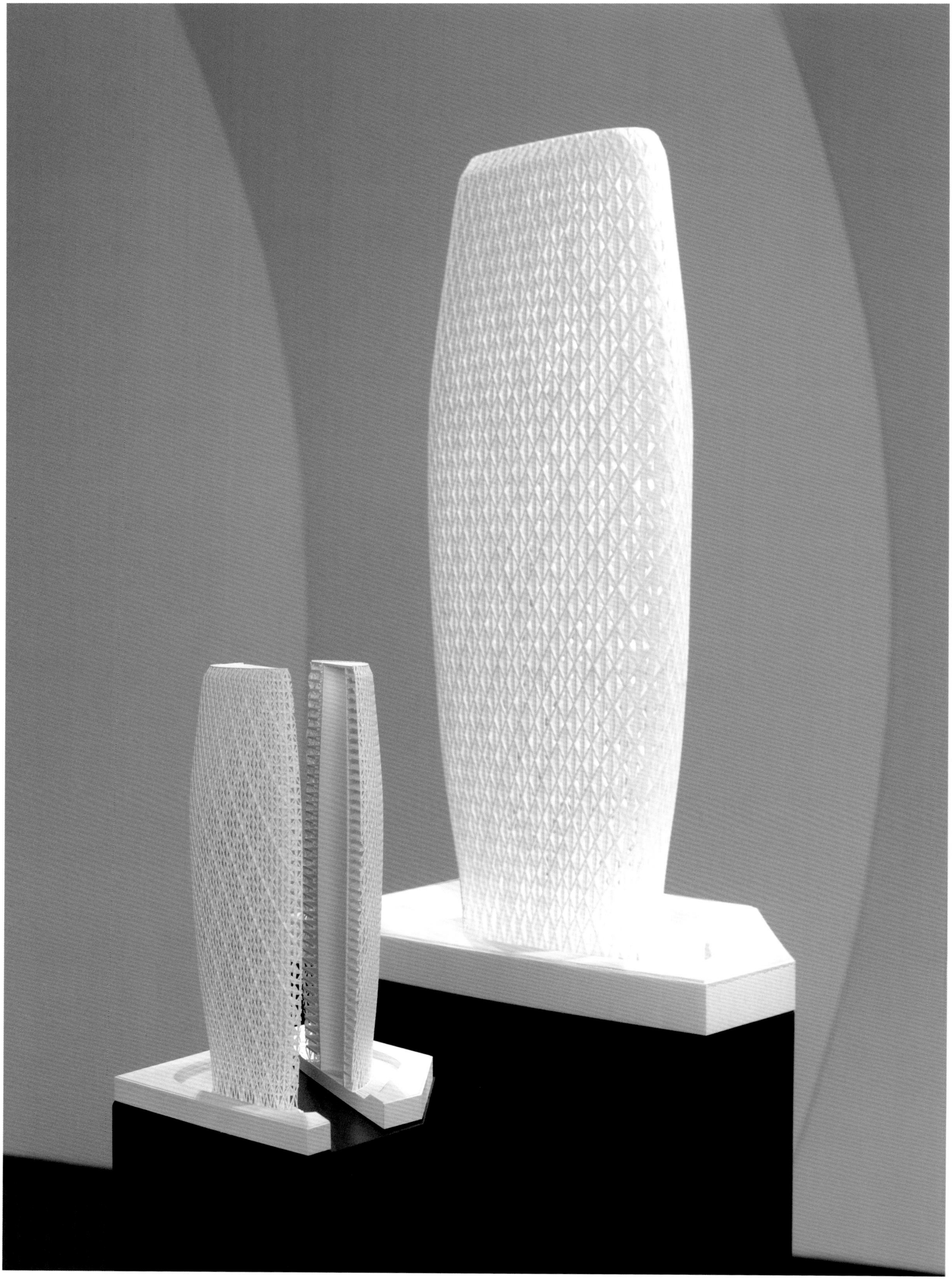

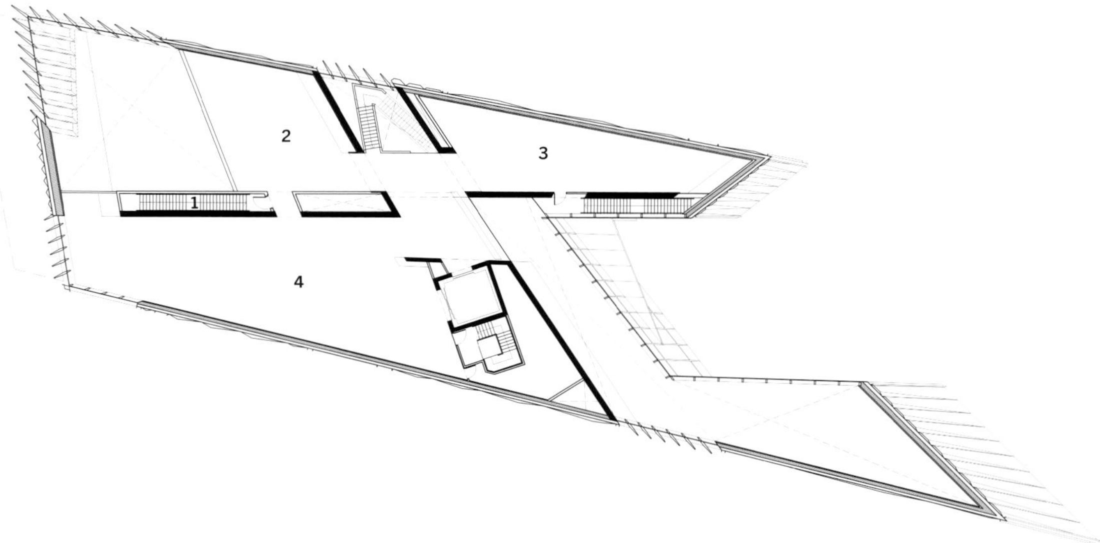

first-floor plan

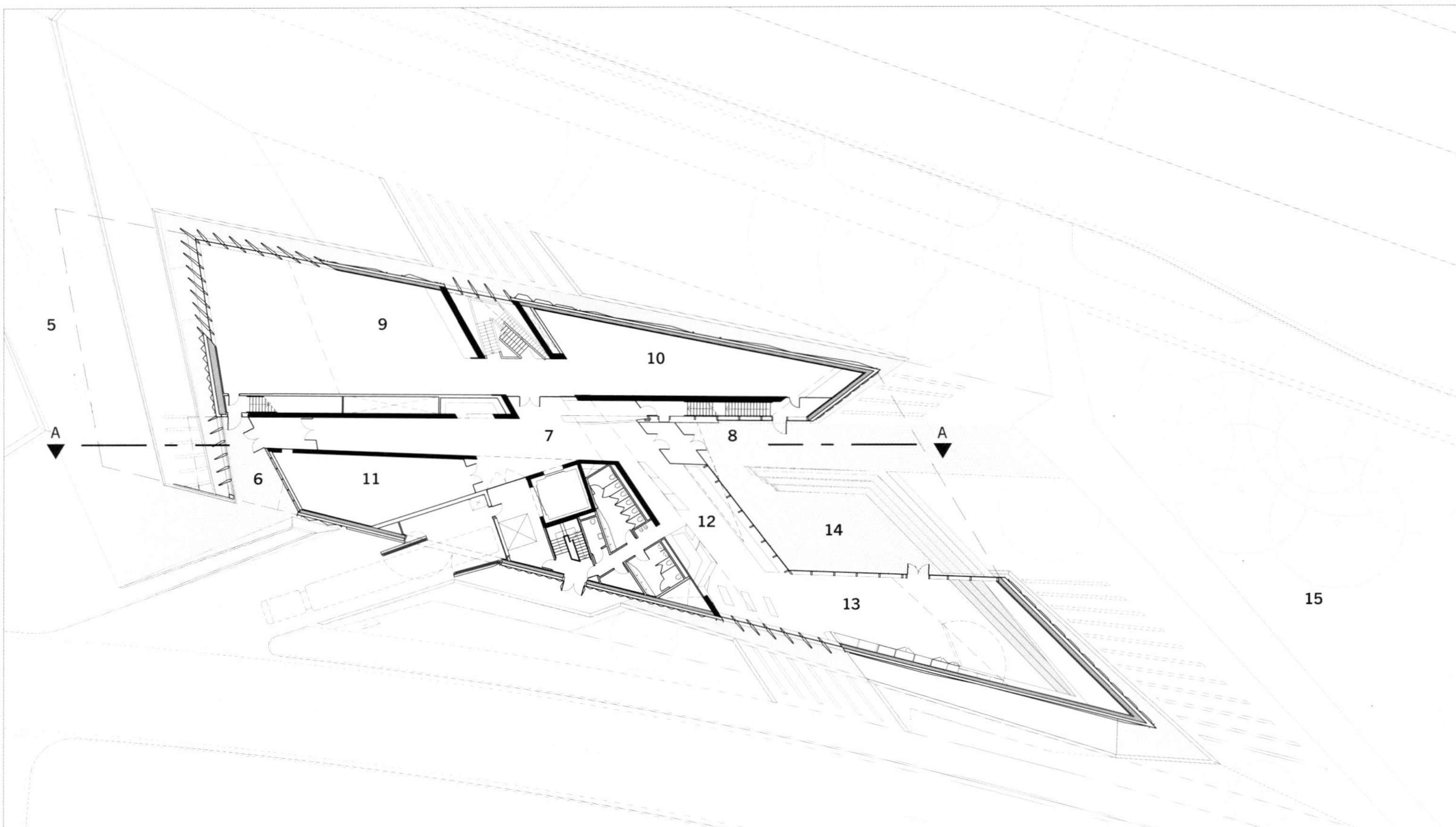

Ground-floor plan

1 Two West Gallery
2 Lobby
3 Two East Gallery
4 Two South Gallery
5 West plaza
6 West entrance
7 Reception/lobby
8 East entrance
9 One West Gallery
10 One East Gallery
11 One South Gallery
12 Café/shop
13 Education wing
14 Courtyard
15 Sculpture garden
16 Administration wing
17 New media gallery
18 Art handling
19 Mechanical room

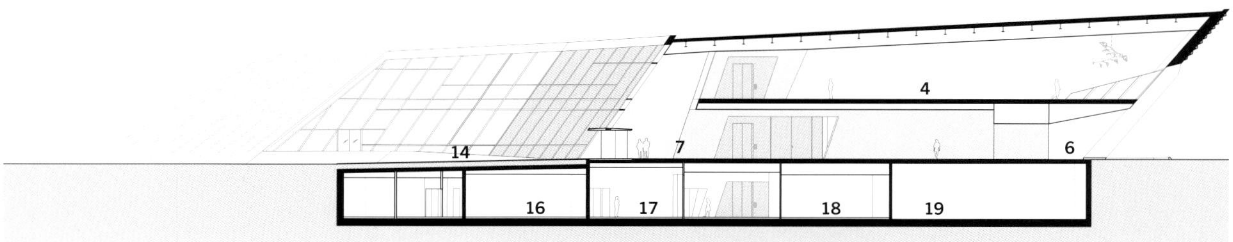

Section A-A

ELI & EDYTHE BROAD ART MUSEUM

The Broad Art Museum features a striking façade of pleated stainless steel and glass, distinguishing the building from the traditional brick Collegiate Gothic north campus, and signaling the museum and the university's forward-looking approach. The building features galleries for special exhibitions, modern and contemporary art, new media, photography, and works on paper. The facility also includes an education wing, a works on paper study centre, shop, and café. Adjacent to the museum is an expansive outdoor sculpture garden and a large pedestrian plaza.

The formal composition of the museum is achieved by defining an interior landscape that brings together and negotiates the different pathways on which people move through and around the site. This dialogue of interconnecting geometries describes a series of spaces that offer a variety of adjacencies; allowing many different interpretations when designing exhibitions. Through this complexity, curators can interpret different leads and connections, different perspectives and relationships.

These detailed investigations and research into the landscape, topography, and circulation of the site, enable us to ascertain and understand these critical lines of connection. By using these lines to inform the design, the museum is truly embedded within the unique context of Michigan State University, maintaining the strongest relationship with its surroundings. The Broad Art Museum presents as a sharp, directed body, comprising directional pleats that reflect the topographic and circulatory characteristics of its surrounding landscape. Its outer skin echoes these different directions and orientations, giving the building an ever-changing appearance that arouses curiosity, yet never quite reveals its content. This open character underlines the museum's function as a cultural hub for the community.

Location East Lansing, United States
Client Michigan State University
Area 46,000 m^2 (495,140 ft^2)
Date 2007–2012

Roof model

ELI AND
BROAD ART MUSEUM
MICHIGAN
UNIVERSITY

ELI AND EDYTHE BROAD ART MUSEUM
MICHIGAN STATE UNIVERSITY

ELI AND EDYTHE BROAD ART MUSEUM
MICHIGAN STATE UNIVERSITY

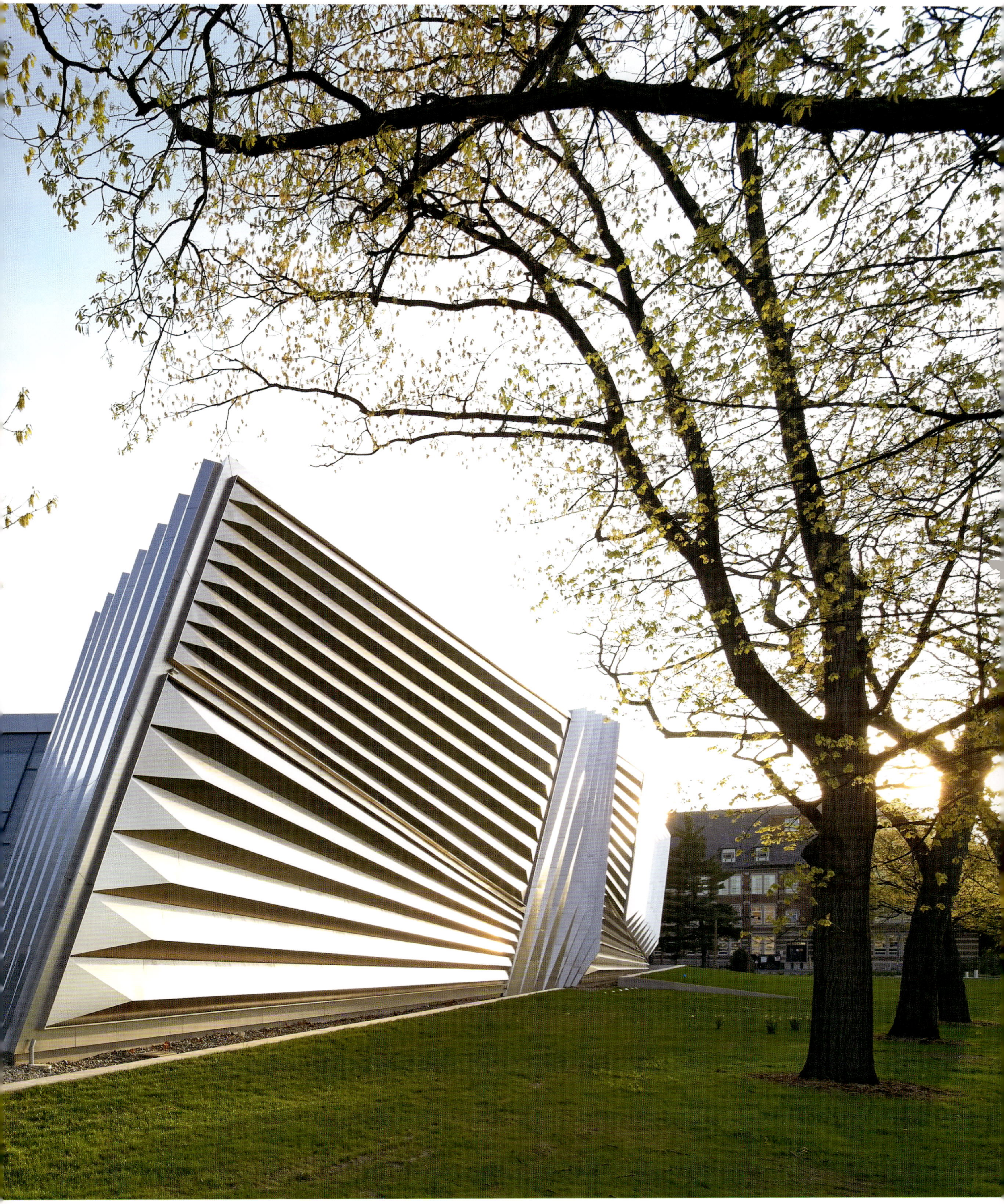

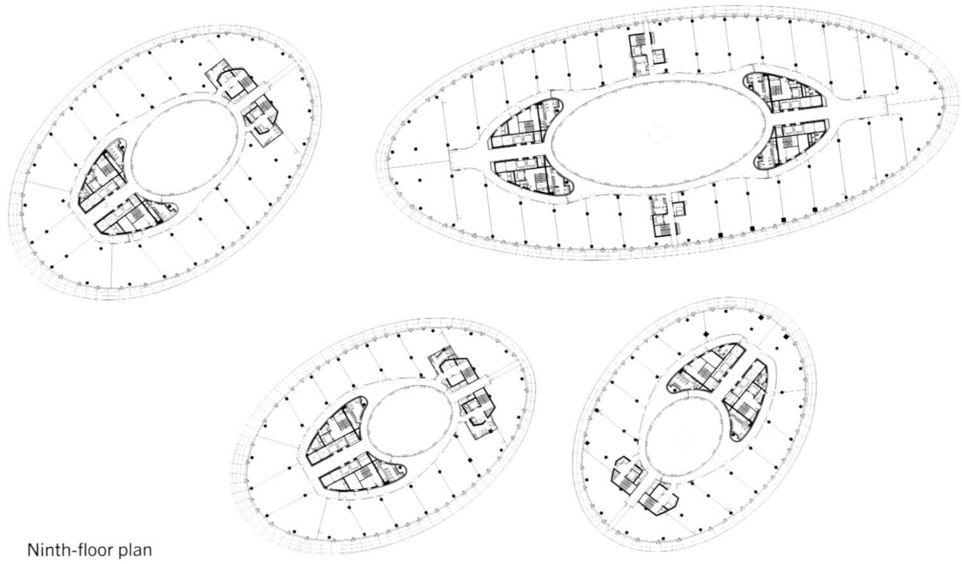

Ninth-floor plan

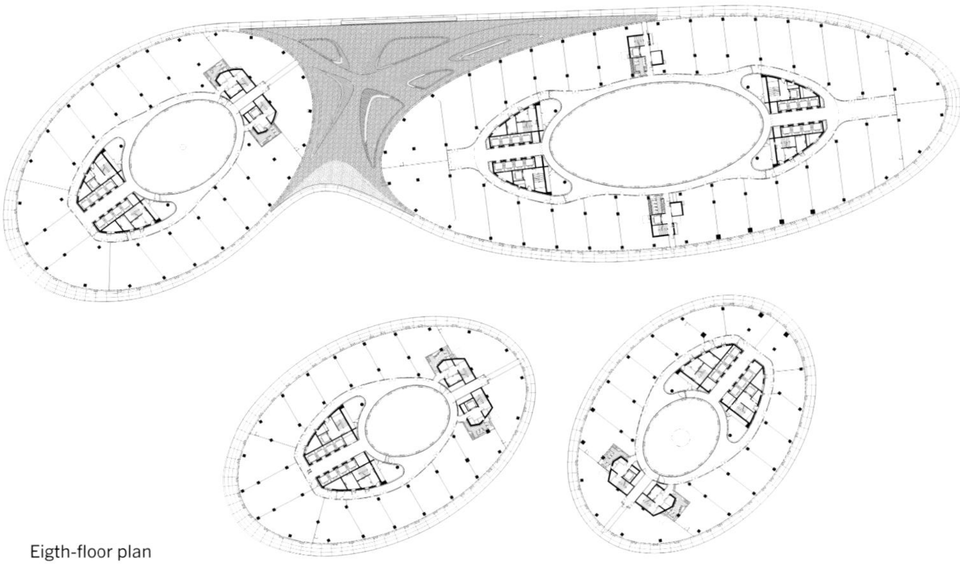

Eigth-floor plan

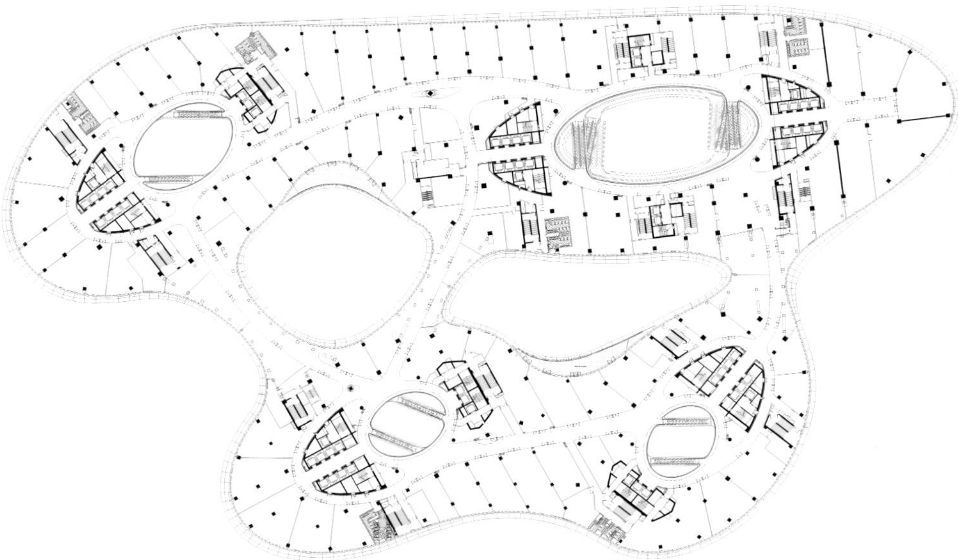

Third-floor plan

0 20m

GALAXY SOHO

The Galaxy SOHO project in central Beijing is an office, retail, and entertainment complex that is an integral part of the city, inspired by the grand scale of Beijing, and designed to create an internal world based on the Chinese theme of the courtyard.

Its architecture is a composition of four towers that are set apart, fused, or linked by stretched bridges. These towers connect to each other in all directions, generating a panoramic architecture without corners or abrupt transitions that could break the fluidity of its formal composition. The four towers each have an atrium, and every floor is serviced by a ring-shaped single-loaded corridor. The rooms, on the other hand, are aligned on a structural grid. The atrium allows daylight into the building, which reaches every room.

The great interior courts of the project are a reflection of traditional Chinese architecture. Here, the architecture is no longer composed of rigid blocks, but instead comprises volumes that coalesce to create a world of continuous mutual adaptation and fluid movement between each building. Shifting plateaus within the design impact upon each other to generate a deep sense of immersion and envelopment. As users enter deeper into the building, they discover intimate spaces that follow the same coherent formal logic of continuous curve linearity.

The lower three levels of Galaxy SOHO house public facilities for retail and entertainment. The levels immediately above provide work spaces for clusters of innovative businesses. The top of the building is dedicated to bars, restaurants, and cafés that offer views along one of the greatest avenues of the city. These different functions are interconnected through intimate interiors that are always linked with the city, helping to establish Galaxy SOHO as a major urban landmark for Beijing.

Location Beijing, China
Client SOHO China
Area 332,857 m^2 (3,582,843 ft^2)
Date 2008–2012

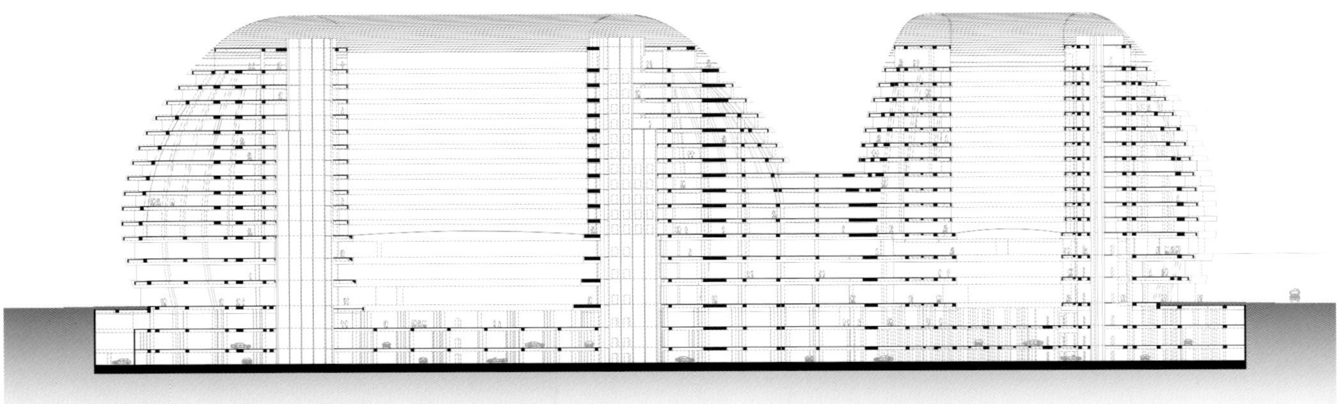

Section

办公室 NO A

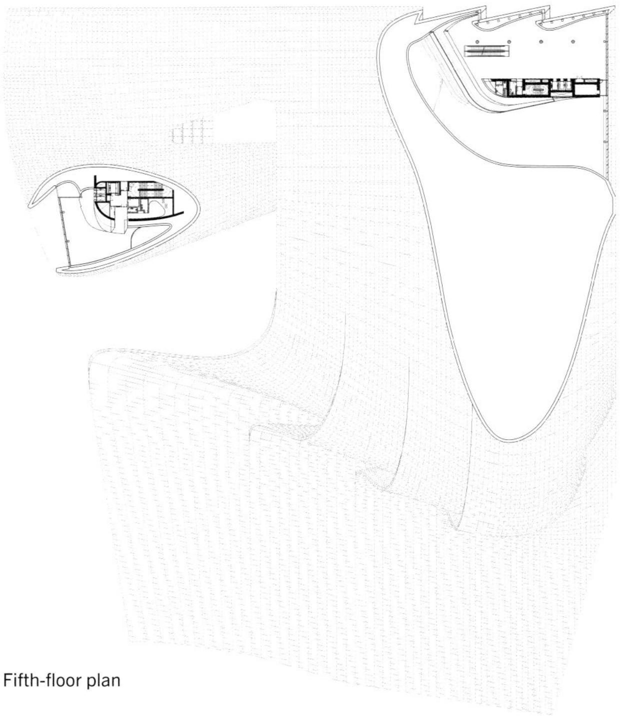

Fifth-floor plan

Seventh-floor plan

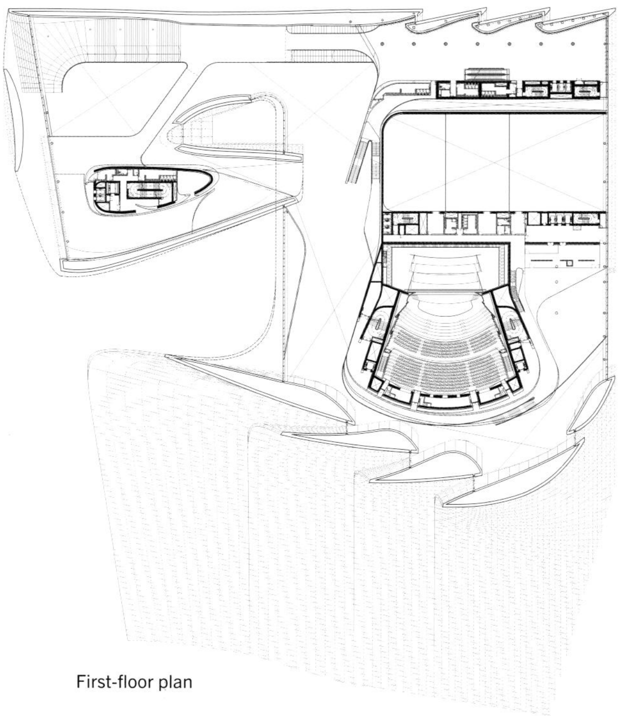

First-floor plan

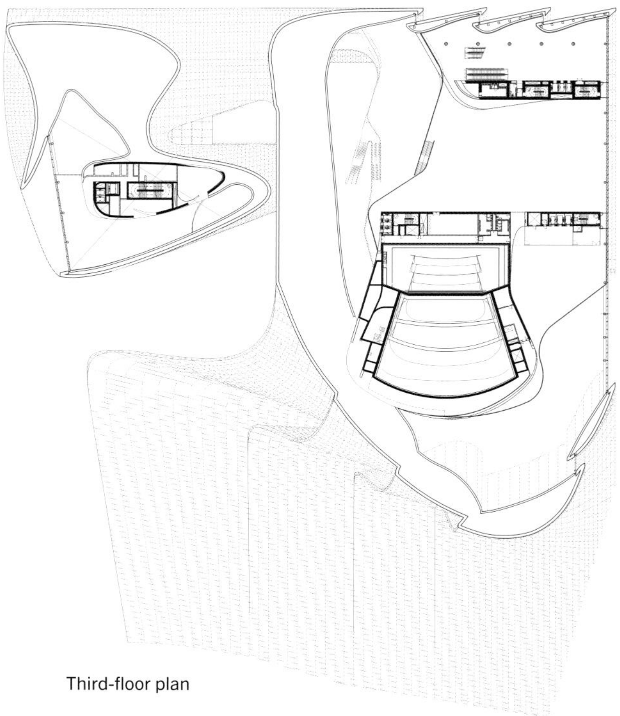

Third-floor plan

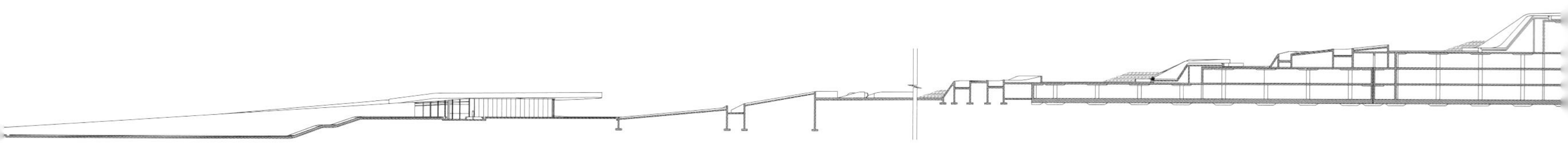

HEYDAR ALIYEV CENTER

The design of the Heydar Aliyev Center establishes a continuous, fluid relationship between its surrounding plaza and the building's interior. The plaza, as the ground surface and accessible to all as part of Baku's urban design, rises to envelop an equally public interior space, and define a sequence of event spaces dedicated to the collective celebration of contemporary and traditional Azeri culture. Elaborate formations such as undulations, bifurcations, folds, and inflections modify this plaza surface into an architectural landscape that performs a multitude of functions: welcoming, embracing, and directing visitors through different levels of the interior.

In order to achieve large-scale, column-free spaces that allow the visitor to experience the fluidity of the interior, vertical structural elements are absorbed by the envelope and curtain wall system. The particular surface geometry fosters unconventional structural solutions, such as the introduction of curved 'boot columns' to achieve the inverse peel of the surface from the ground to the West of the building, and the 'dovetail' tapering of the cantilever beams that support the building envelope to the east of the site.

To emphasise the continuous relationship between the building's exterior and interior, the lighting of the Heydar Aliyev Center has been very carefully considered. The lighting design strategy differentiates the day and night reading of the building. During the day, the building's volume reflects light, constantly altering the centre's appearance according to the time of day and viewing perspective. The use of semi-reflective glass gives tantalising glimpses within, arousing curiosity without revealing the fluid trajectory of spaces inside. At night, this character is gradually transformed by means of lighting that washes from the interior onto the exterior surfaces, unfolding the formal composition to reveal its content and maintaining the fluidity between interior and exterior.

Location Baku, Azerbaijan
Client The Republic of Azerbaijan
Area 101,801 m^2 (1,095,777 ft^2)
Date 2007–2012

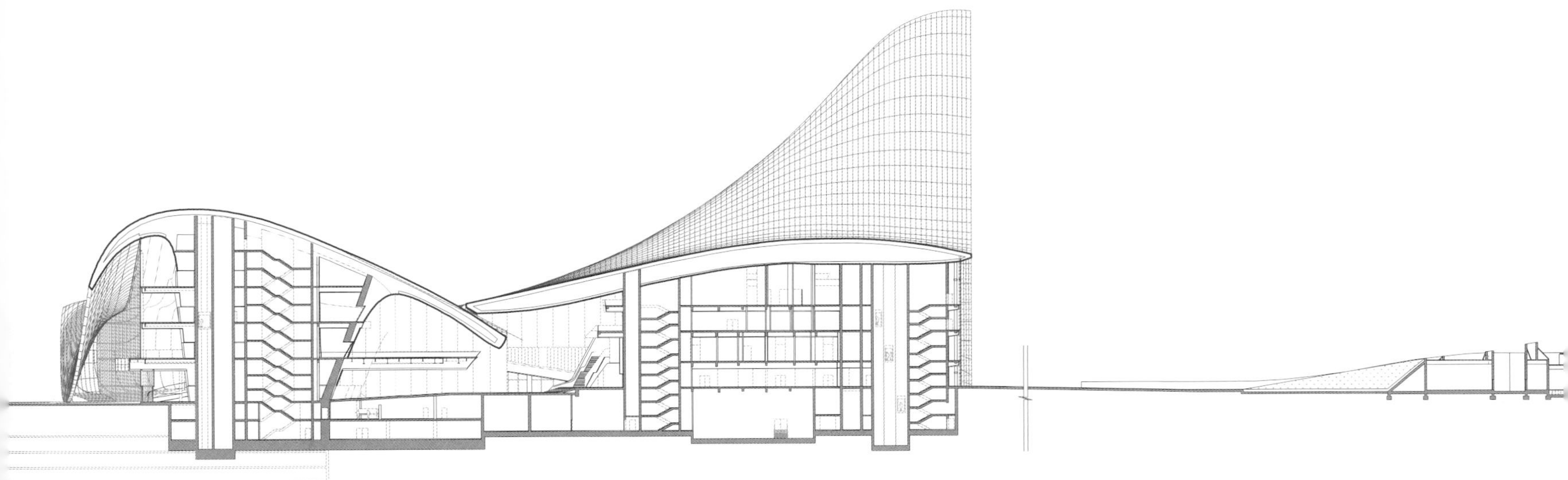

Section

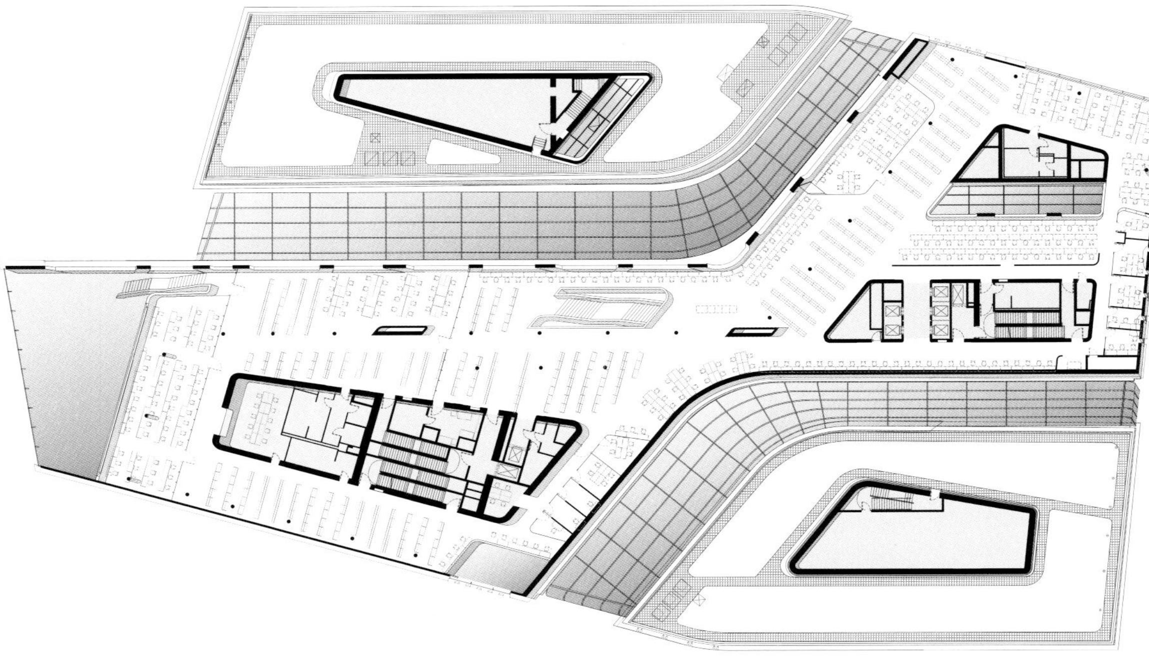

Fifth-floor plan

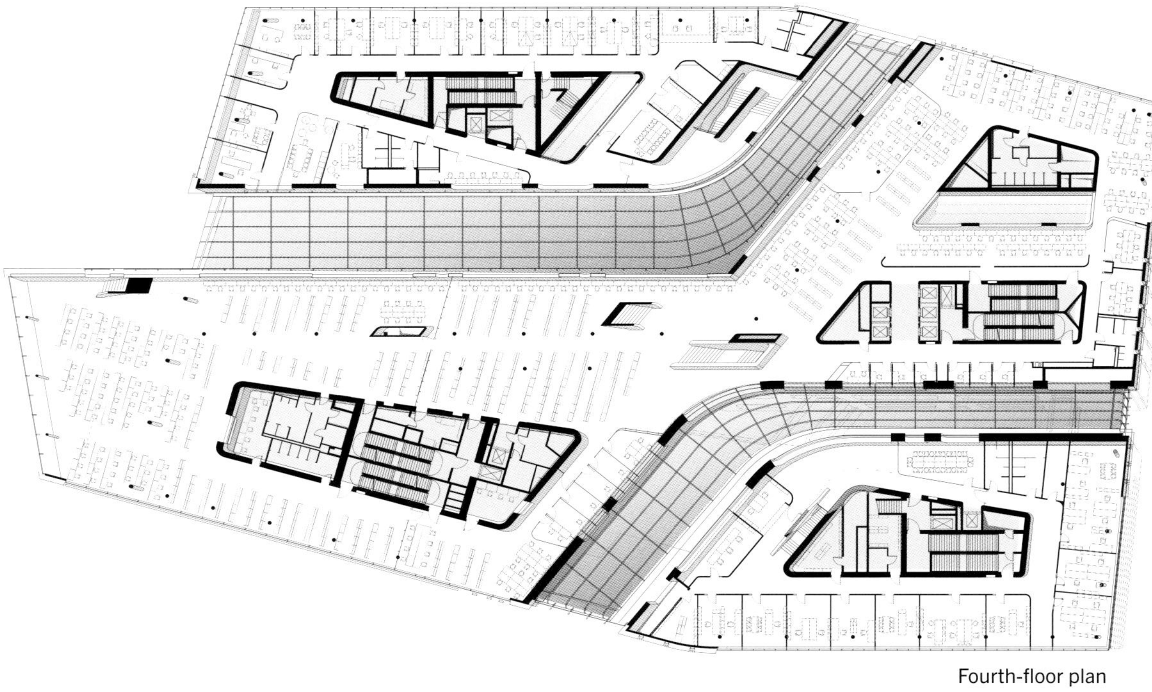

Fourth-floor plan

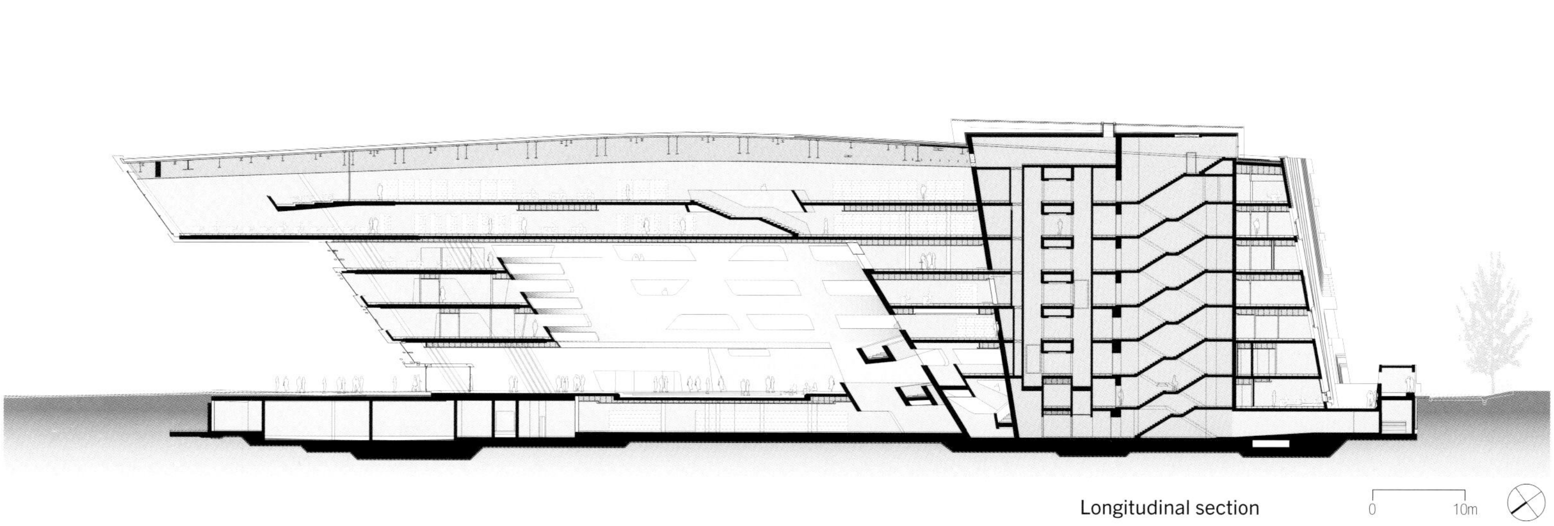

Longitudinal section

LIBRARY AND LEARNING CENTRE—UNIVERSITY OF ECONOMICS VIENNA

The new Library and Learning Centre rises as a polygonal block in the heart of the new university campus. The interior is informed by the external landscape of the master plan, which maps out the different levels. The straight lines of the building's exterior are cut sharply, and their alignment contrasts with the site edges specified on the master plan and with the position of the adjacent buildings. They separate as they move inward, becoming curvilinear and fluid to generate a free-form interior canyon that serves as the principal public plaza of the centre, as well as generating corridors and bridges ensuring smooth transitions between different levels.

The main block of the building houses the Service Area, the Learning Centre and the Economics Library, with Student Services and Library Management located in the smaller block.

The external appearance of the LLC is characterised by two elements of contrasting colours separated by a glass joint: shell and shadow. These different colours facilitate the orientation and understanding of the two primary areas of the building from the exterior.

From the main entrance, visitors can walk directly to the central auditorium, which also functions as a large atrium flooded by natural light. A system of ramps leads from the auditorium to the library entrance and the central services on the first floor. The security and locker areas are located on the mezzanine below.

Visitors can access the library and the student management offices via ramps and stairways spiralling upwards from the ground floor. The different areas on the upper levels are connected via platforms, bridges, terraces, and galleries.

Location Vienna, Austria
Client University of Economics Vienna
Area 28,000 m^2 (301,390 ft^2)
Date 2008–2013

Models

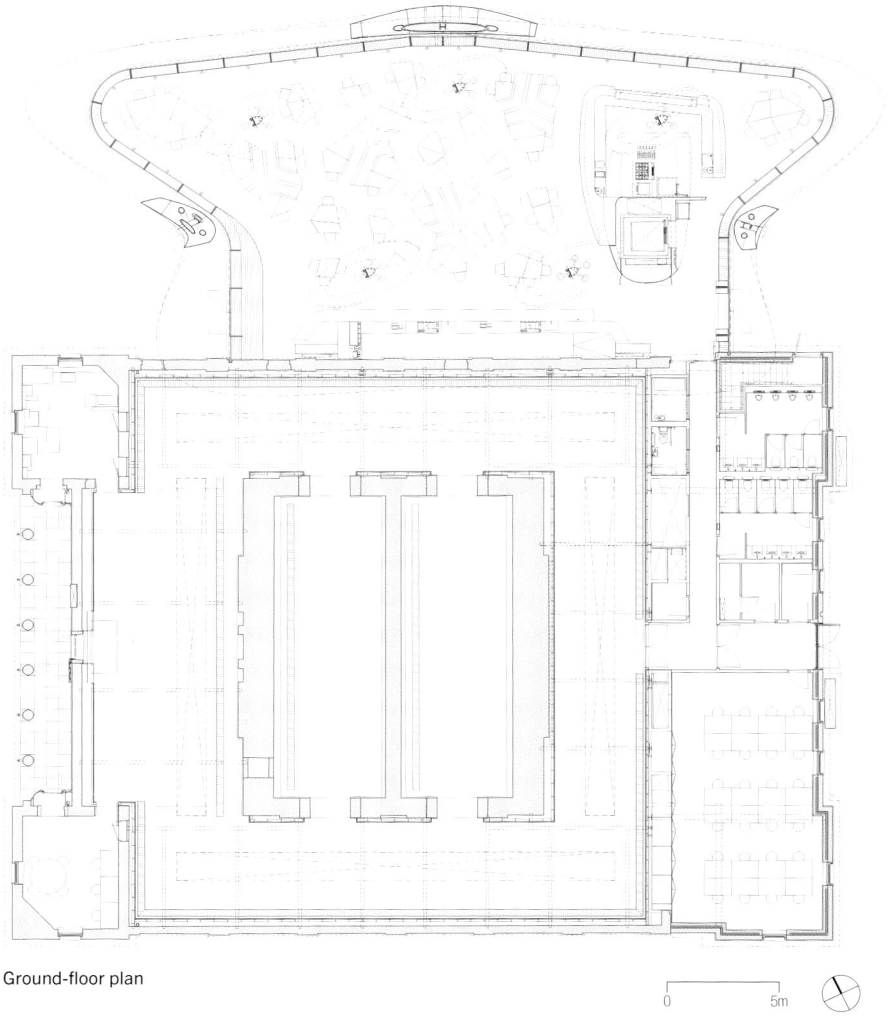

Ground-floor plan

North elevation

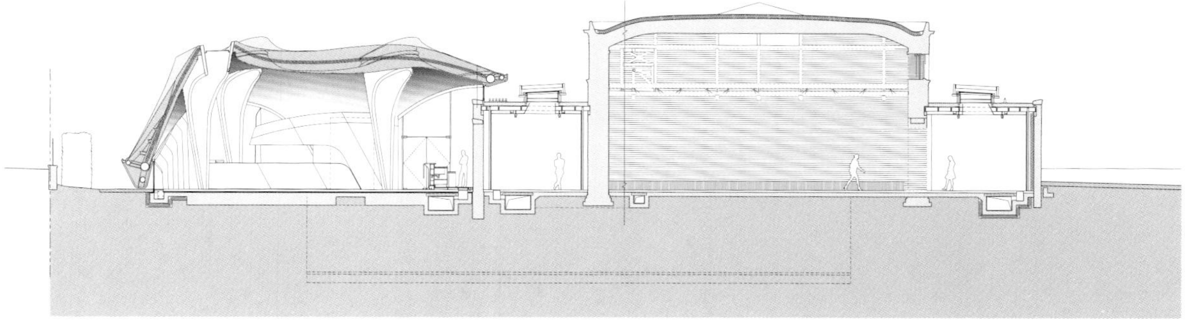

West-east section

0 5m

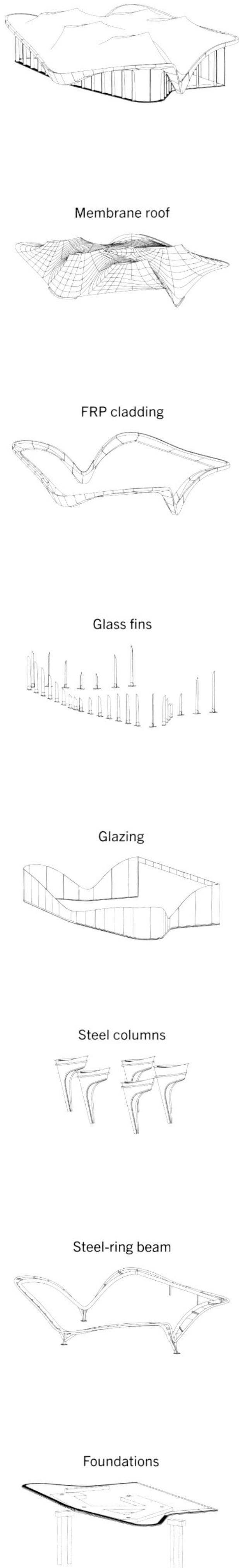

Structural diagram

THE SERPENTINE SACKLER GALLERY

The Serpentine Sackler Gallery consists of two distinct parts: the conversion of a classical 19th-century brick structure—The Magazine—and a 21st-century tensile structure.

The historic arrangement of the Magazine building was redesigned, whereby the former courtyards were covered to become internal exhibition spaces. Longitudinal skylights deliver natural daylight into the gallery surrounding the central vaults, and with a fixed louvre system, they create perfectly lit exhibition spaces. Necessary services and lighting were discreetly integrated as to not interfere with the 'as found' quality of the spaces. Retractable blinds allow for a complete black-out of the galleries.

The extension has been designed to complement the solid classical building with a light and distinctly contemporary space of the 21st century. The glass-fiber woven textile membrane stretches between and connects a perimeter ring beam and a set of five interior columns that articulate the roof's high points. The edge beam—a twisted ladder truss supported on three points—dips down to the supporting ground in front, in the back, and on the free west side. On the east side, this edge beam (and thus the roof of the extension) swings above the parapet of the Magazine. A linear strip of glazing gives the appearance that the roof is hovering above the Magazine without touching. The Magazine's western exterior brick wall becomes an interior wall within the new extension without losing its original function and beauty.

The envelope is completed by a curved, frameless glass wall that cantilevers from the ground to reach the edge beam and fabric roof. The interior of the extension is a bright, open space with light pouring in from all sides. The only fixed elements are the kitchen island and a long bar counter along the Magazine's wall. The tables, banquets, and chairs are designed as a continuous Voronoi pattern, reminiscent of organic cell structures.

Location London, England
Client The Serpentine Trust
Area 1566 m^2 (16,856 ft^2)
Date 2009–2013

THE MAGAZINE

THE MAGAZINE

THE MAGAZ

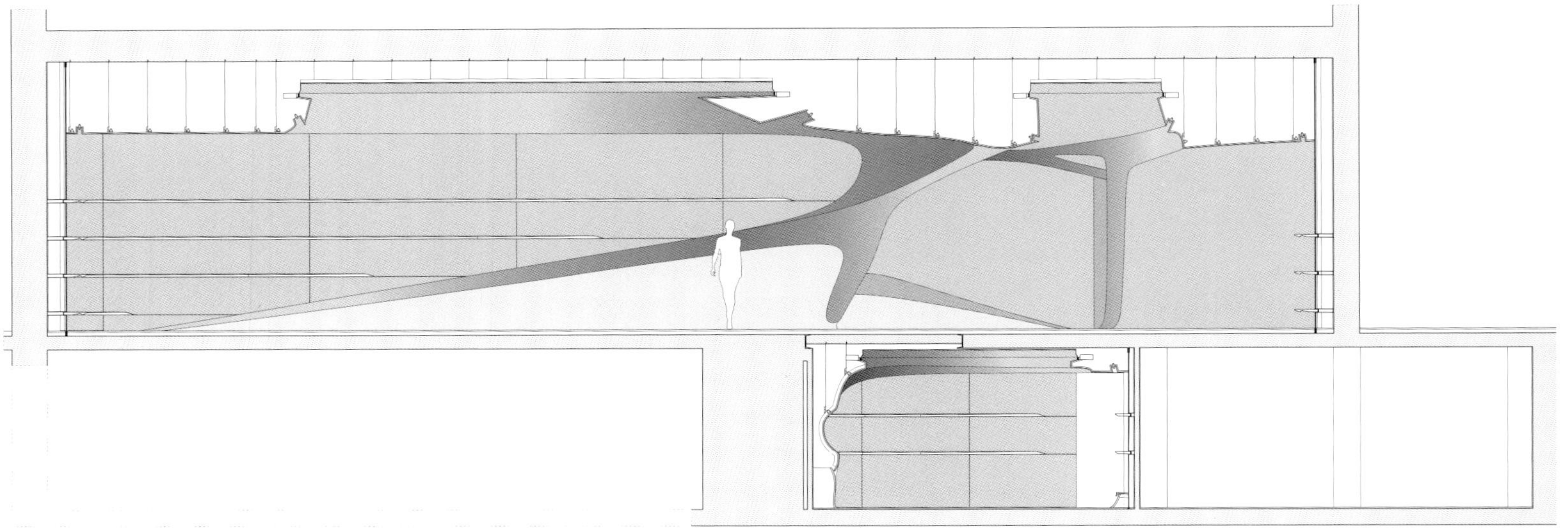

Section Milan store

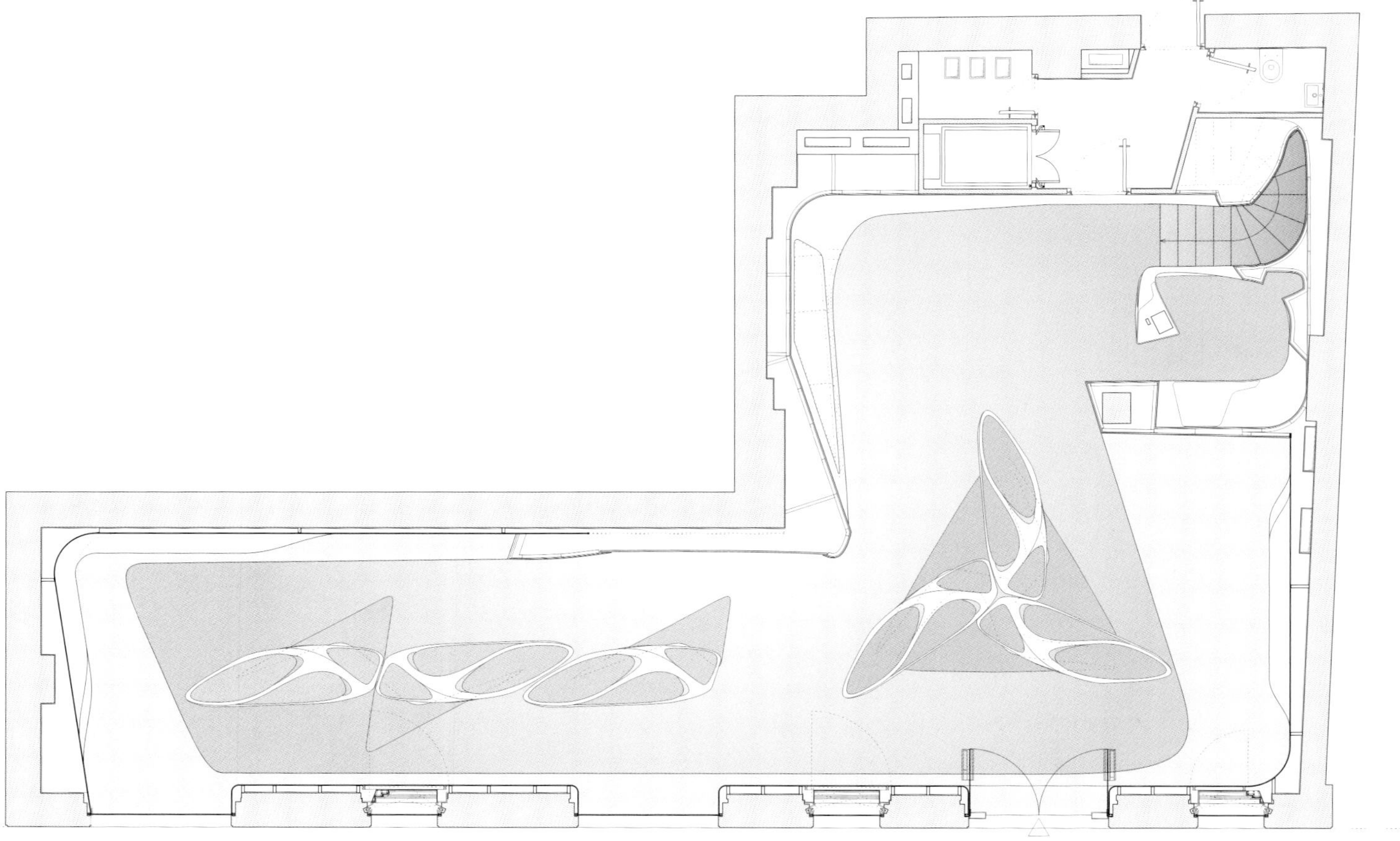

Ground-floor plan Milan store

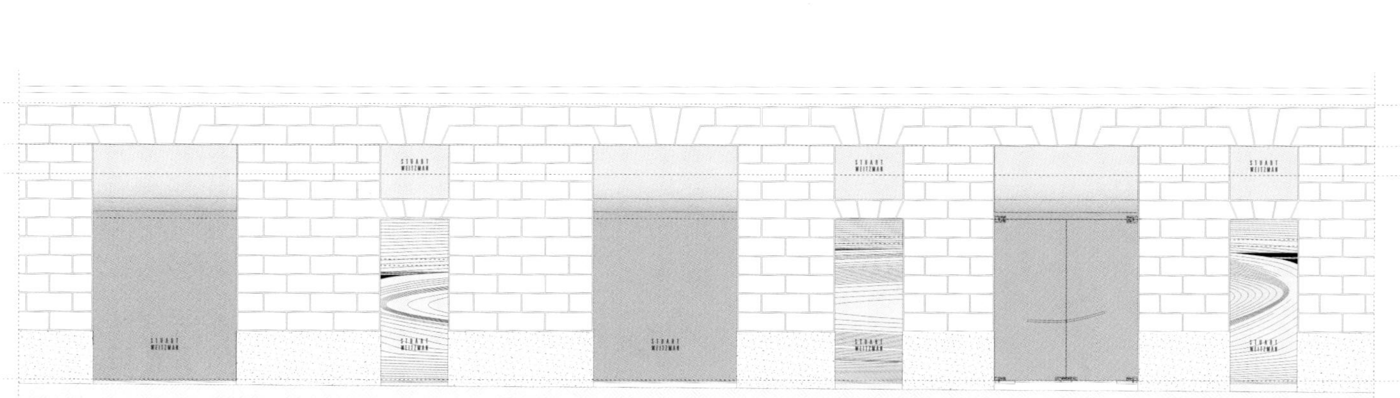

Façade Milan store

STUART WEITZMAN FLAGSHIP STORE

Location Milan/Hong Kong/Rome
Client Stuart Weitzman
Area 280 m^2 (3014 ft^2) | Milan
Date 2013–2014

The design concept for Stuart Weitzman worldwide is a playful dialogue of geometries, creating a rhythm of folds and recesses that have been shaped further by functional and ergonomic considerations. The store's central display units have been designed to showcase the Stuart Weitzman collection and also provide seating. The juxtaposition of these distinct elements of the design defines the different areas of the store. Rooted in a palette of subtle monochromatic shades, the design creates an interior landscape of discovery centred on two separate zones to enhance the relationship between the customer and the collection.

An intricate combination of materials and construction technologies have further defined the spatial experience. The curved modular seating and free-standing display elements have been constructed from fiberglass dipped in rose gold, a technique similar to that used in boat manufacturing. Also, the glass-reinforced concrete of the store's walls and ceiling expresses solidity, while at the same time the precision of complex curvatures generate focal points and areas for display.

The Stuart Weitzman design concept is divided into invariant and adaptive elements. This enables the design to establish unique relationships within each worldwide location, yet also enables every store to be recognised as a Stuart Weitzma6n space. Additional flagship stores are planned over the next few years and will be strategically located around the globe.

This is a major new initiative that will help achieve the next phase of growth and raise brand recognition worldwide. The combination of incredible architecture and Stuart Weitzman's collection will create a one-of-a-kind retail experience.

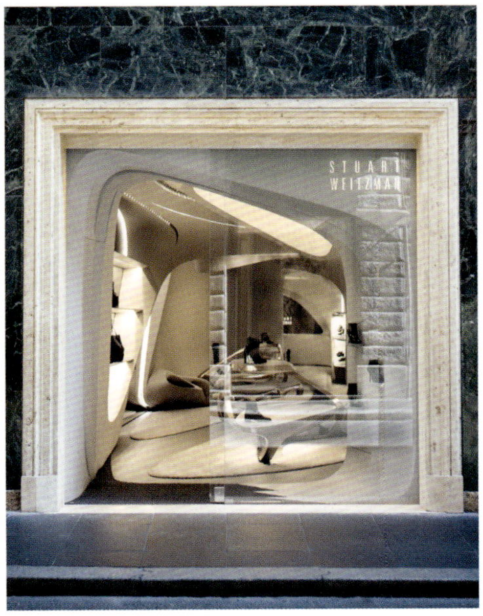

Façade detail

1 Researcher's office
2 Seminar room
3 Lobby
4 Toilets
5 Electrical room
6 Lift
7 Stairs
8 Kitchenette
9 Electrical room
10 Void
11 Hardscape
12 Softscape

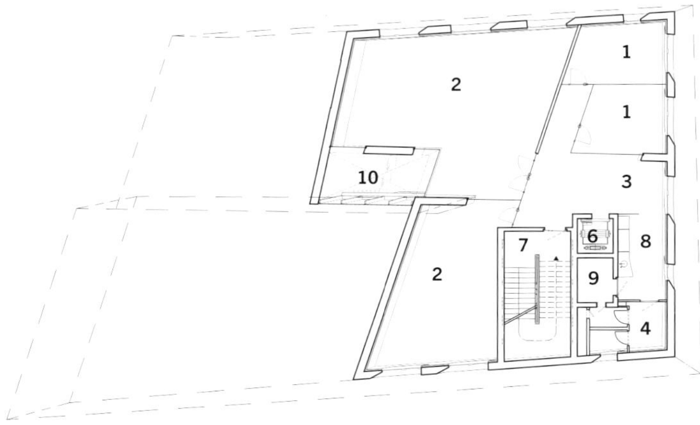

Third-floor plan

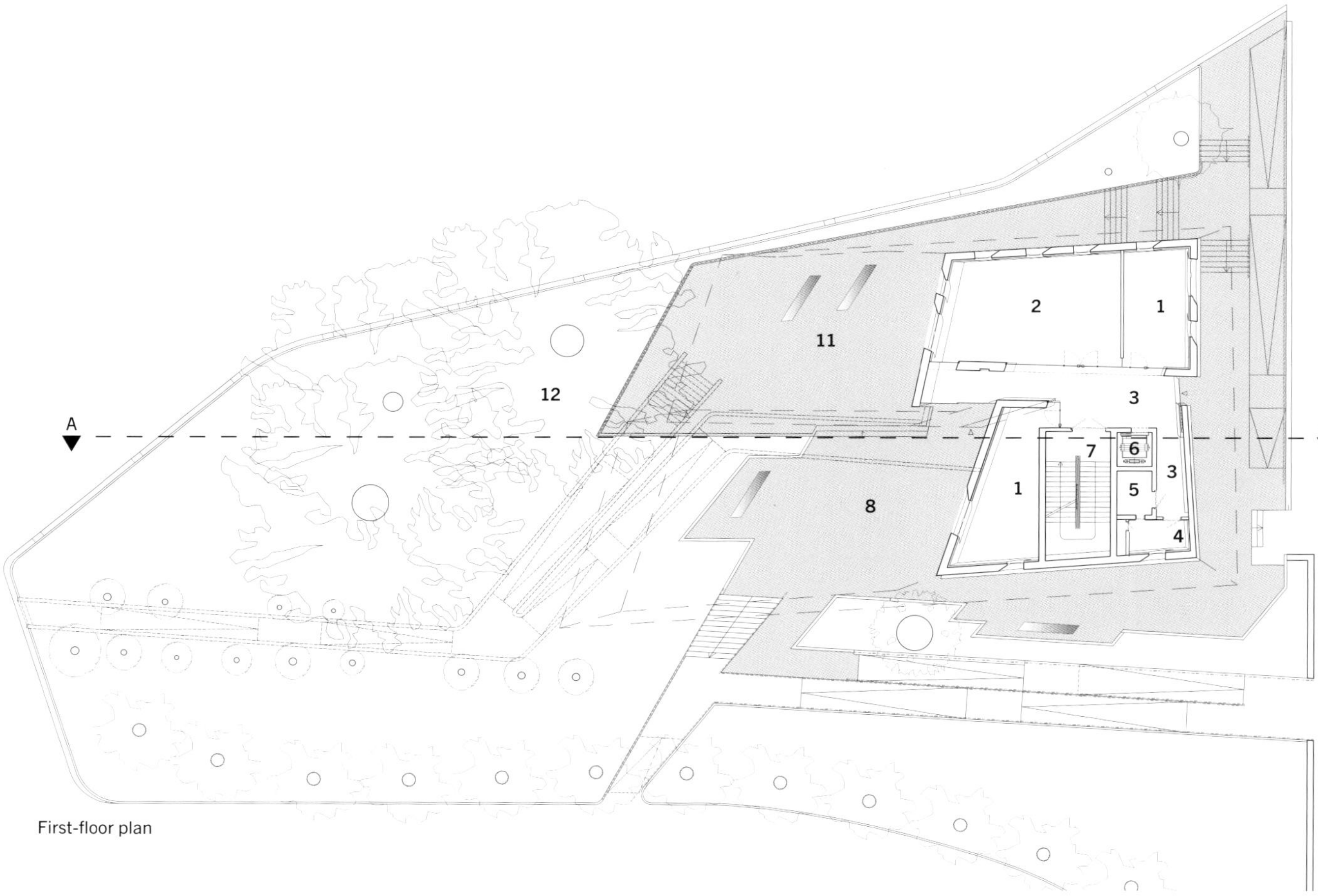

First-floor plan

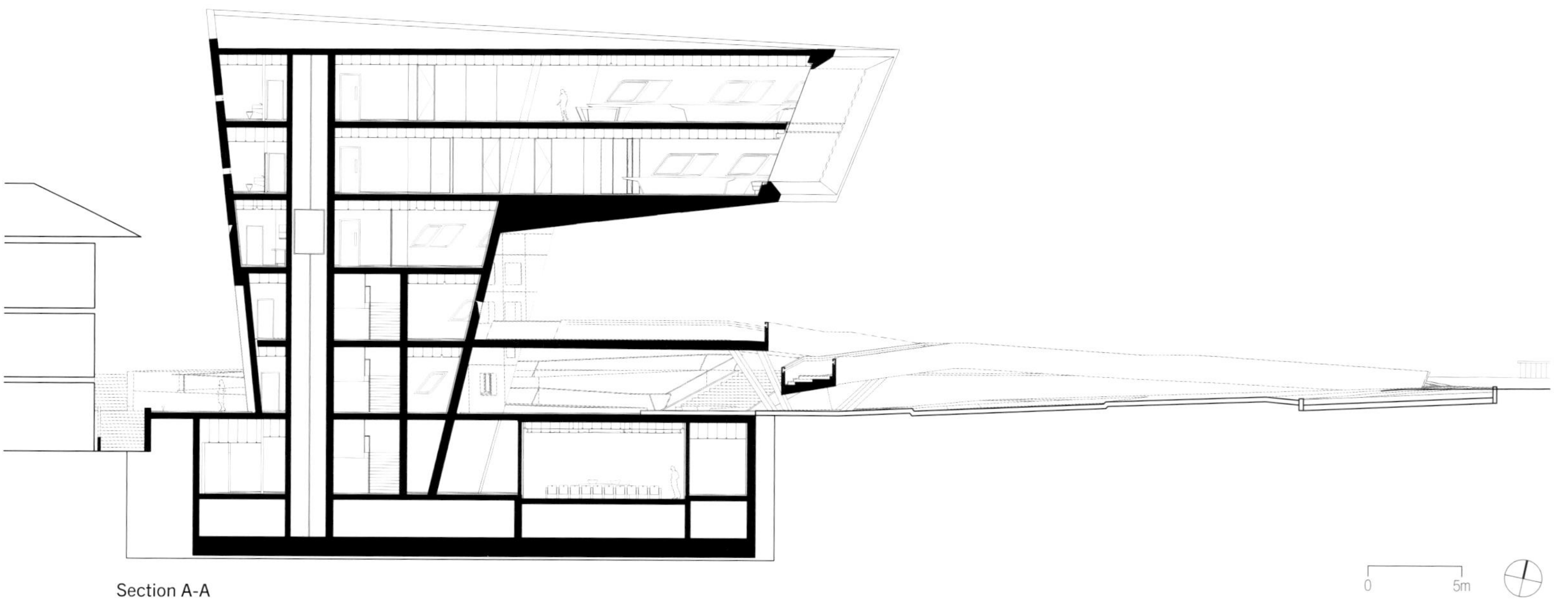

Section A-A

ISSAM FARES INSTITUTE FOR PUBLIC POLICY & INTERNATIONAL AFFAIRS

The Issam Fares Institute building design introduces new links between the Central Oval with the forested area of the Middle Campus and sea beyond. Existing ficus and cypress trees on the site (aged between 120 and 180 years old) are integral to the design. The building emerges from the geometries of intersecting routes as a series of interlocking platforms and spaces.

The institute invites the community inside via the many connections and paths that converge at its double-height entrance courtyard. This new civic space for the university is a covered outdoor terrace and extension of the shaded area beneath the existing trees—a place for chance meetings and informal discussion—located at the nexus of pathways that traverse the site.

A ramp leads between the trees to connect the research lounges on the second floor directly with the campus, while the first-floor seminar room and offices are accessed at grade from the east, and the public courtyard to the west. These routes meet at the atrium hall of the building, establishing the institute as a crossroads—a central hub for students, faculty, researchers, and visitors.

The IFI's reading room, conference workshops, and research rooms 'float' above the exterior courtyard. The 100-seat auditorium is on the lowest level with its own entrance to the north, enabling the institute to host larger conferences and presentations without disrupting students, fellows, and researchers working throughout the building. Internal partitions are in ink-pigmented glass to enable communication and interaction.

The building takes full advantage of the region's tradition and expertise of working with in-situ concrete. Passive design measures, high-efficiency active systems, and recycled water technologies minimise the building's impact on the local and wider environment.

Location Beirut, Lebanon
Client Issam Fares Institute for Public Policy & International Affairs
Area 7000 m^2 (75,347 ft^2)
Date 2002–2014

ISSAM FARES INSTITUTE
for Public Policy and International Affairs

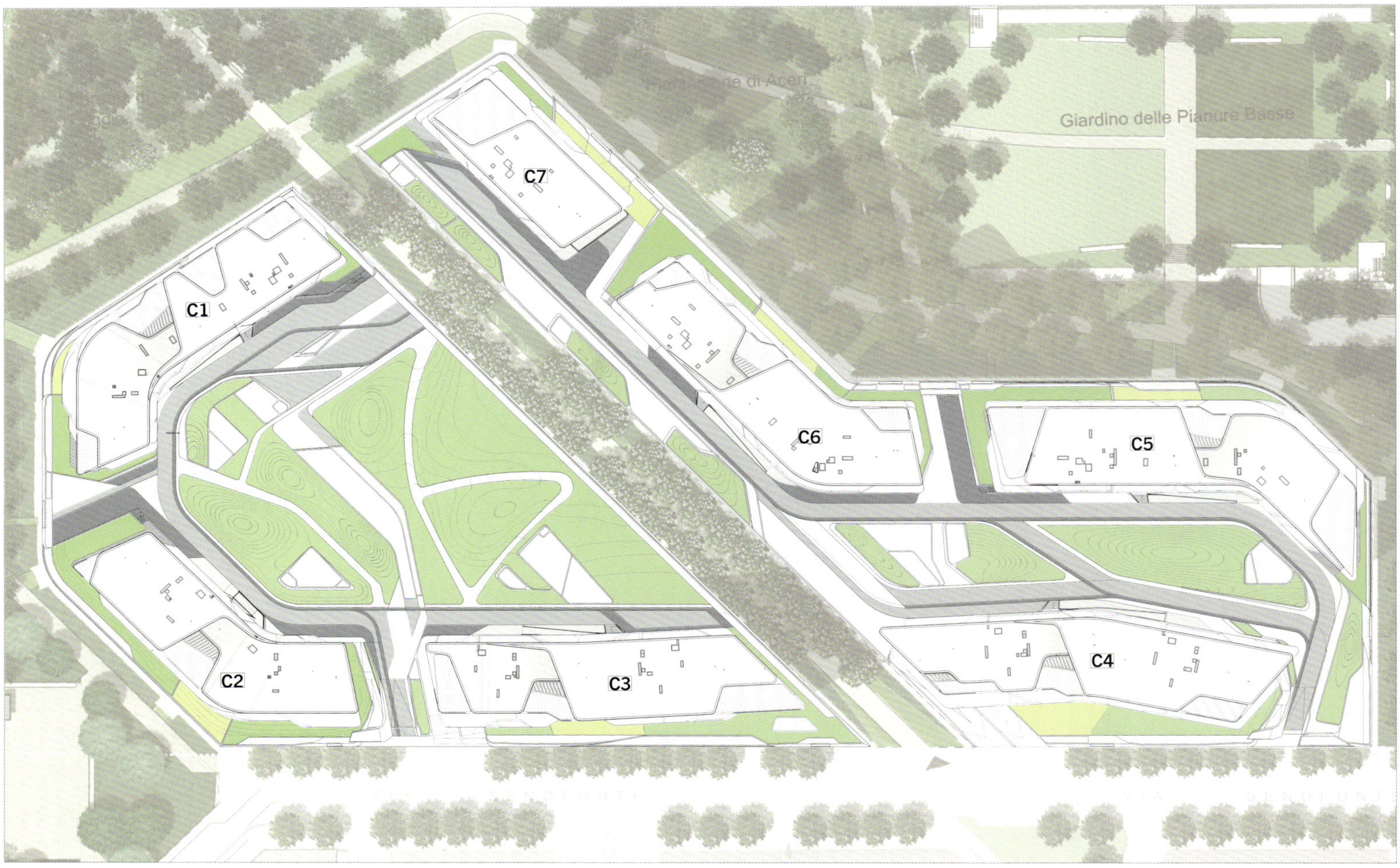

Site plan

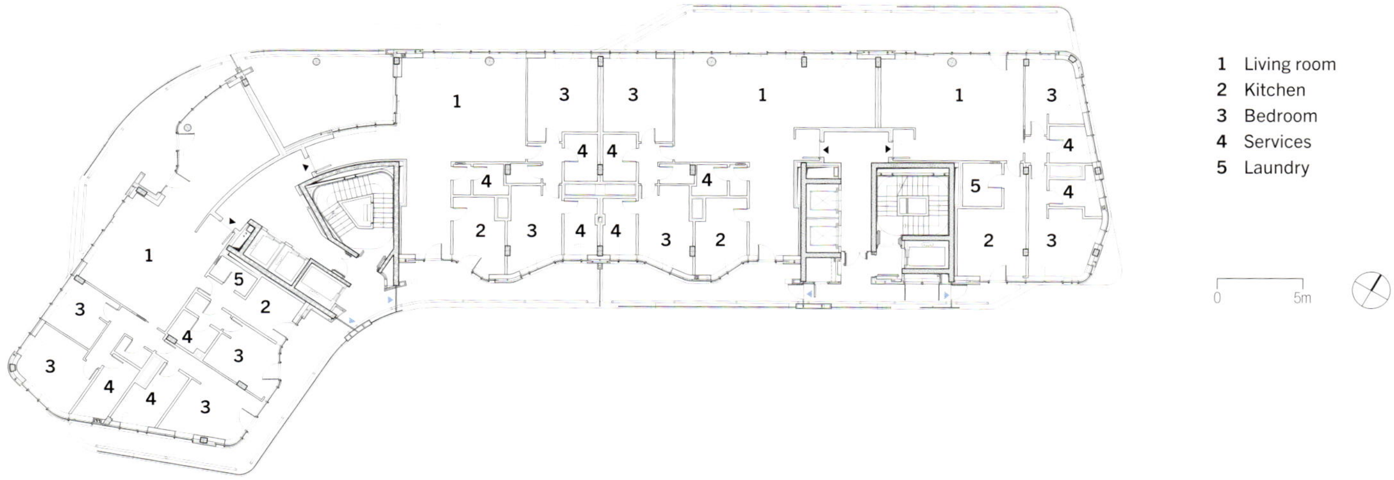

Typical floor plan (building C1)

South elevation

CITY LIFE MILANO RESIDENTIAL COMPLEX

The residential plot is composed by seven linear buildings set along a continuous path around two land areas divided by a strip of public park. The skyline of the residential complex is defined and characterised by a sinuous fluid line. The roof outline raises continuously from building to building. Most apartments face southeast and at the same time, the best views from the terraces are towards the city or the public park.

The façades design involves continuity and fluidity: the volumetric envelope of the buildings is defined by a curvilinear movement of balconies and terraces, opening up into a rich variety of private spaces, both interior and exterior, echoing the landscape below. The façade materials—fiber concrete panels and natural wood panels—emphasise this complex, volumetric movement, and at the same time give a private and 'domestic' quality to the interior of the residential courtyard.

At ground level, the double-height lobbies are flooded with light by large openings stretching from floor to ceiling, designed to confer strong visual continuity with the park. Although great consideration has been given to the ground-floor design and morphology, the project is formally defined mainly by the roof profile and the intense urban horizon it generates. This strategy was determined by the awareness of forthcoming towers looking upon the residential roofs and by the strong will to engender, within the inner courtyard, a completely new residential landscape, reassuring yet dynamic.

Location Milan, Italy
Client City Life Consortium
Area 38,000 m^2 (409,029 ft^2)
Date 2004–2014

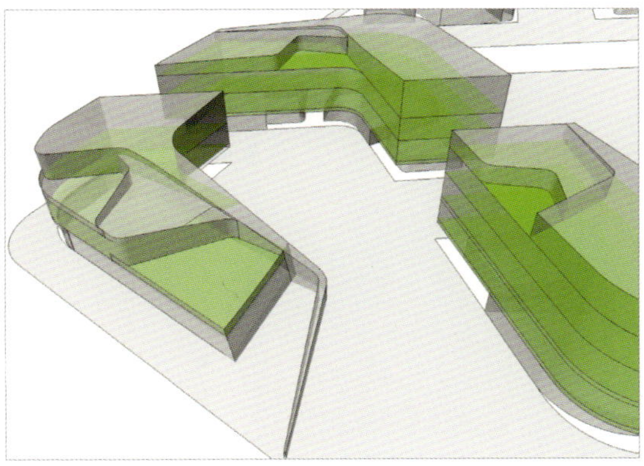

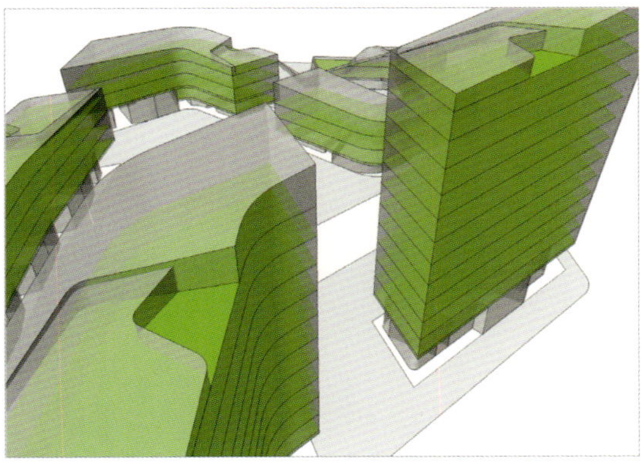

3D studies

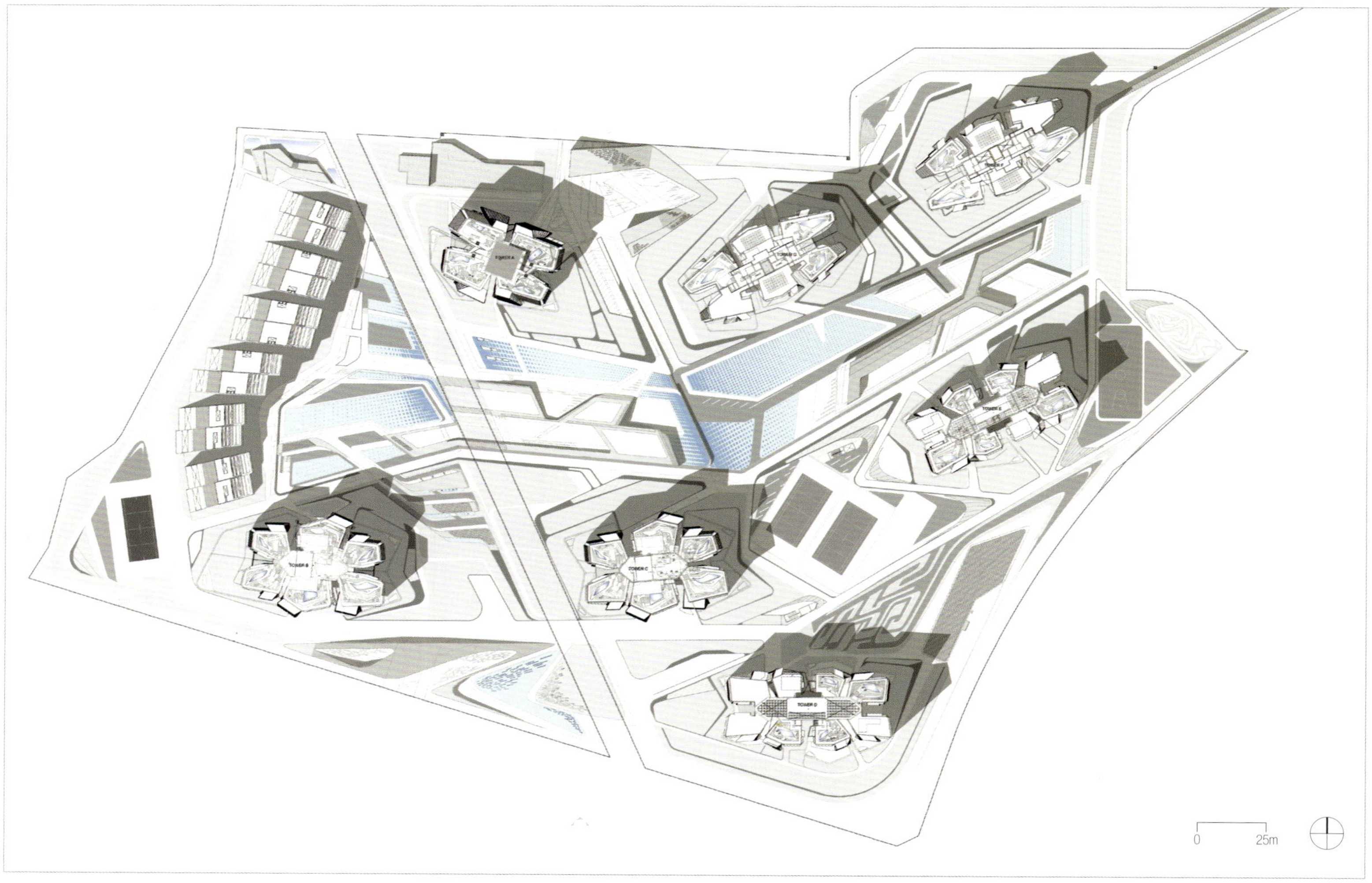

Site plan

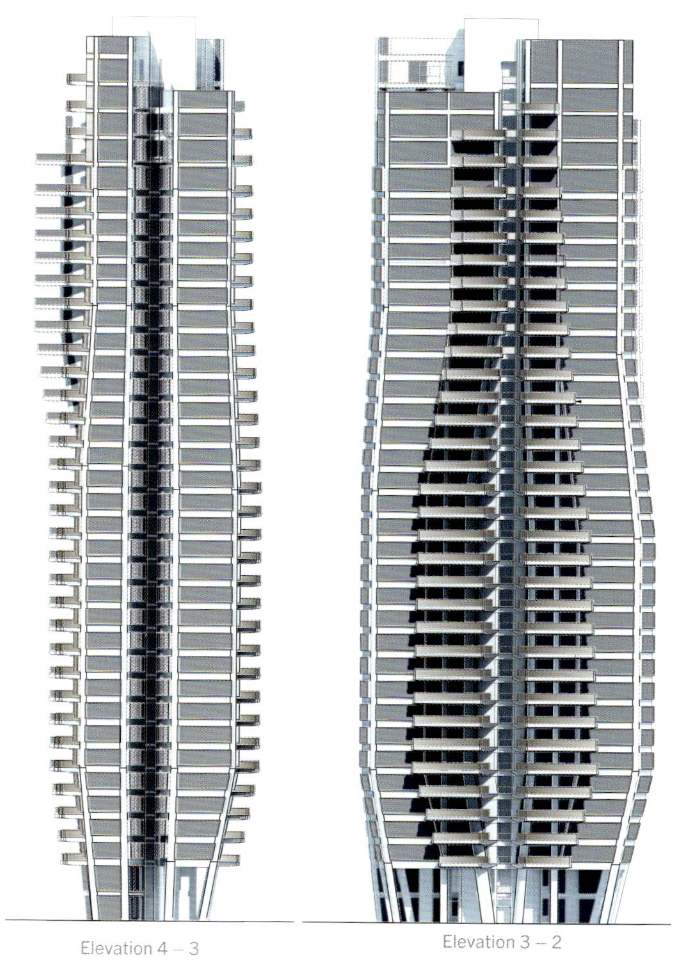

Tower A: elevations

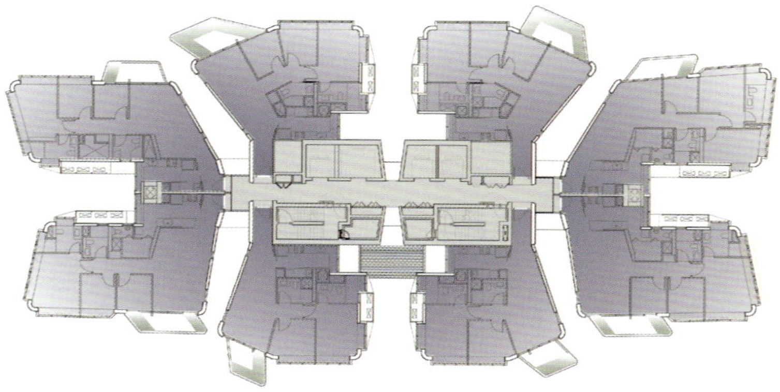

Tower D: Typical floor plan

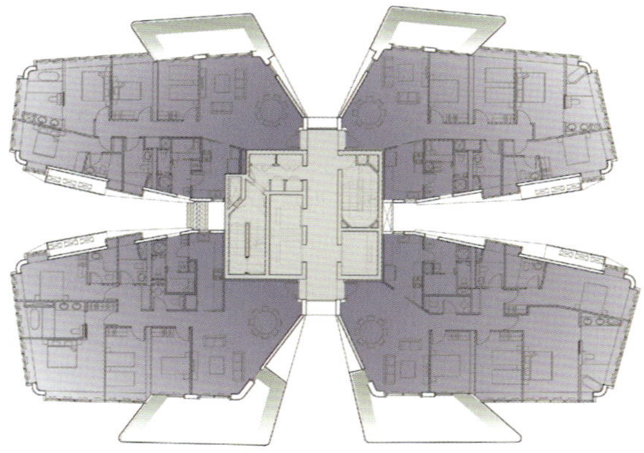

Tower A: Typical floor plan

D'LEEDON

d'Leedon, Singapore comprises seven residential towers, 12 semi-detached villas, and integrated landscaping with recreation facilities. Towers taper inwards as they reach the ground to optimise public space. Varied balcony geometries and the integrated landscaping create a unique project defined by its site conditions and context.

The towers are subdivided into 'petals' according to the number of residential units per floor, which informs the plan layout. Each petal creates one unit, maximising façade area for each apartment with a three-sided exposure. This provides for over 270-degree views, cross-ventilation, and functional openings for back-of-house areas, with living rooms exposed to the largest façade, bedrooms around the corners, and kitchen and bathroom in the cut areas.

The petals are expressed in three dimensions thanks to vertical cuts, which give definition to the buildings' façades and allow for cross-ventilation of the flats. Through rotating the buildings across the site and the careful use of balconies and façade panelling, a combination of towers produce an incredible amount of diversity across the development, giving each unit a unique and distinguishable location and appearance, both externally and internally.

The towers culminate at the top with a series of fingers at different heights. This feature creates fantastic opportunities for penthouses with rooftops gardens and pools. Garden units at the base of the towers have private parking underground, higher ceilings, and private gardens.

The interior of the residential unit is organised with entry and views in mind. The entrance leads directly to both living and service areas. The lifts are finished in solid surface material, with bespoke list panelling and buttons.

One of the strongest features of d'Leedon is a park that makes the project resemble a holiday destination resort where people can live year-round in the centre of Singapore.

Location Singapore
Client CapitaLand Residential, Hotel Properties, Morgan Stanley, Wachovia
Area 78,043 m² (840,049 ft²)
Date 2007–2014

Four-petal tower

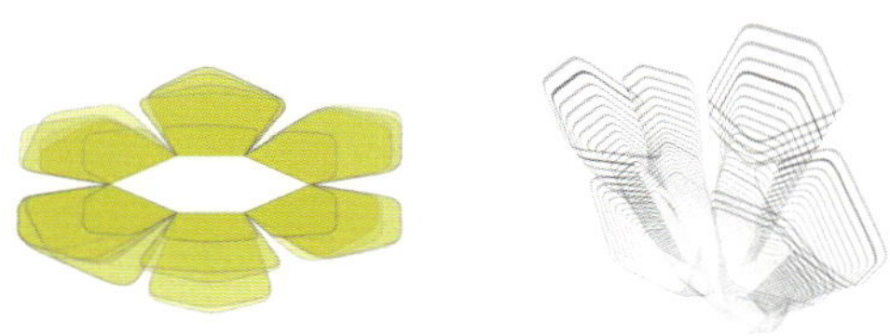
Six-petal tower

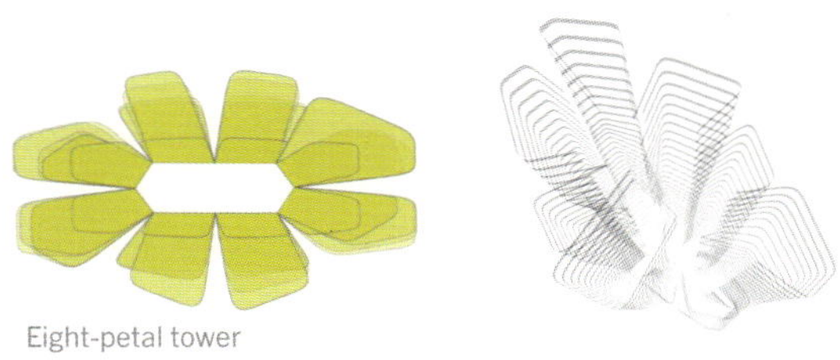
Eight-petal tower

Tower types: petal layout comparisons

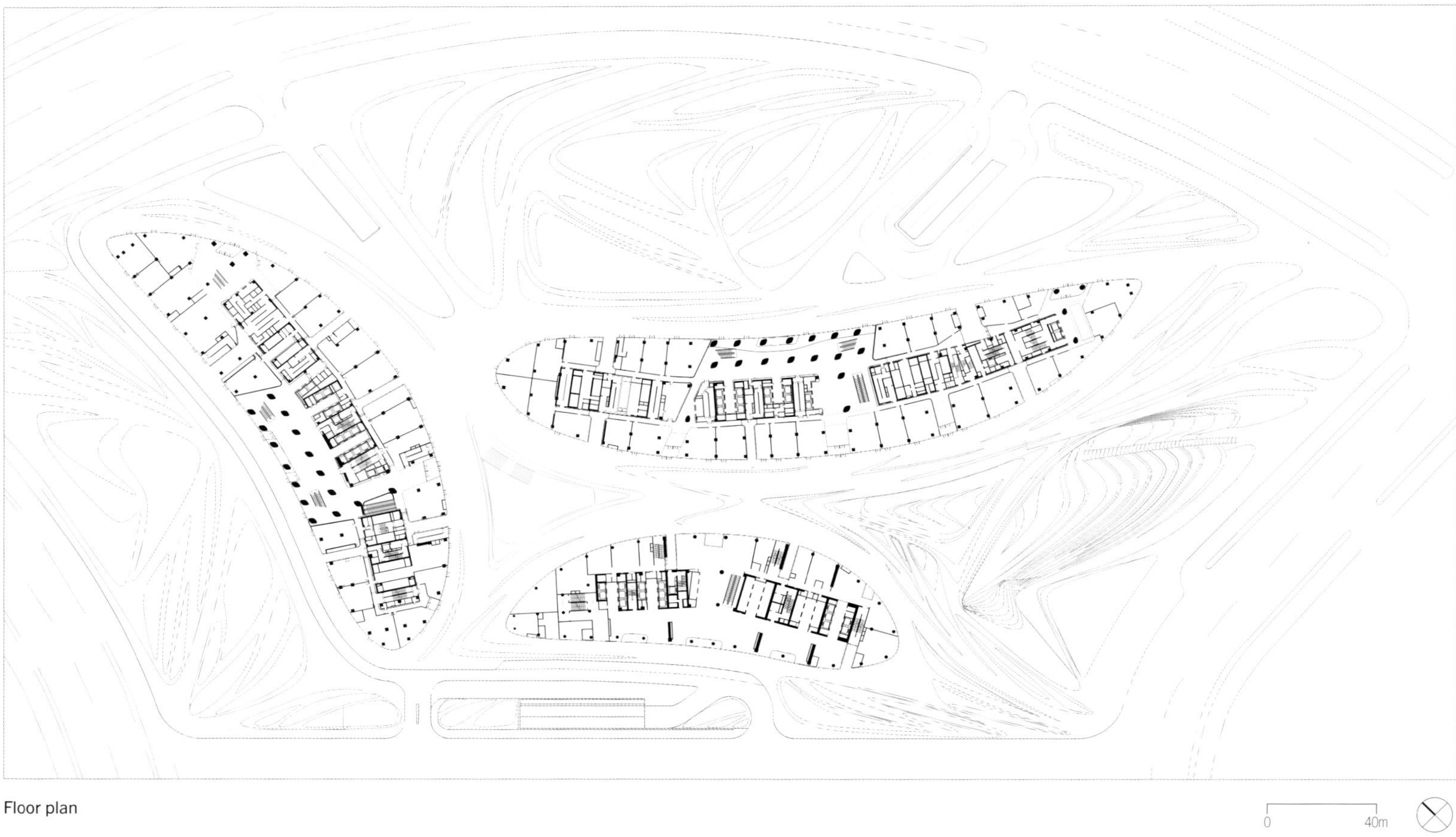

Floor plan

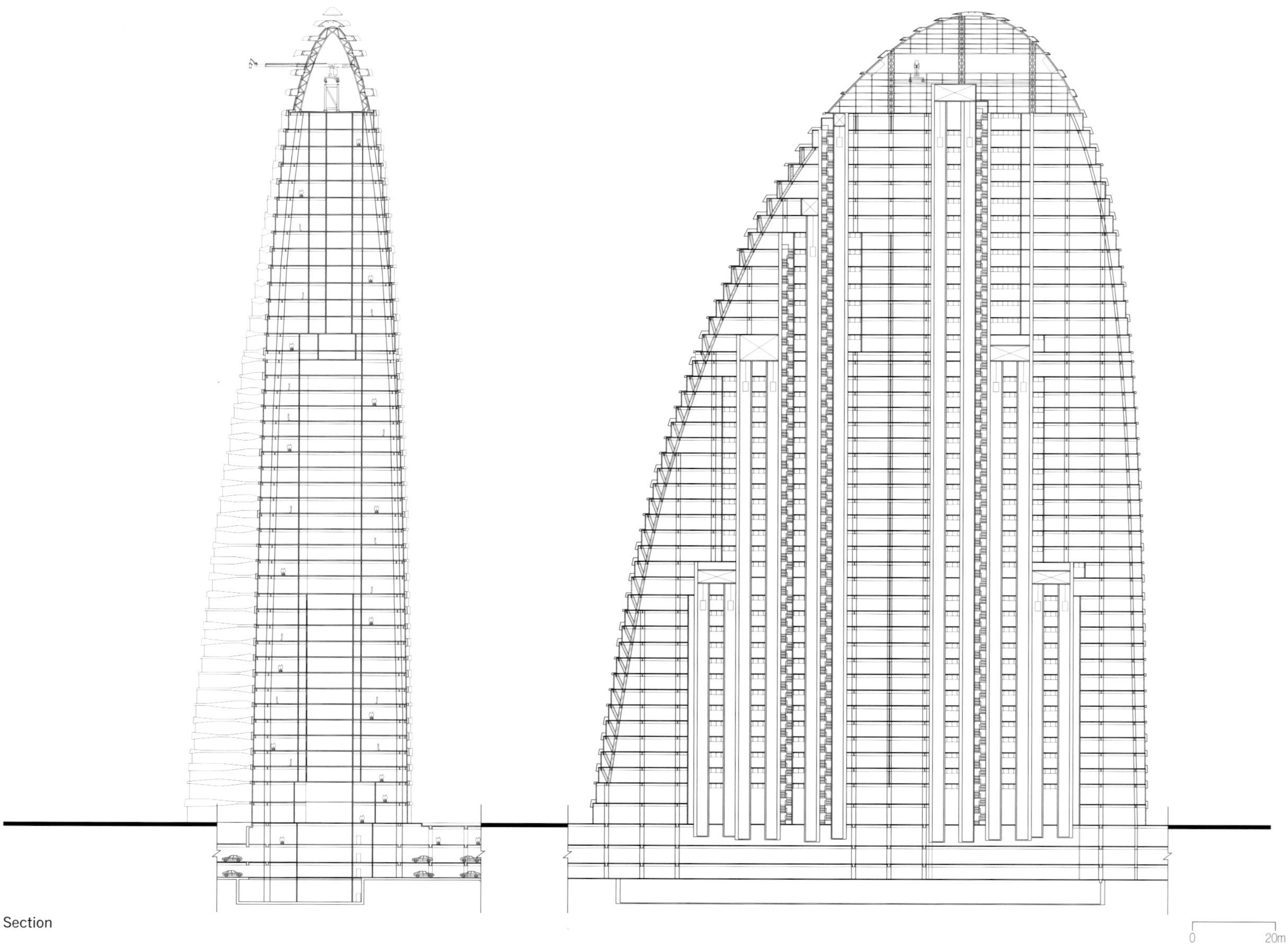

Section

WANGJING SOHO

Wangjing SOHO is a mixed-use development consisting of three towers designed as three interweaving 'mountains' that fuse building and landscape to bring together the surrounding community with a new public park.

The design responds to the flow of the city and allows natural daylight into each building from all directions. The juxtaposition of the tower's fluid forms continuously changes when viewed from different directions; appearing as individual buildings in some views, or as a connected ensemble in others. The orientation and composition of the towers directs visitors and staff to the various transport links that surround the site.

The cohesive design of the project creates an anchor and identity for the growing Wangjing community. Large public spaces open 24 hours a day and include a park to the south, and landscaped gardens to the north, east, and west with activity zones and water features that have already become popular areas for the local community.

The large entrance lobbies for each tower face out towards the city and extend through each building to the central shopping street and plaza between the towers, which in turn flow into public gardens and courtyards.

The thin floor plates provide flexible, open plan office space, and the tapering section of each tower provides extensive natural daylight to each office, retail space, and lobby. Windows on every floor of the towers can be opened to enable each office to be naturally ventilated whenever appropriate. Double-insulated unitised low-e glazing systems, and horizontal ribbons of white aluminium external louvres provide overhangs for sun shading as well as maintenance terraces and water collection. The envelope insulation reduces heating/cooling requirements, and systems are also designed to reduce emissions, potable-water usage, and energy consumption.

Location Beijing, China
Client SOHO China Ltd
Area 521,265 m^2 (5,610,850 ft^2)
Date 2009–2014

Digital sketch: tower volumes

望京SOH
SOHO

B
F21-F30

B
F1-F20

SOHO

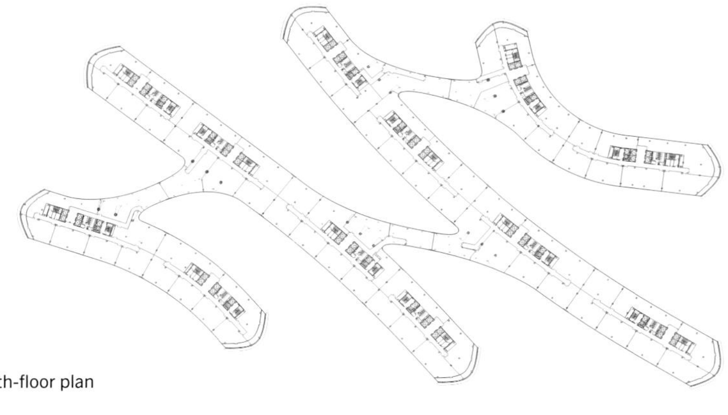

10th-floor plan

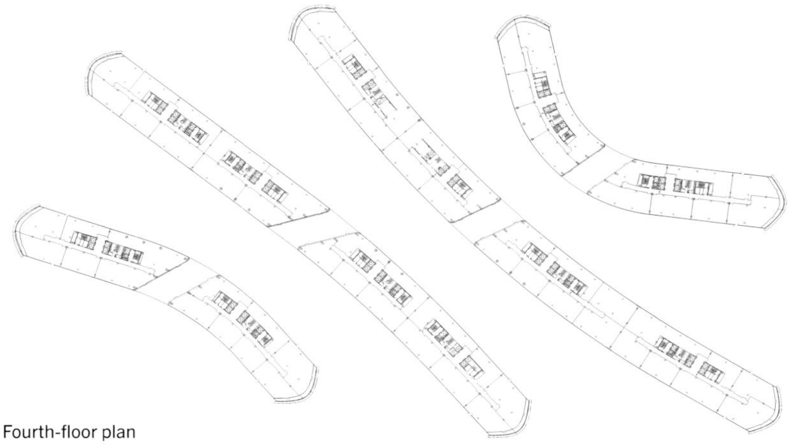

Fourth-floor plan

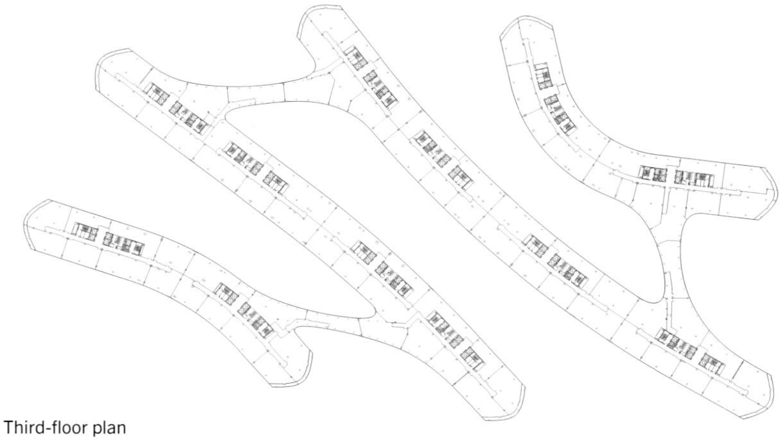

Third-floor plan

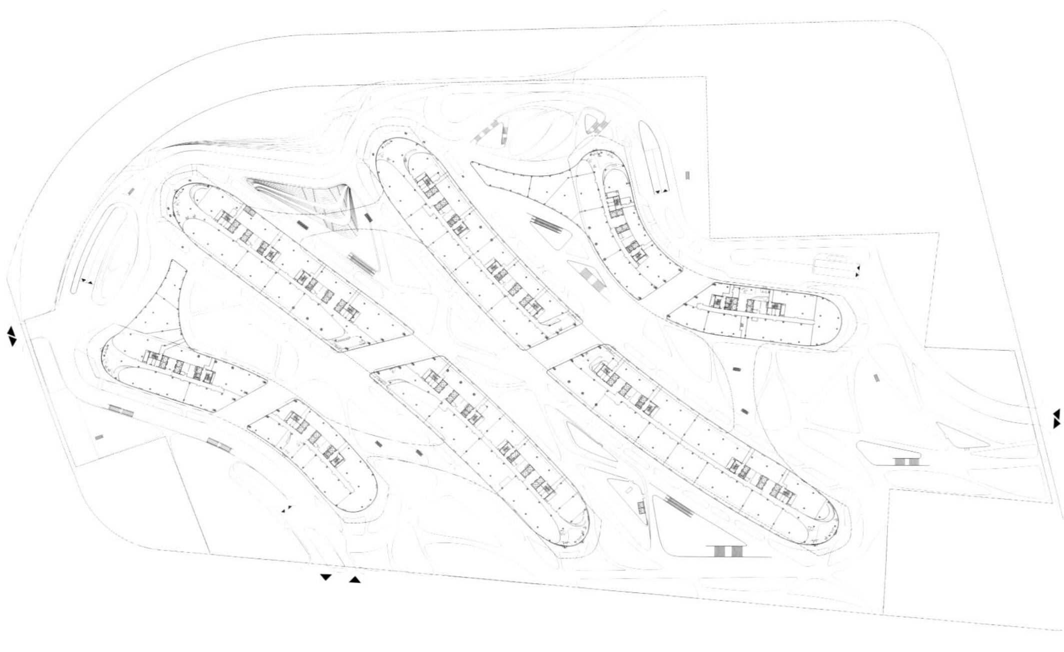

Ground-floor plan

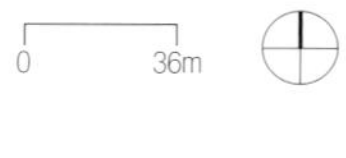

SKY SOHO

Located in the Linkong Economic Park within the Hongqiao Business Zone, and served by its transportation hub, Sky Soho connects multinational, national, and local enterprises with local residents.

The concept for the new mixed-use building is the underlying simplicity of four parallel slabs. This design provides the convenience and flexibility of a simple modular system based on a 8.4-metre (27.6-foot) grid and a building depth of approximately 18 metres (59 feet). The envelope is defined by four main components: four elongated elements tied together by a sinuous retail podium and continuous metallic ribbon that connects them, and a green roof, like calligraphy. These four primary elements are 'squeezed' together in their centre to create intimate courtyards framed by connecting bridges that create a wholly integrated spatial experience with dynamic interior and exterior public spaces.

Location Shanghai, China
Client SOHO China Ltd
Area 521,265 m^2 (5,610,850 ft^2)
Date 2010–2014

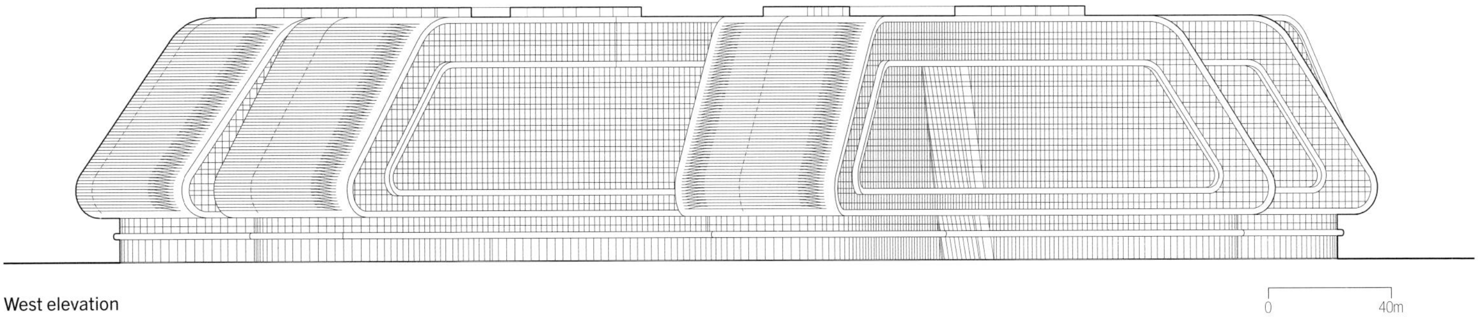

West elevation

SOHO
2

11

Second-floor plan

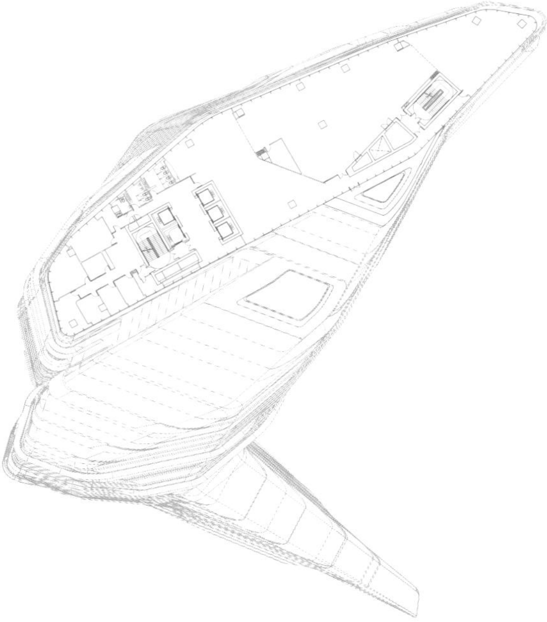

13th-floor plan

Ground-floor plan

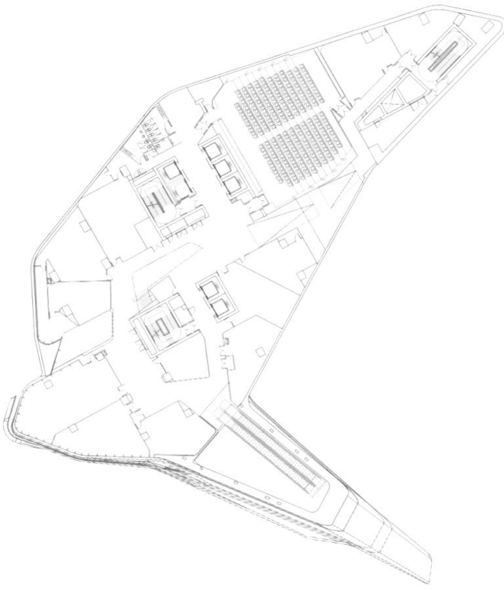

Third-floor plan

0 15m

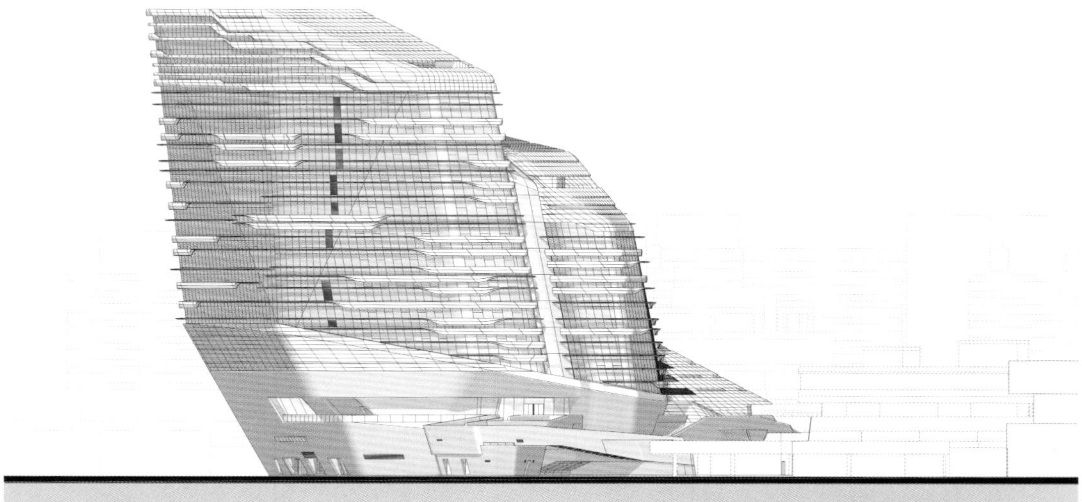

West elevation

0 15m

JOCKEY CLUB INNOVATION TOWER

The 15-storey tower accommodates more than 1800 students and staff, with facilities for design education and innovation that include design studios, labs and workshops, exhibition areas, multi-functional classrooms, a lecture theater, and a communal lounge.

The tower creates a new urban space that enriches the diversity of university life and expresses the dynamism of an institution looking to the future. The design dissolves the typical typology of the tower/podium into a more fluid composition. Interior and exterior courtyards create informal spaces to meet and interact, complementing the large exhibition forums, studios, theater, and recreational facilities.

The tower's design promotes a multi-disciplinary environment by connecting the variety of programs within the School of Design; establishing a collective research culture where many contributions and innovations can feed off each other.

With a unique building geometry, a unique three-dimensional metal cladding was selected for the curved 3D façade. A multiple layer of panelling allows the top layer of cladding to have open joints, while a hidden lower layer provides functional weatherproofing and drainage functions. The key façade design challenge on the project was the detailing and interface resolution of the cladding. A series of catwalks were designed behind the façade cladding with removable access panels to the interior to access glass that could not be reached by the building maintenance unit's normal operation.

Interior glazing and voids bring transparency and connectivity, while circulation routes and communal spaces have been arranged to encourage interaction between the many learning clusters and design disciplines.

The building has also incorporated energy-efficient features in building services installations, including evaporative cooling towers for water-cooled chillers, energy wheels provided to the primary air unit to enable energy recovery between exhaust air and fresh air intake, and carbon-dioxide sensors in general teaching facilities and offices to modulate the volume of fresh air.

Location Hong Kong, China
Client Hong Kong Polytechnic University
Area 15,000 m^2 (161,459 ft^2)
Date 2007–2014

Louvre study

李嘉誠樓
LI KA SHING TOWER
SLOW

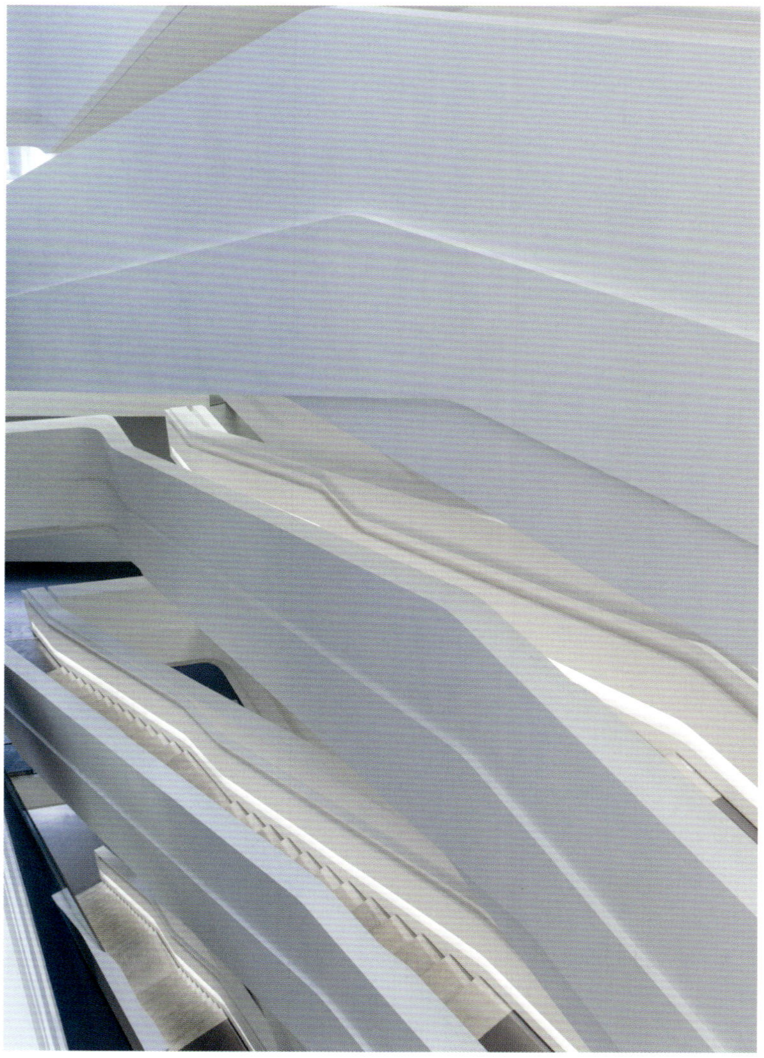

邵 逸 夫 樓
SHAW AMENITIES BUILDING
TAXI

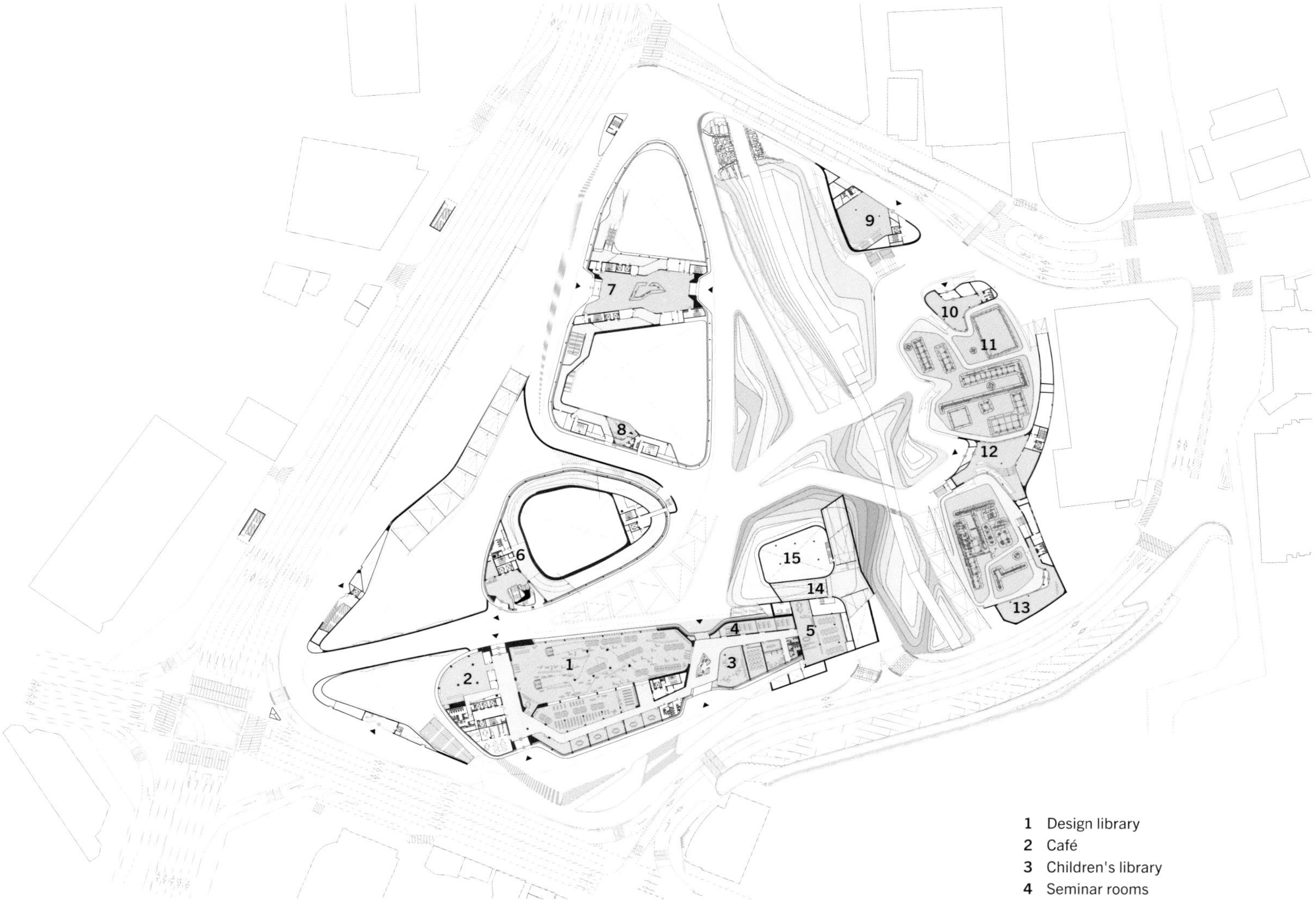

Level F1 floor plan

1 Design library
2 Café
3 Children's library
4 Seminar rooms
5 DDP operation office
6 Exhibition ramp
7 Convention hall lobby
8 VIP room
9 Exhibition gallery
10 Sport memorial
11 Relic park
12 Relic museum
13 Design gallery
14 Parking/loading dock entrance
15 Energy centre
16 Convention hall #1
17 Convention hall #2
18 Press room
19 Break-out space
20 Information/ticket centre
21 Retail area
22 Exhibition hall #1
23 Underground plaza
24 Information
25 Subway entrance
26 Parking facilities
27 Event hall
28 Energy centre
29 Storage

Level B2 floor plan

0 40m

DONGDAEMUN DESIGN PLAZA

The Dongdaemun Design Plaza is an architectural landscape that revolves around the ancient city wall and newly discovered cultural artefacts that form the central element of the composition linking the park and plaza together. The fluid design encourages the greatest degree of interaction between the park and the people of Seoul.

The new DDP park is a place for leisure, relaxation, and refuge, a green oasis within the busy urban surroundings of Dongdaemun. The design integrates the park and plaza seamlessly as one, blurring the boundary between architecture and nature in a continuous, fluid landscape that connects the city, park, and architecture. Voids and inflections in the park's surface give visitors glimpses into the innovative world of design below, making the DDP an important link between the city's contemporary culture, emerging nature, and history.

The design is the very specific result of how the context, local culture, programmatic requirements, and innovative engineering come together. The design blurs the boundaries between architecture and urban landscape, solid and void, interior and exterior. It is an architectural landscape where concepts of spatial flow are made real, creating a whole new kind of civic space for the city.

The façade cladding system is exemplary. Construction of the exterior envelope was a challenge as the cladding system consists of more than 45,000 panels in various sizes and degrees of curvature.

The DDP comprises a design museum, library, and educational facilities, while the park reinterprets the celebrated spatial concepts of traditional Korean garden design: layering, horizontality, blurring relationship between the interior and the exterior—with no single feature dominating the perspective. This approach is further informed by historic local painting traditions that depict grand visions of the ever-changing aspects of nature.

Location Seoul, Korea
Client Seoul Metropolitan Government / Seoul Design Foundation
Area 86,574 m² (931,875 ft²)
Date 2007–2014

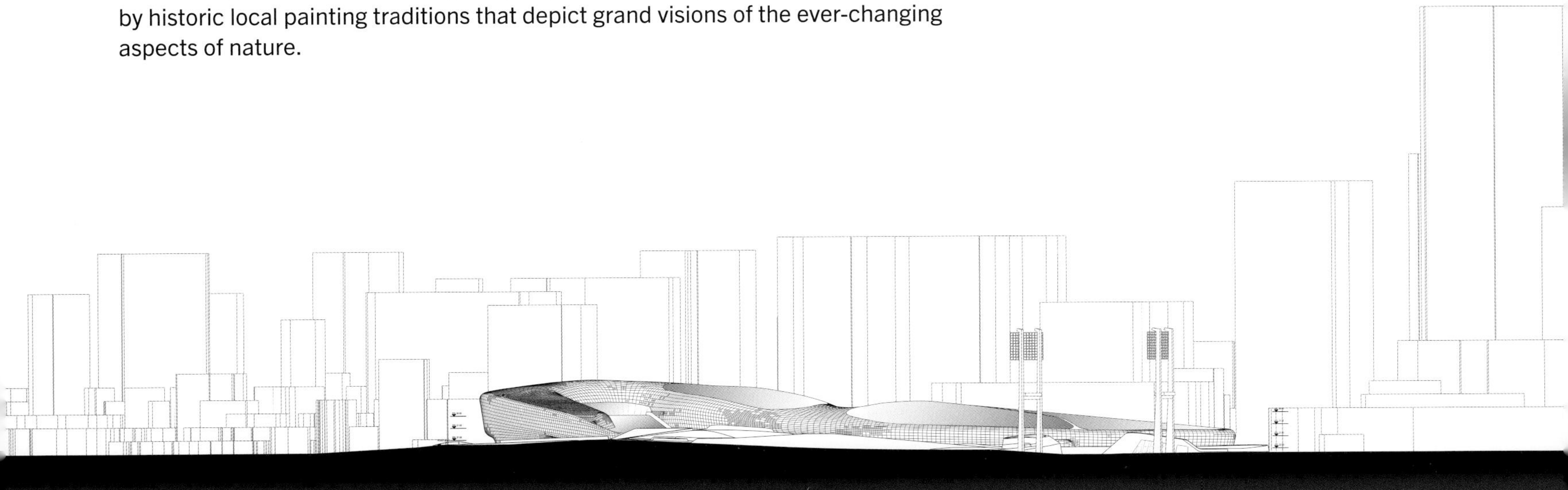

East elevation

maxtyle
holiday
hollys

60

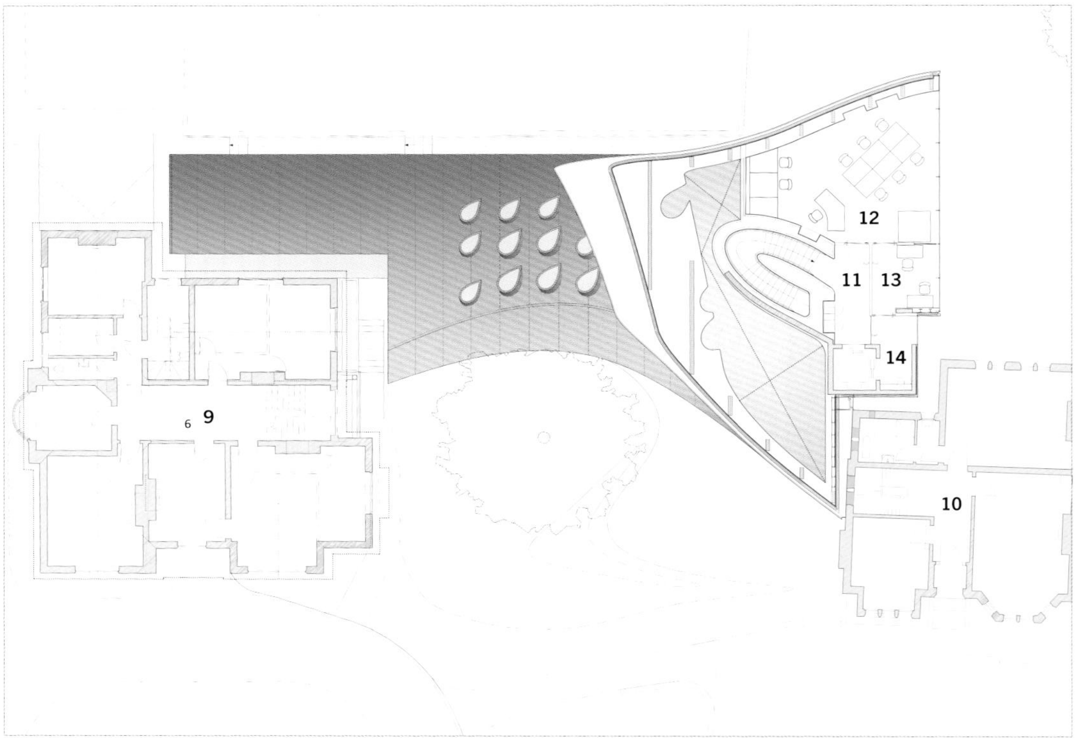

Second-floor plan

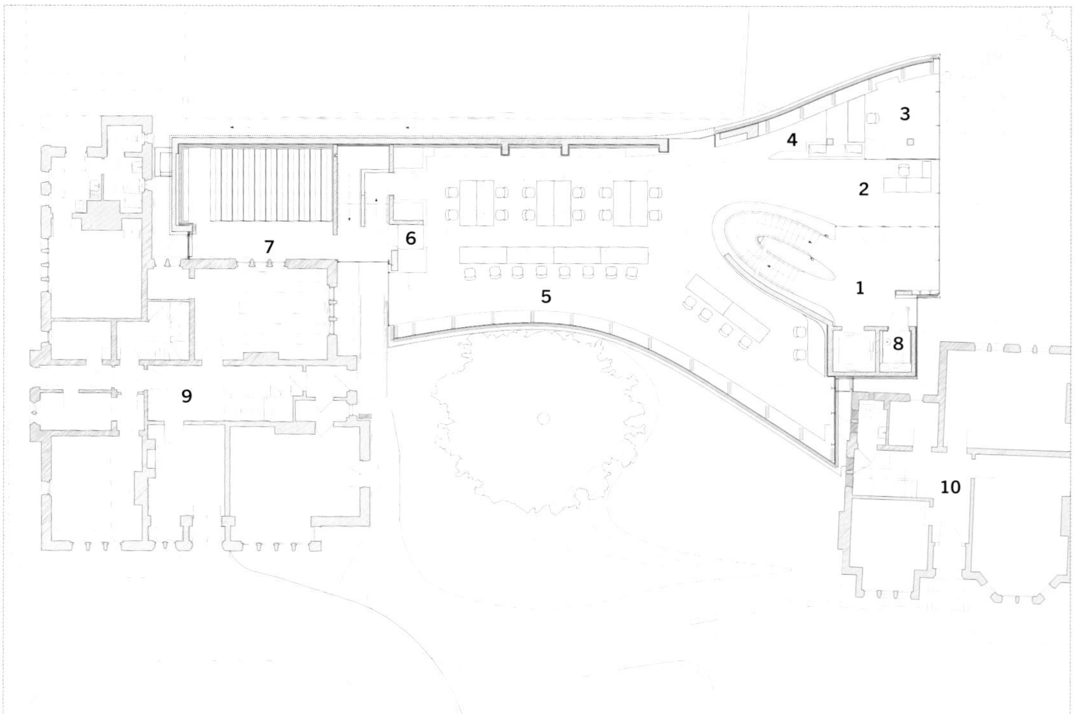

First-floor plan

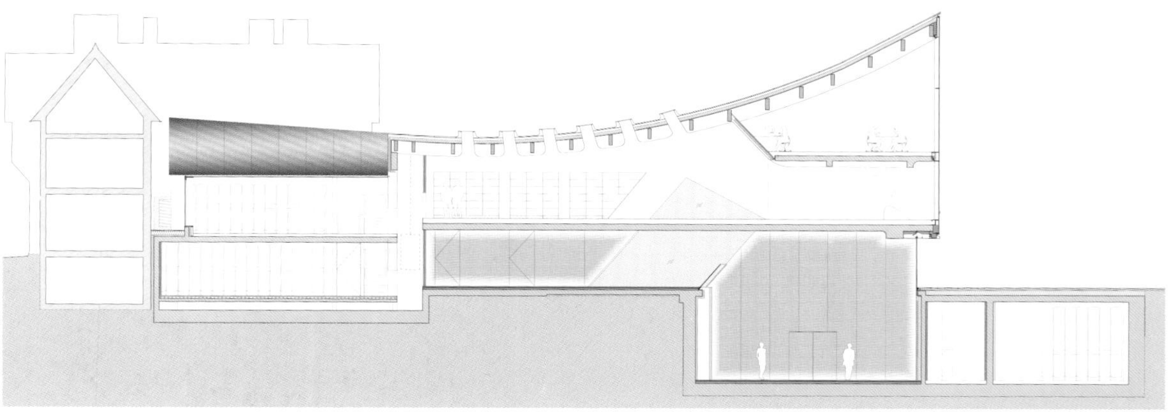

Section

1 First-floor hall
2 Circulation desk
3 Librarian's offfice
4 IT Resource
5 Library reading room
6 Book hoist
7 Library rolling stack
8 Toilets
9 68 Woodstock Road
10 66 Woodstock Road
11 Hall
12 Archive reading room
13 Archive office
14 Lift lobby

INVESTCORP BUILDING

Location Oxford, England
Client Oxford University
Area 1127 m^2 (12,131 ft^2)
Date 2013–2015

The Middle East Centre holds the University of Oxford's primary collection on the modern Middle East, a world-class archive of private papers and historic photographs used by scholars and researchers with an interest in the region. As an integral part of the college's on-going expansion plans, the new Investcorp Building for the Middle East Centre provides 1127 square metres (12,131 square feet) of additional floor space and a new 117-seat lecture theatre; doubling the space available for the Middle East Centre's expanding library and archive, with essential new facilities to meet the centre's increasing demand for research and academic activities. The new lecture theatre will allow the centre to expand its popular program of seminars, lectures and debates—much of which is open to both the university and the general public.

The Investcorp Building complements the college's ongoing development. Its design weaves through the restricted site at St Antony's College to connect and incorporate the existing protected buildings and trees, while its stainless steel façade softly reflects natural light to echo the building's context. The building integrates new academic and research facilities within a design defined by the existing built and natural environment of the college. The project maintains the detached character of the college's current buildings, allowing them to be read as separate elements, while introducing a contemporary building that conveys the past, present and future evolution of the college, university and city.

To the west, the project's scale defers to existing buildings of 66 and 68 Woodstock Road. The curved form of the library reading room's western façade accommodates the century-old Sequoia tree and its extensive root network; while a drainage system has been installed below the foundation slabs to ensure the tree receives enough moisture. To the east, the archive reading room and librarians' offices rise towards the height of the 1970 Brutalist Hilda Besse Building it faces, yet the new Investcorp Building remains below the roofline of the adjacent 66 Woodstock Road.

The new lecture theatre is located below ground and is ventilated through a thermal labyrinth. A similar labyrinth exists beneath the library archive room to achieve the essential environmental controls and mitigate the need for mechanical air-handling. A ground-source heat pump provides active ground coupling controlled for both temperature and humidity, creating a secure environment to conserve the centre's renowned collection.

The work of the Middle East Centre contributes to the global discourse and greater understanding of the region. The new Investcorp Building connects disparate buildings within the college, defining a series of spaces for the centre's renowned archive, library and seminar program; allowing the Middle East Centre to expand its commitment as a vital forum of research, understanding and open debate.

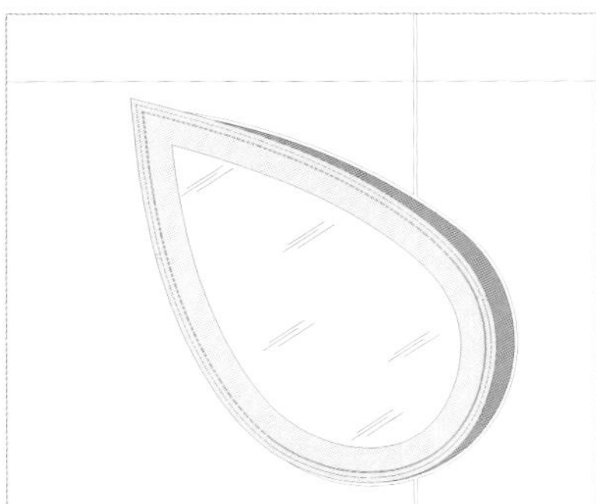

Skylight detail

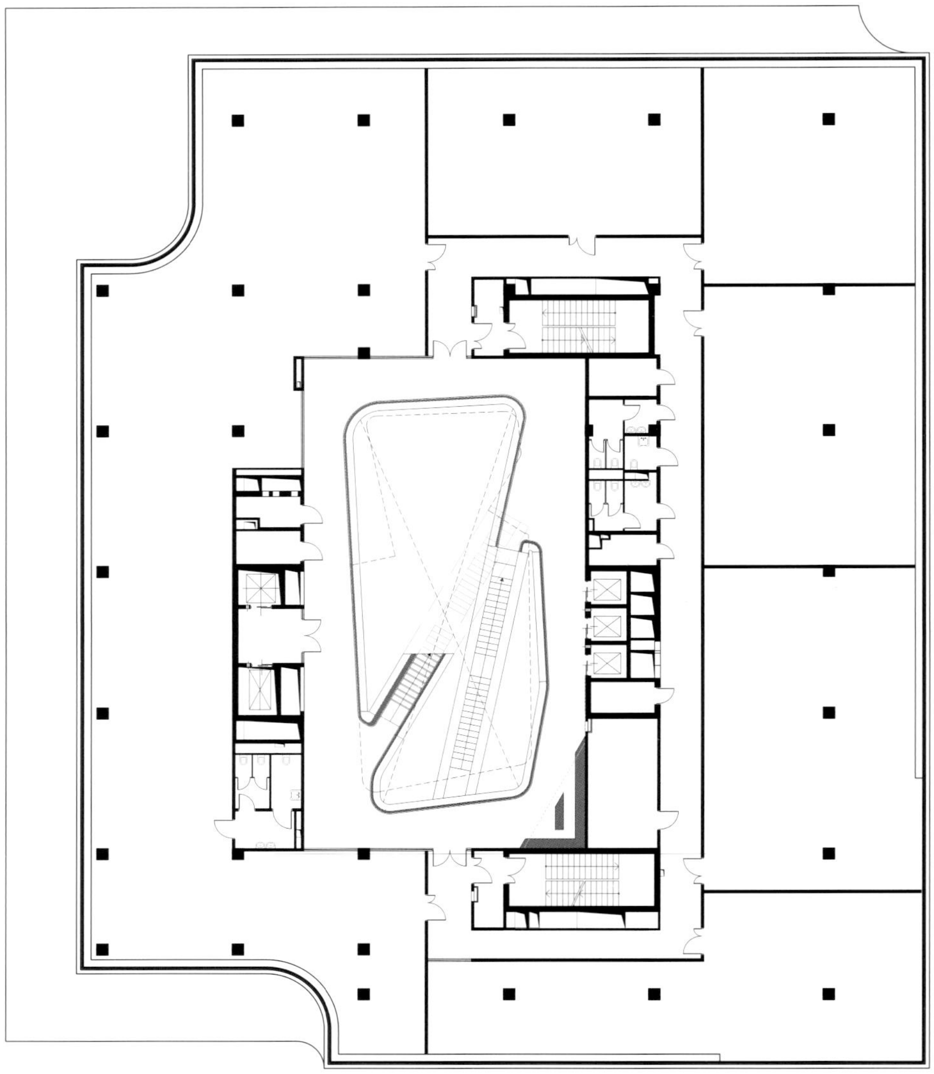

Third-foor plan

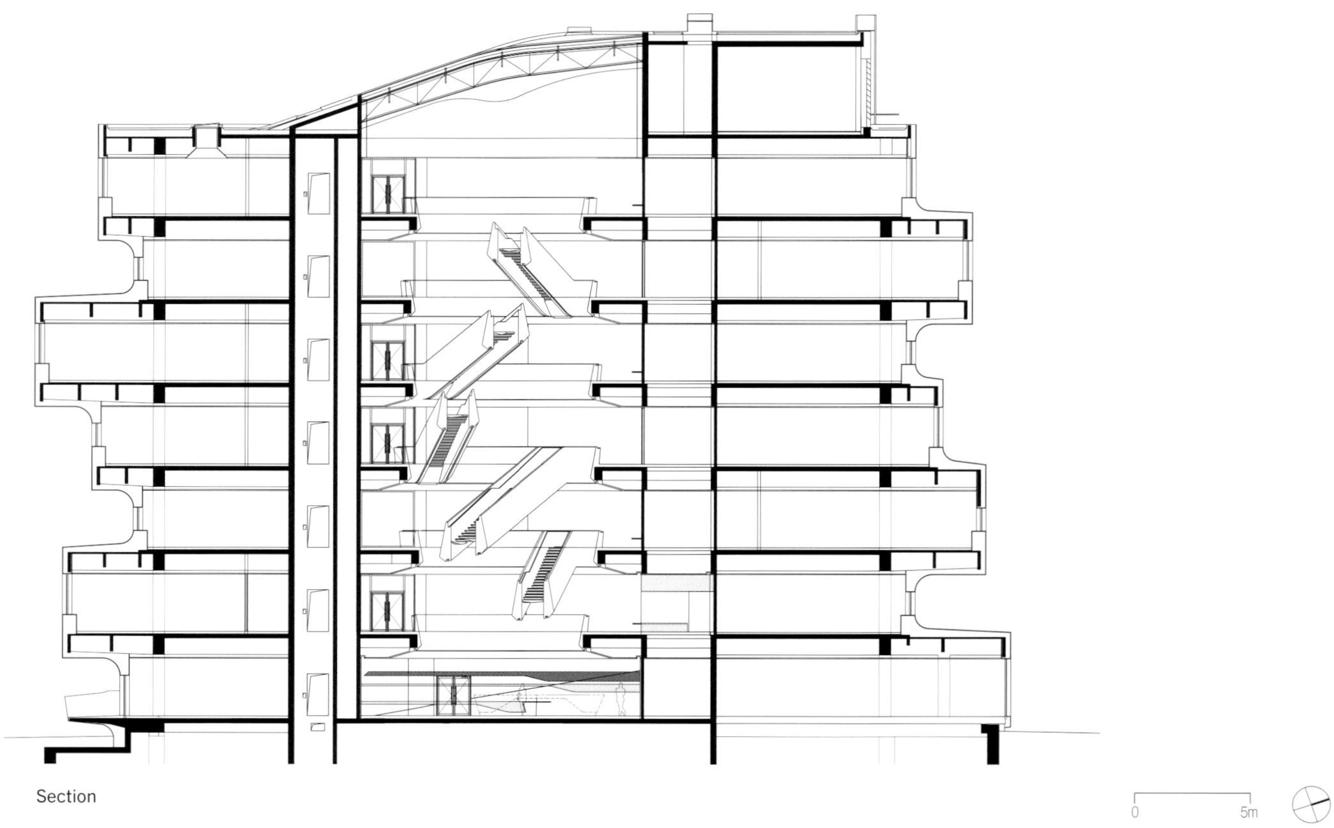

Section

DOMINION OFFICE BUILDING

Located in Moscow's Sharikopodshipnikovskaya Street, the Dominion Office Building is among the first of the new projects to be built for the growing creative and IT sectors in this primarily industrial and residential district in the southeast of the city.

Conceived as a series of vertically stacked plates offset at each level with connecting curved elements, a central atrium rises through all levels to bring natural light into the centre of the building. Balconies at each level project into the atrium and correspond to the displacement of the outer envelope, and a series of staircases interconnect through this central space.

With the ground-floor restaurant linking the atrium to the outdoor terrace and Sharikopodshipnikovskaya Street beyond, and coffee/snack areas and relaxation zones on the balconies, the atrium becomes a shared space over many levels that encourages interaction between the employees of the different companies within the building. This integration also encourages collaboration between companies of different services and disciplines. Many IT and creative-industry start-up companies regard this collective research culture as vital for progress and development.

The office spaces are arranged within a system of standard rectilinear bays to offer many different possibilities for small, expanding or large companies. Located on the periphery of the atrium and housing the lifts, fire escapes, washrooms and service shafts, the service cores provide a degree of privacy from the separate office spaces, with gaps in-between these cores giving some transparency and allowing light to penetrate into the office areas from the central shared atrium space. This service core ring around the atrium, together with an additional bay of columns close to the outer envelope of the building, provides the central structure. In some areas, columns are removed and replaced with transfer beams to increase the uninterrupted floor space for larger tenants or public programs.

Location Moscow, Russia
Client Peresvet Group/Dominion-M Ltd
Area 21,184 m^2 (228,022 ft^2)
Date 2012–2015

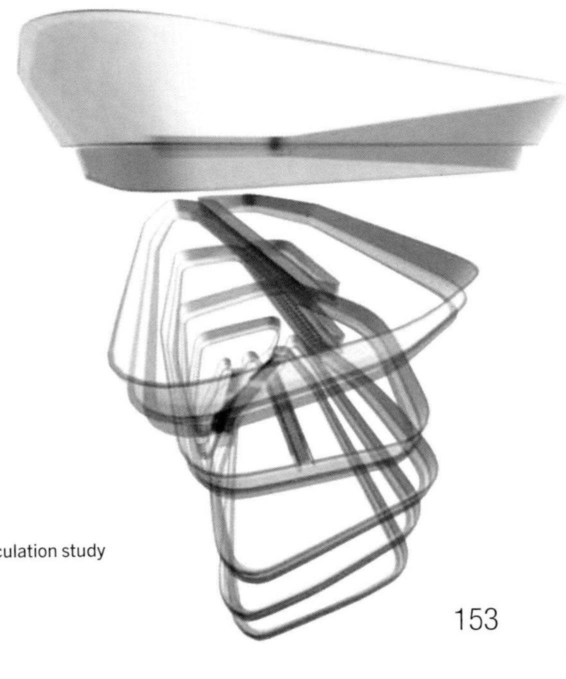

Circulation study

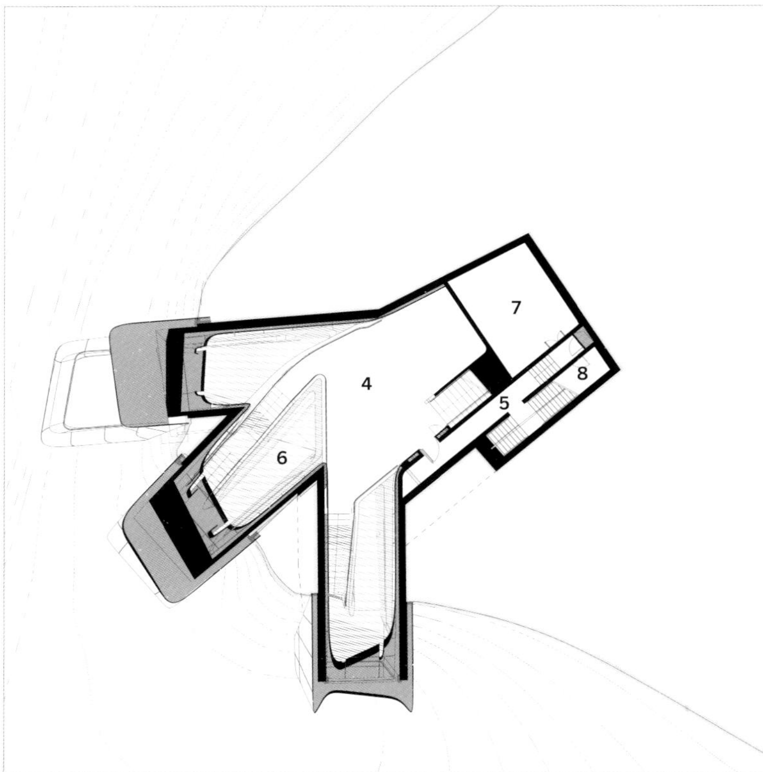

Second-underground-floor plan

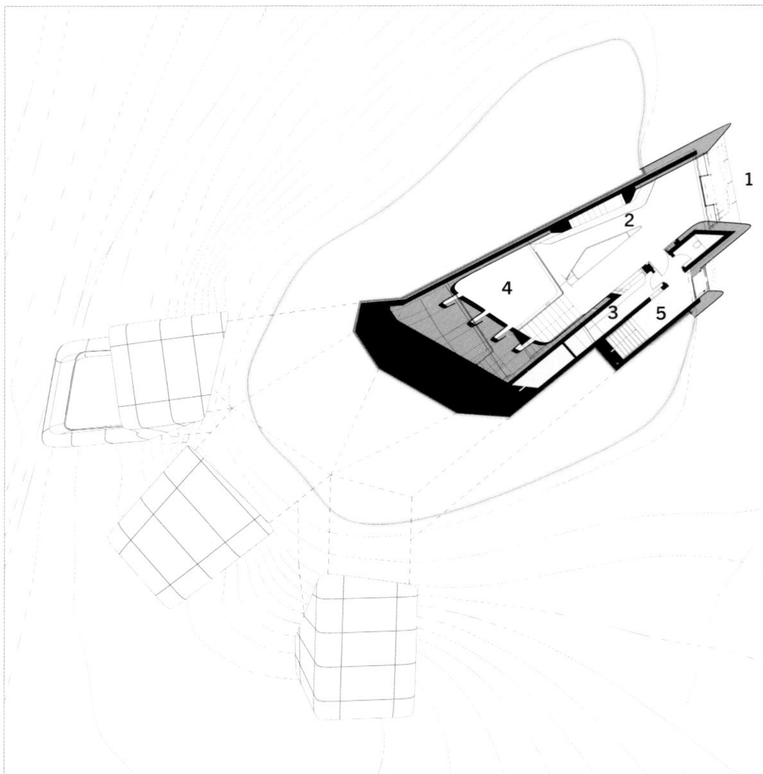

Ground-floor plan

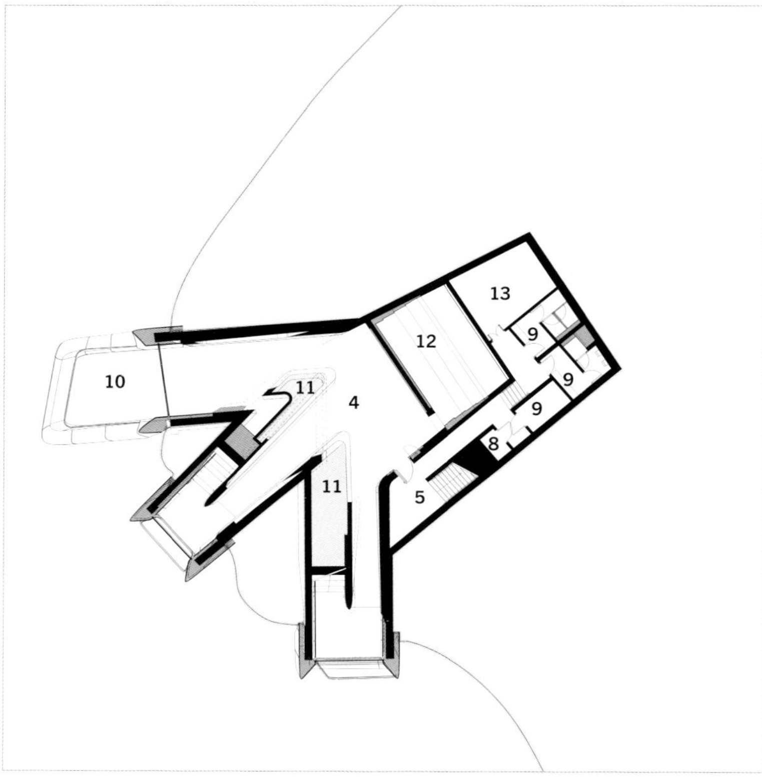

First-underground-floor plan

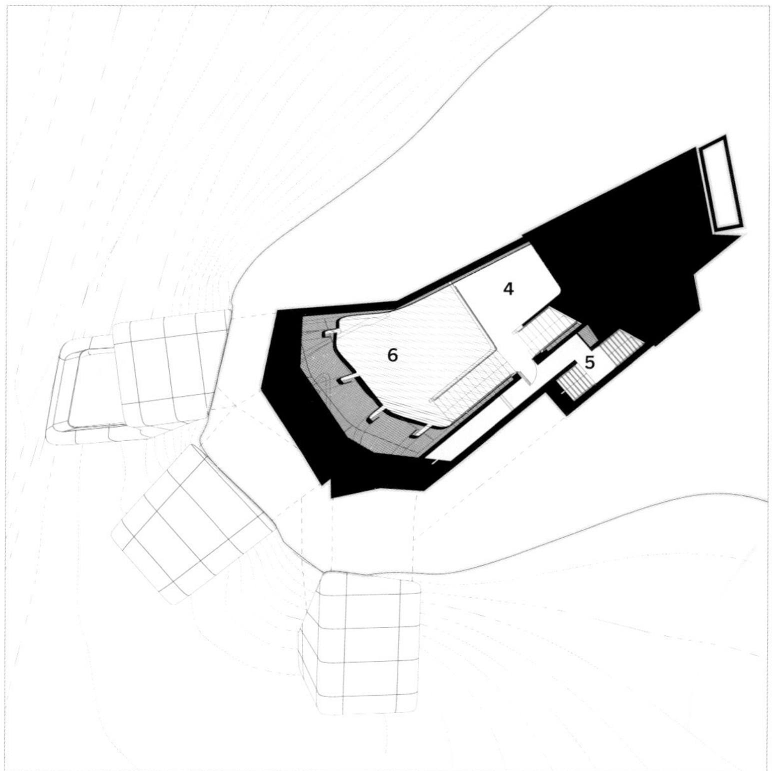

Third-underground-floor plan

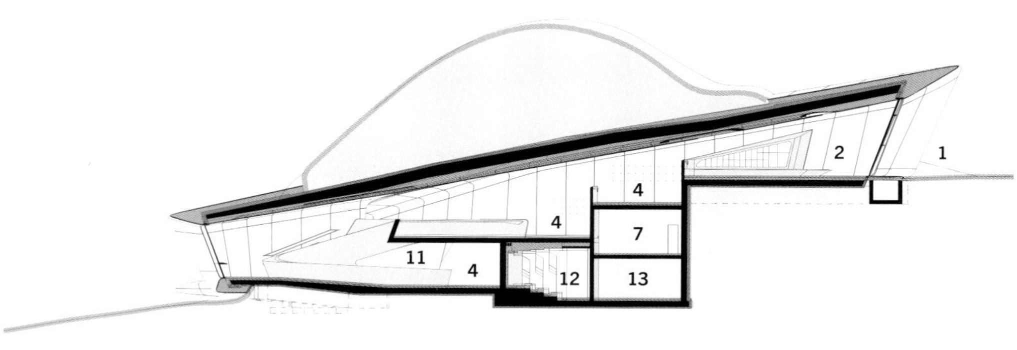

Longitudinal section

1 Main entrance
2 Lockers
3 Ticket counter
4 Exhibition area
5 Escape staircase
6 Void
7 Plant room
8 Storage
9 Toilets
10 Terrace
11 Display cases
12 Cinema
13 Main storage

0 10m

MESSNER MOUNTAIN MUSEUM CORONES

Embedded within the summit of Mount Kronplatz, 2275 metres above sea level at South Tyrol's most popular ski resort, here, visitors can descend within the mountain to explore the museum's caverns and grottos, before emerging through the mountain wall on the other side, out onto the terrace overhanging the valley far below with spectacular, panoramic views.

The museum's structure has walls between 40 and 50 centimetres (15 and 20 inches) thick, and most of its exterior and interior panels are made from in-situ reinforced concrete, with a formwork of tapered surfaces used to generate the peaks and abutments of the exterior panels that convey the shards of rock and ice formations of the surrounding landscape. The museum's roof, which supports excavated and replaced earth and rock that embeds the museum into the mountain, is up to 70 centimetres (28 inches) thick, helping to maintain a more constant internal temperature. A scaffold of steel sections with adjustable brackets to offset tolerances forms the museum's substructure. Counter-plates for the connecting brackets are laminated directly within each panel during the prefabrication process.

Reflecting the lighter colours and tones of the jagged limestone peaks of the surrounding Dolomites, the exterior panels are formed from a lighter shade of glass-reinforced fibre concrete and fold within the museum to meet the darker interior panels that have the luster and colouration of anthracite found deep below the surface. A series of staircases, like waterfalls in a mountain stream, cascade through the museum to connect the exhibition spaces and describe visitors' circulation over three levels. At the lowest level, visitors traverse through the galleries, drawn by the wide windows allowing natural light, to emerge out onto the cantilevered terrace that projects 6 metres (20 feet) from the mountainside, giving a 240-degree panorama across the Alps and over the valley far below.

Location South Tyrol, Italy
Client Skirama Kronplatz/Plan de Corones
Area 1000 m^2 10,764 ft^2)
Date 2013–2015

Mountains are finite and fragile.

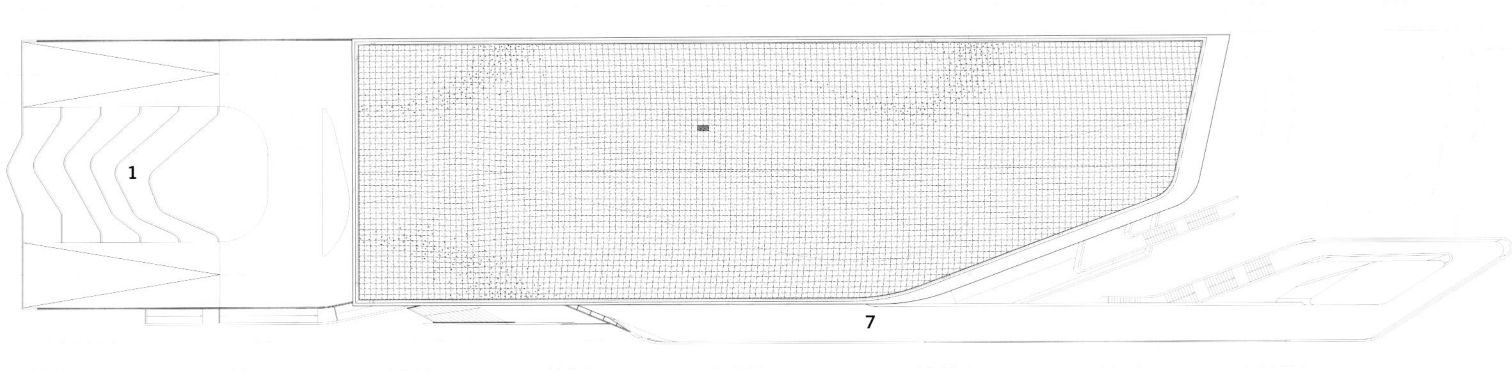

Roof plan

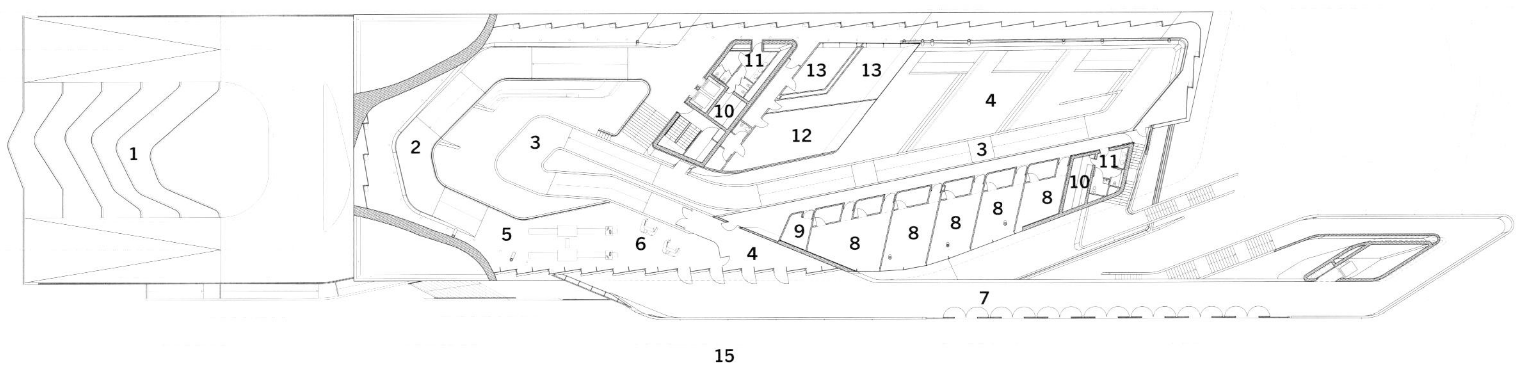

First-floor plan

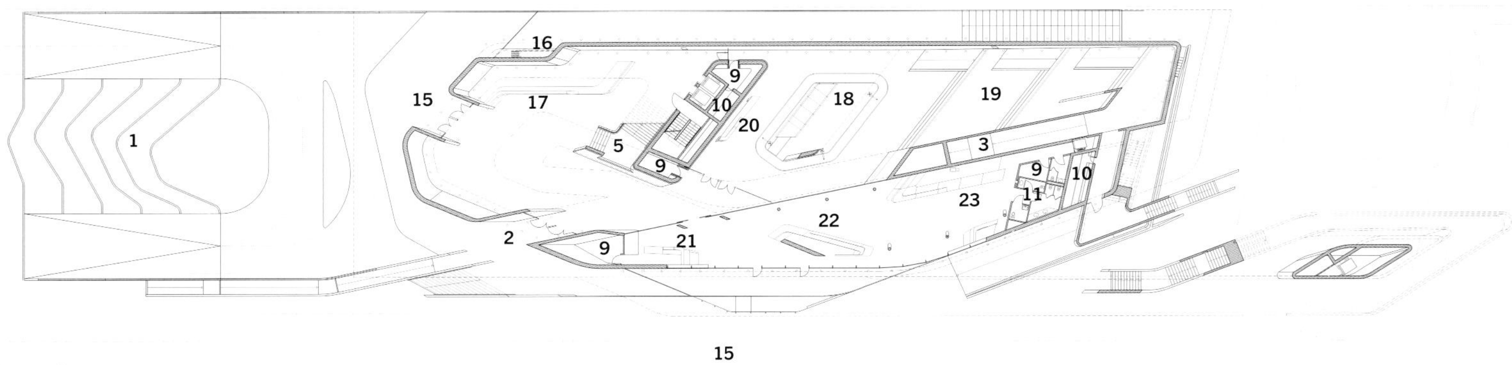

Ground-floor plan

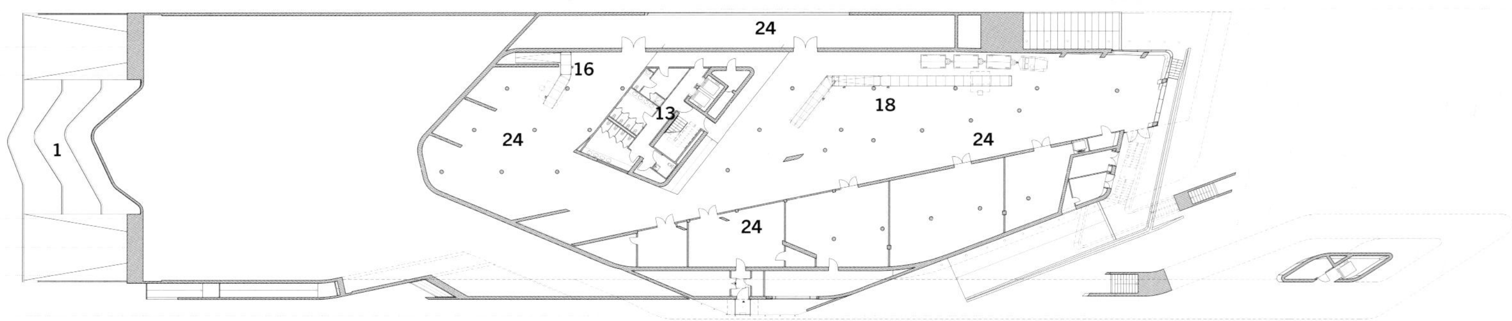

Underground-floor plan

1 Access ramp
2 Departure ramps
3 Arrivals ramp
4 Arrivals hall
5 Departure hall
6 Passport control
7 Boarding bridge
8 Offices
9 Storage
10 Shaft
11 Toilets
12 Surgery
13 Control room
14 Mooring quay
15 Entrance
16 Conveyor belt | check-in
17 Check-in
18 Conveyor belt | arrivals
19 Arrivals lounge
20 Customs
21 Ticketing
22 Information
23 Bar
24 Plant rooms

0 10m

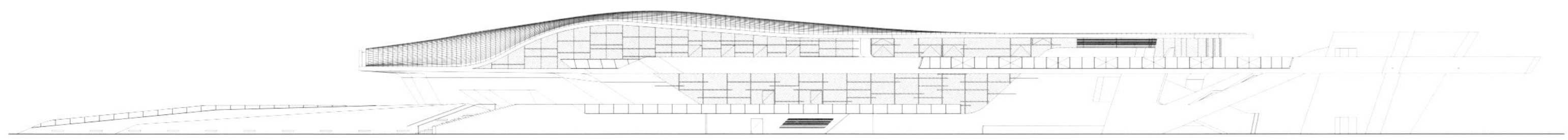

Elevation

MARITIME TERMINAL SALERNO

The new Salerno maritime terminal by Zaha Hadid Architects is integral to the city's urban plan, which targeted the development of essential projects and programs for the social, economic and environmental regeneration of the city. Located on the public quay that extends into Salerno's working harbour and marina, the new maritime terminal continues the city's relationship with the sea and establishes new links; connecting Salerno's rich maritime traditions with its historic urban fabric and beyond to the hills that frame the city.

Like an oyster, the terminal's hard, asymmetric shell protects the softer elements within; sheltering passengers from the intense Mediterranean sun during the popular tourist season.

The new maritime terminal is composed of three primary interlocking components: administration offices for national border controls and shipping lines; the terminal for international ferries and cruise ships from around the world; and the terminal for the local and regional ferries.

The quayside gently rises as passengers approach the terminal from the city, indicating the gradually sloping path of ramps within the building, which raise passengers to the embarking level of large ships and ferries. The terminal's interior arrangement orientates and leads passengers through a sequence of interior spaces that flow into each other and are organised around focal points, such as the restaurant and the waiting lounge.

Local and regional ferry commuters move through the terminal quickly, arriving at ground level and ascending via ramps to reach the upper and vessel entrance. Passengers travelling on international ferries and cruise ships are guided seamlessly through check-in, passport, security and customs controls to their ship. Arriving passengers follow a similar progression through the terminal with the inclusion of the luggage reclaim area.

At night, the glow of the terminal near the harbour entrance will act as a lighthouse to the port, welcoming visitors to the city.

The new terminal operates, both functionally and visually, as a smooth transition between land and sea; a coastal land formation that mediates between solid and liquid. From its terraces and windows, the terminal offers spectacular views of the Amalfi Coast, the Gulf of Salerno and the Cilento.

The new Salerno Maritime Terminal will enable the port of Salerno to increase arrivals of ferry and cruise ships by 500,000 additional passengers each year, which would create up to 2000 new jobs in the city's hospitality, services and retail sectors.

Location Salerno, Italy
Client Comune di Salerno Palazzo di Citta'
Area 4500 m^2 (48,438 ft^2)
Date 2000–2016

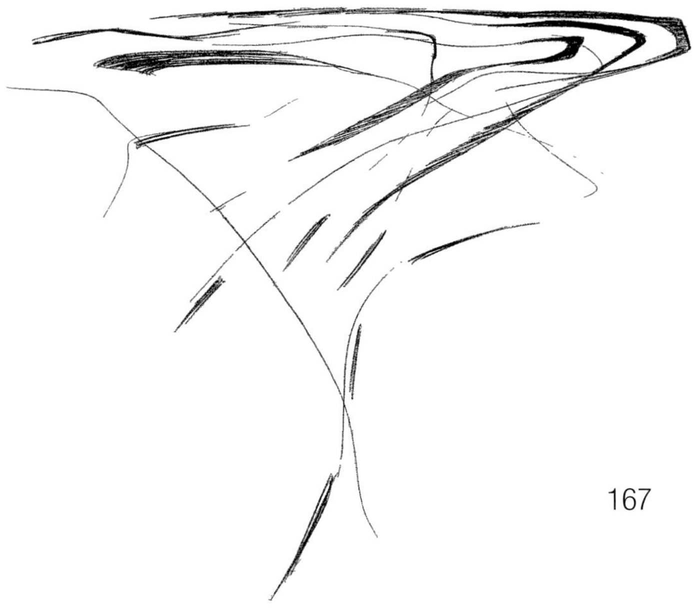

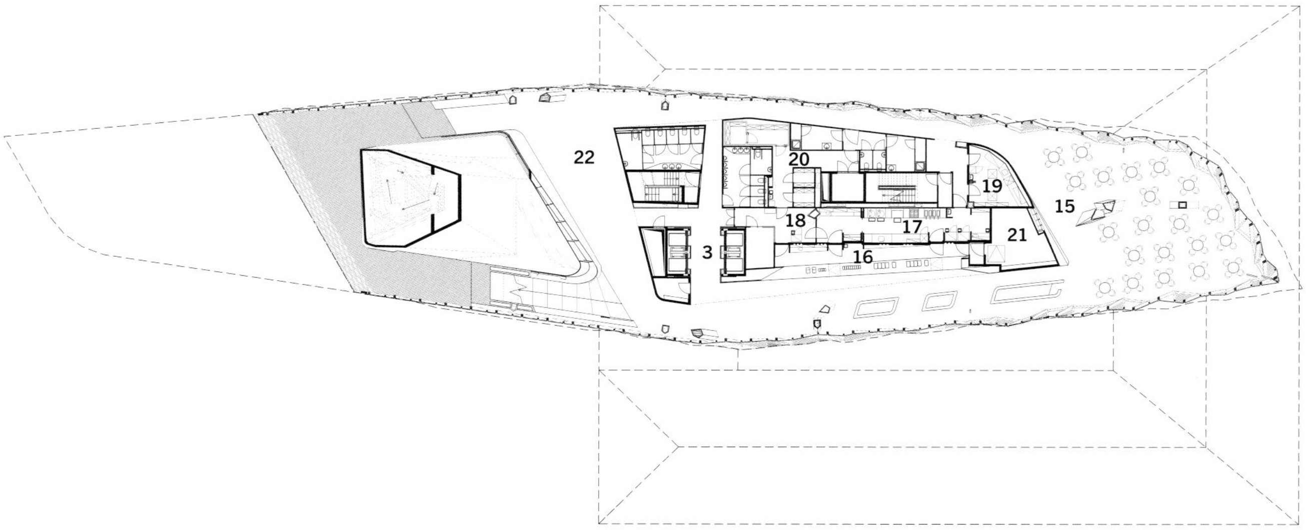

Sixth-floor plan

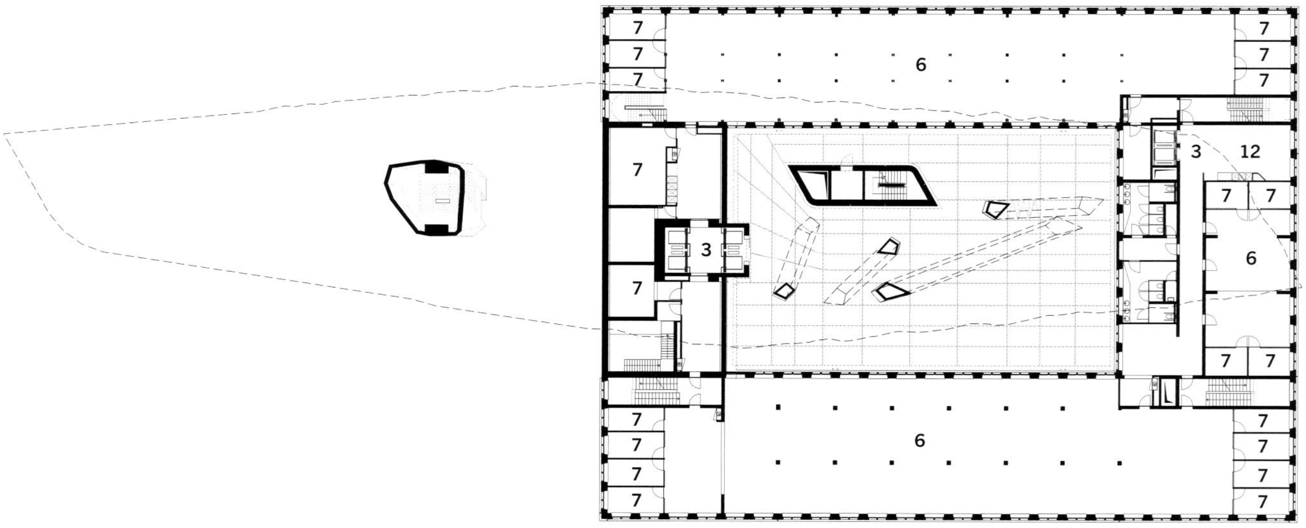

Second-floor plan

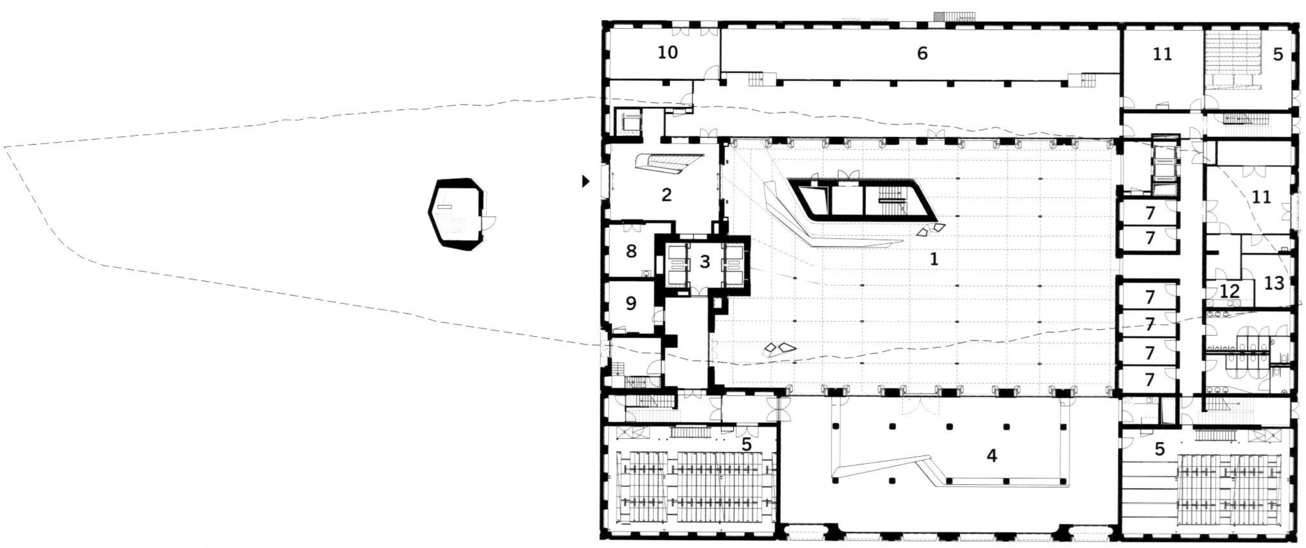

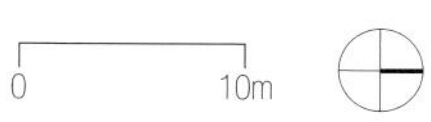

Ground-floor plan

1 Courtyard
2 Main entrance hall
3 Lift lobby
4 Libray
5 Archive
6 Offices
7 Meeting room
8 First aid
9 Lockers
10 Print room
11 Storage
12 Coffe corner
13 Control room
14 UPS/Data/Local
15 Restaurant
16 Self-service counter
17 Cold kitchen
18 Warm kitchen
19 Washing-up
20 Kitchen storage
21 Technical room
22 Foyer

PORT HOUSE

The new Port House in Antwerp repurposes and extends a derelict fire station into the city's new port headquarters. The design is an elevated extension that 'floats' above the old building, respecting each of the old façades. Like the bow of a ship, the new extension points towards the Scheldt, connecting the building with the river on which Antwerp was founded.

The new extension's façade is a glazed surface that ripples like waves and reflects the changing tones and colours of the city's sky. The building's sparkling appearance reinterprets Antwerp's moniker as the city of diamonds, and its carefully cut form changes its appearance with the shifting intensity of daylight. Triangular facets allow the apparently smooth curves at either end of the building to be formed with flat sheets of glass. They also facilitate the gradual transition from a flat façade at the building's south end to a rippling surface at the north. A calibrated mix of translucent and opaque facets ensures sufficient sunlight within the building and controls solar load for optimal working conditions; the alternation of the façade panels breaks down the extension's volume, giving panoramic views of its surroundings, as well as providing enclosure.

The old fire station's central courtyard has been enclosed with a glass roof and is transformed into the main reception area for the new Port House. From this central atrium, visitors access the historic public reading room and library within the newly restored fire truck hall. Panoramic lifts provide direct access to the new extension with an external bridge between the existing building and new extension giving panoramic views of the city and port. An activity-based office structure is integrated within the design, with common areas such as the restaurant, meeting rooms and auditorium located at the centre of the upper levels of the existing building and the bottom floors of the new extension; the remaining floors more remote from the centre, comprise open plan offices.

Despite the challenges of integrating with a protected historic building, high standards in sustainable design were achieved, including a bore-hole energy system, waterless lavatory fittings and motion detectors to minimise water consumption and building automation and optimal daylight to minimise artificial lighting.

Location Antwerp, Belgium
Client Antwerp Port Authority
Area 12,800 m^2 (137,778 ft^2)
Date 2009–2016

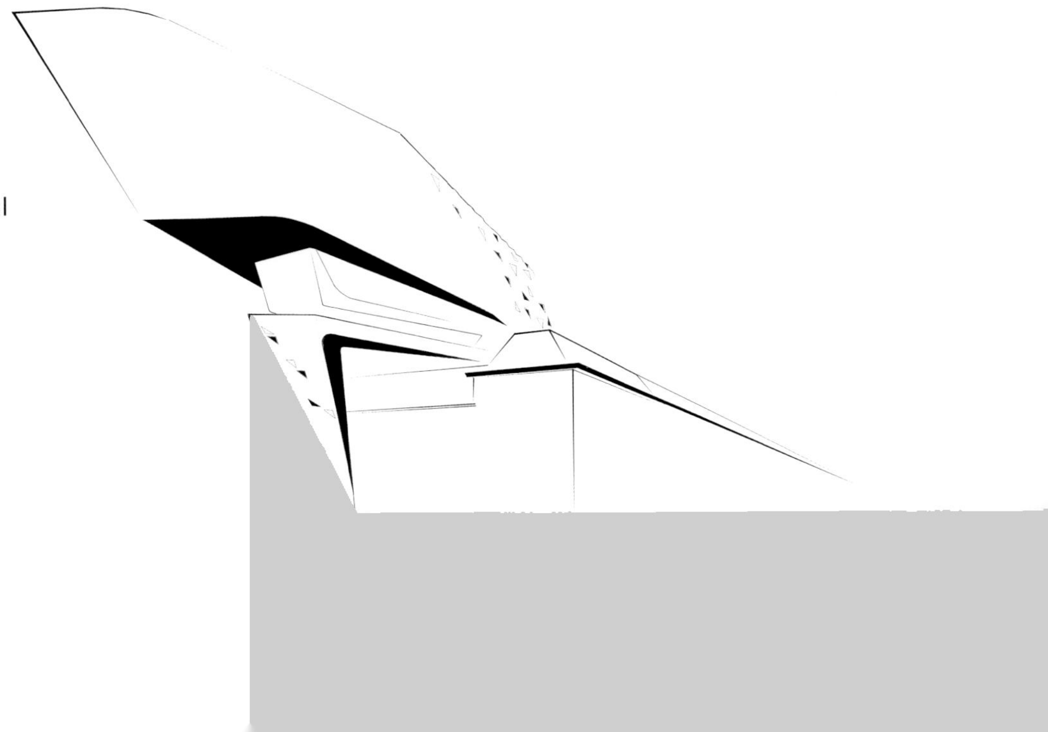

MAES

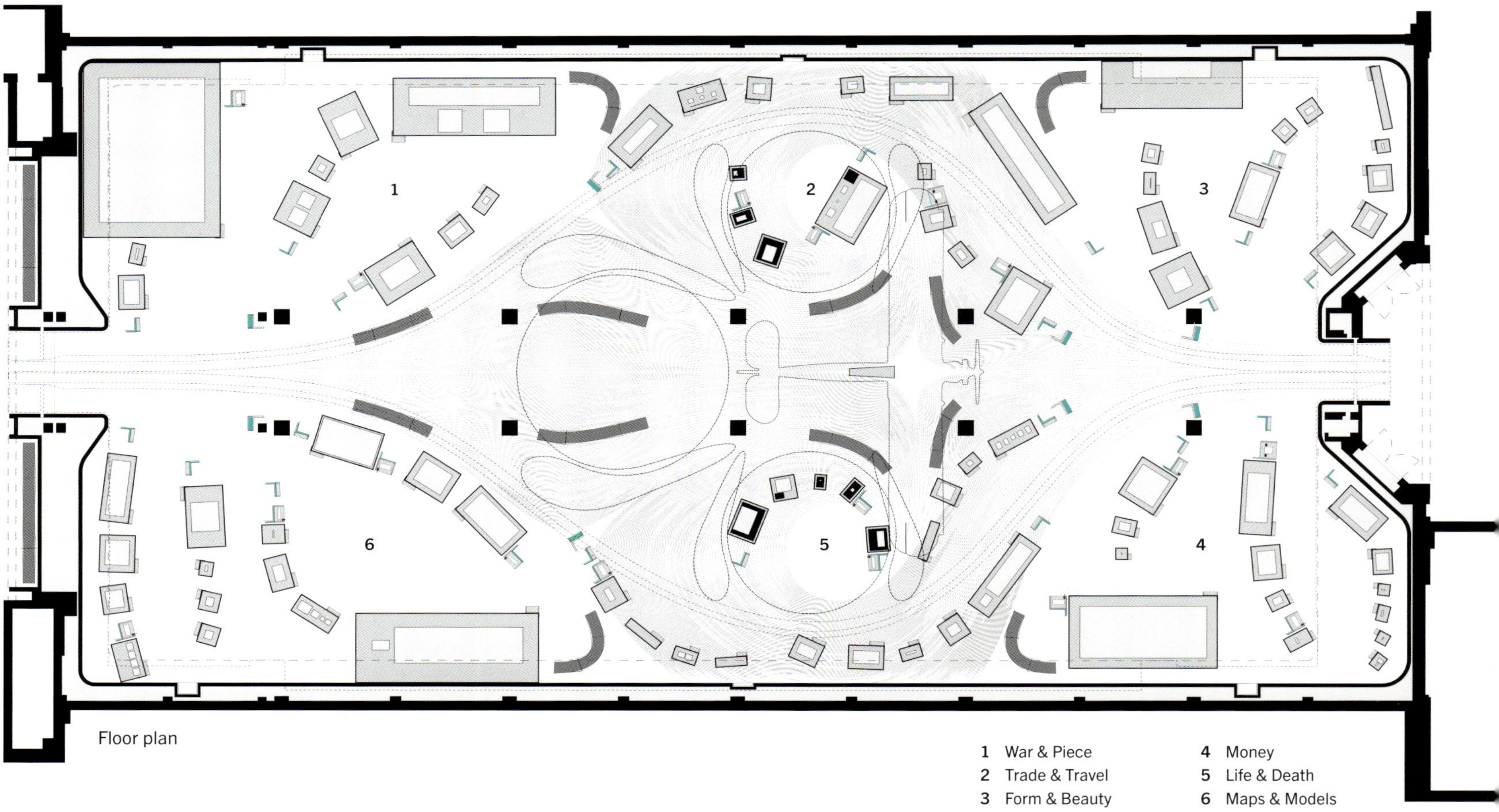

Floor plan

1 War & Piece
2 Trade & Travel
3 Form & Beauty
4 Money
5 Life & Death
6 Maps & Models

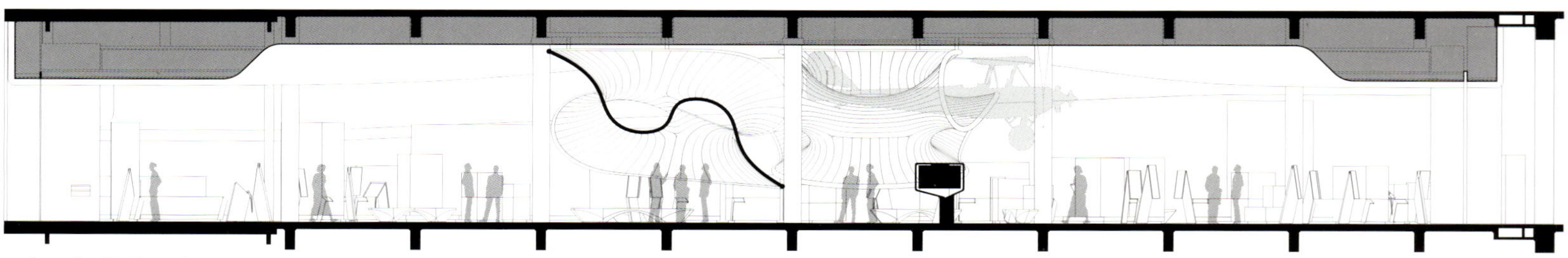

Longitudinal section

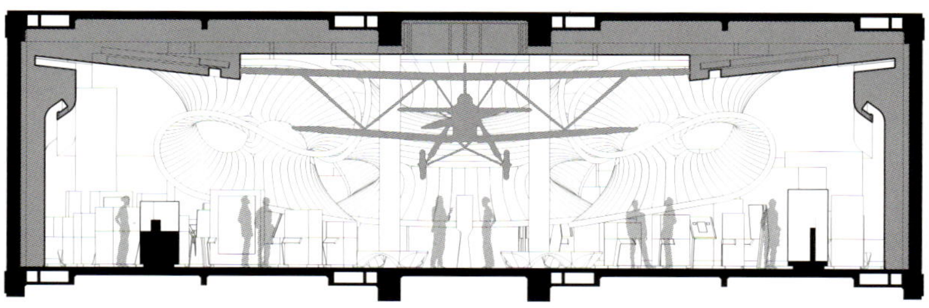

Short section

0 5m

MATHEMATICS: THE WINTON GALLERY

In December 2016 the Science Museum opened an inspirational new mathematics gallery, designed by Zaha Hadid Architects. Mathematics: The Winton Gallery brings together remarkable stories, historical artefacts and design to highlight the central role of mathematical practice in all our lives, and explores how mathematicians, their tools and ideas have helped build the modern world over the past four centuries.

More than 100 treasures from the Science Museum's world-class science, technology, engineering and mathematics collections have been selected to tell powerful stories about how mathematics has shaped, and been shaped by, some of our most fundamental human concerns—from trade and travel to war, peace, life, death, form and beauty.

Curator Dr David Rooney said, "At its heart this gallery reveals a rich cultural story of human endeavour that has helped transform the world over the last four hundred years. Mathematical practice underpins so many aspects of our lives and work, and we hope that bringing together these remarkable stories, people and exhibits will inspire visitors to think about the role of mathematics in a new light."

Positioned at the centre of the gallery is the Handley Page 'Gugnunc' aeroplane, built in 1929 for a competition to construct safe aircraft. Ground-breaking aerodynamic research influenced the wing design of this experimental aeroplane, helping to shift public opinion about the safety of flying and to secure the future of the aviation industry. This aeroplane encapsulates the gallery's overarching theme, illustrating how mathematical practice has helped solve real-world problems and in this instance paved the way for the safe passenger flights that we rely on today.

Location London, United Kingdom
Client Science Museum
Area 913 m^2 (9827 ft^2)
Date 2014–2016

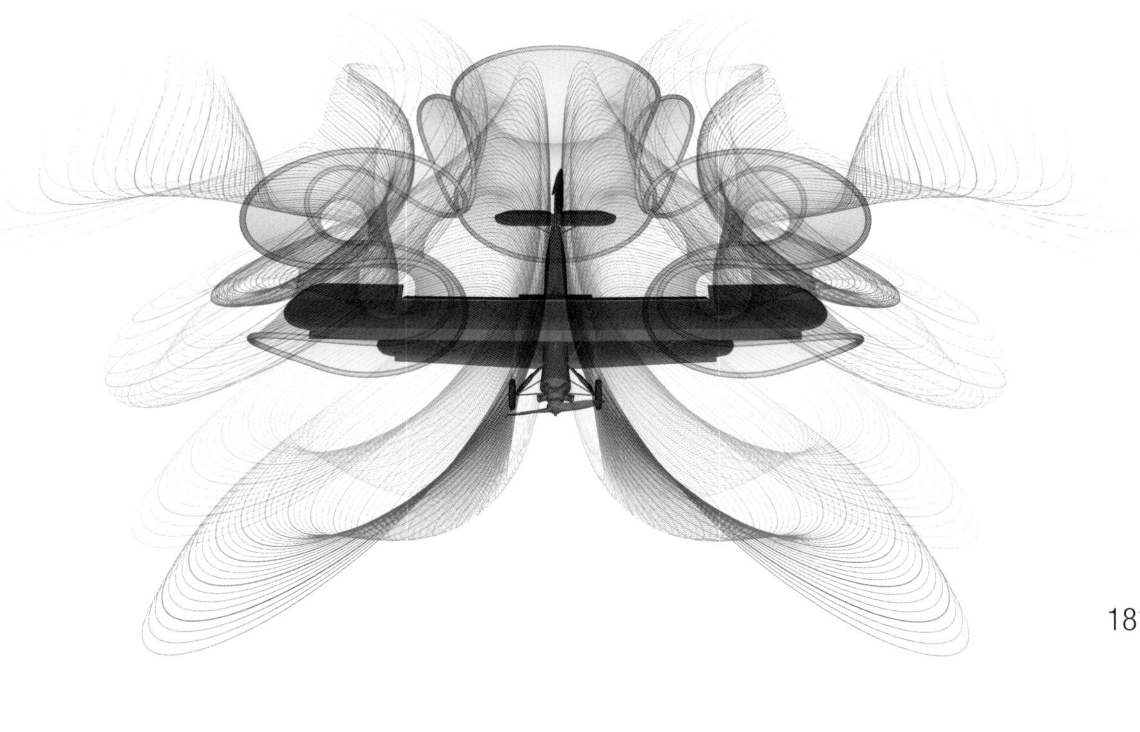

LIFE AND DEATH
We have created remarkable medical tools and techniques to cure illness, ease pain and live longer.
In parallel we use mathematics to spot trends, understand statistics and help people reach their life's potential, as well as make provisions for the inevitable end.

TRADE AND TRAVEL
The modern global economy is based on our ability to trade with other countries, ship vast quantities of goods, and travel readily around the world.
Mathematics has underpinned this activity for centuries, whether helping us navigate safely, design efficient ships, communicate in private or transact goods fairly.

IN PROGRESS

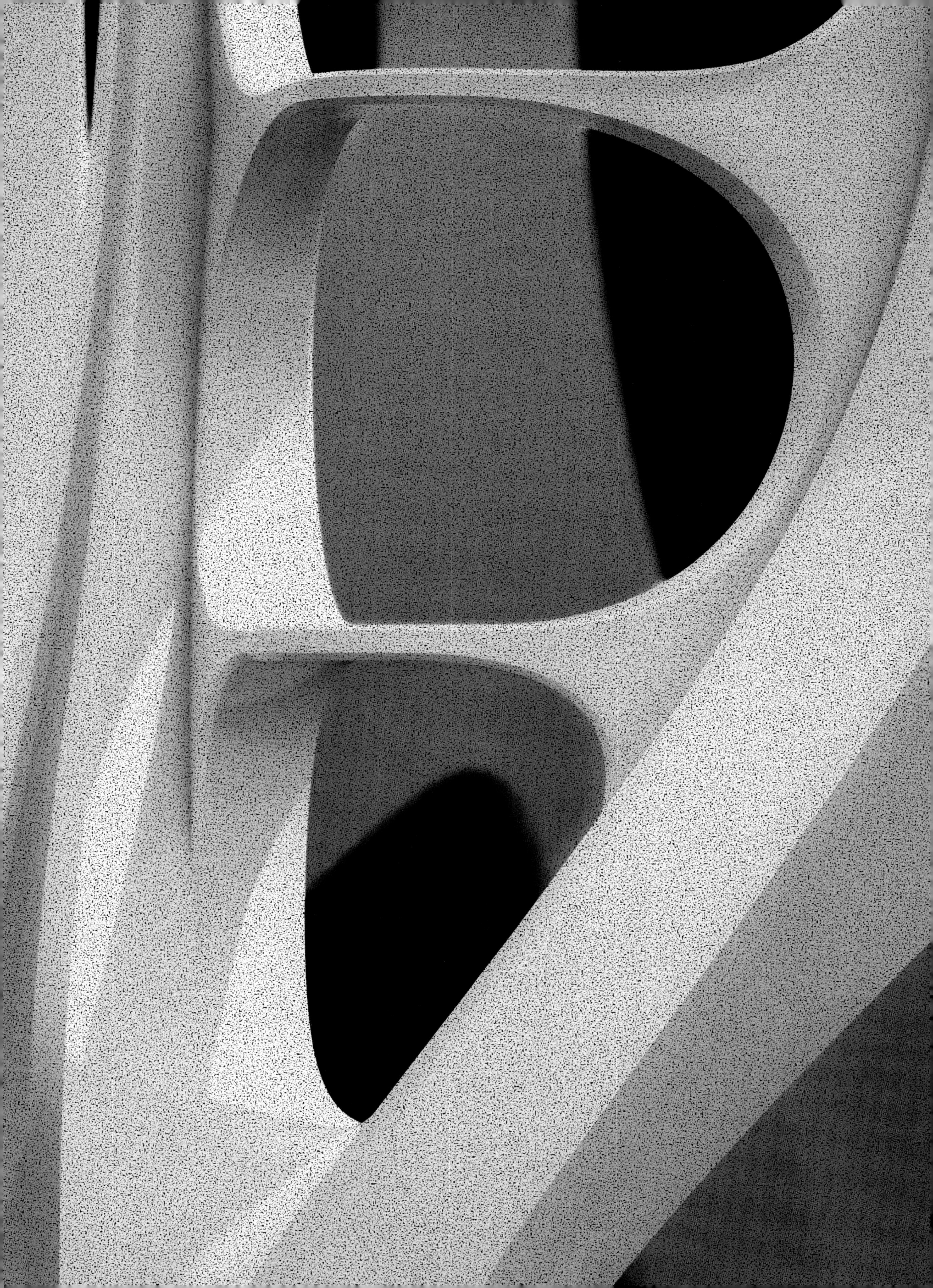

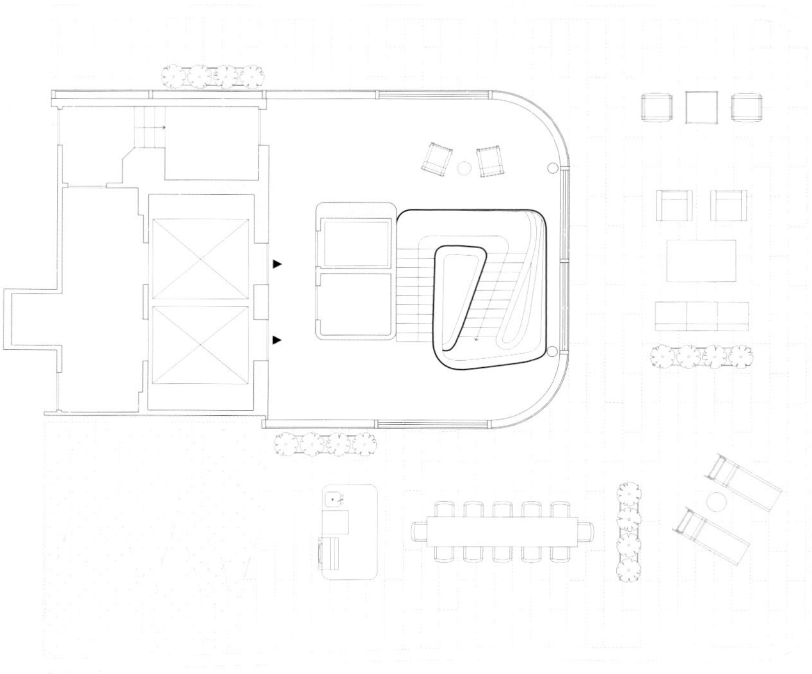

Floor plan roof level (residence 37)

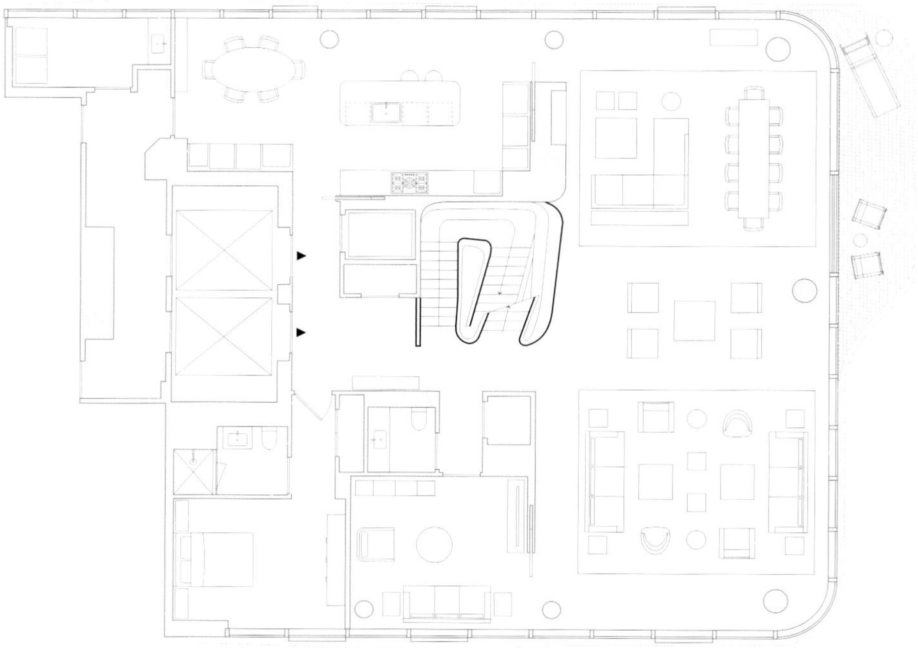

Floor plan upper level (residence 37)

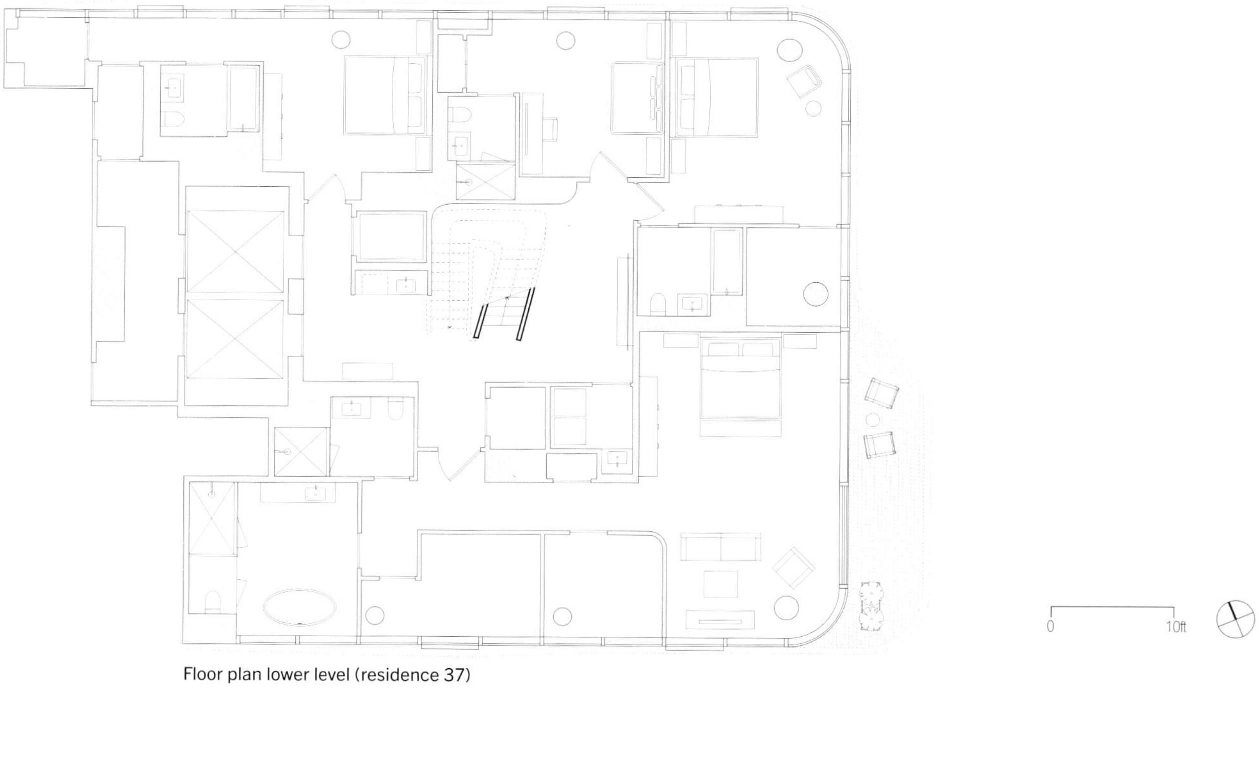

Floor plan lower level (residence 37)

520 WEST 28TH STREET

520 West 28th Street is located in the heart of West Chelsea's thriving arts district and is the first residential building in New York that was designed by Zaha Hadid. Stretching from Whitney Museum at its south to Hudson Yards at its north, this highly anticipated design takes a sculptural sensibility that is inherent to Zaha Hadid's style, instead of the city's traditionally rectangular residential landscape. The 11-storey development, with 21 interlaced floors, features 39 distinctive residences of up to a sprawling 594 square metres (6390 square feet) and ceiling heights up to nearly 3.3 metres (11 feet).

This project demonstrates Zaha Hadid's seamless vision for residential interiors that reflect the distinctive nature of the exterior façade. The building's organic curve and chevron patterns on the outside create generous outdoor spaces and enhance the privacy between residences, simultaneously merging and separating the interior and exterior. Each residence will also feature a distinct Zaha Hadid sculptural element that creates dramatic feature walls, ensuring that every apartment has a profound design statement in its interiors. 520 West 28th Street is also strategically situated on the High Line, within two blocks from Hudson Yards development—the innovative combination of 5.5 hectares (14 acres) of open public space with a new arts venue known as The Culture Shed. For residents, this wholly unique and contemporary project will augment the West Chelsea precinct, and create dynamism in one of Manhattan's most exciting neighborhoods with its unique combination of lifestyle services and amenities.

Location New York, United States
Client Related Companies
Area 1700– 5500 m^2 (18,299– 59,202 ft^2)
Date 2014–2017

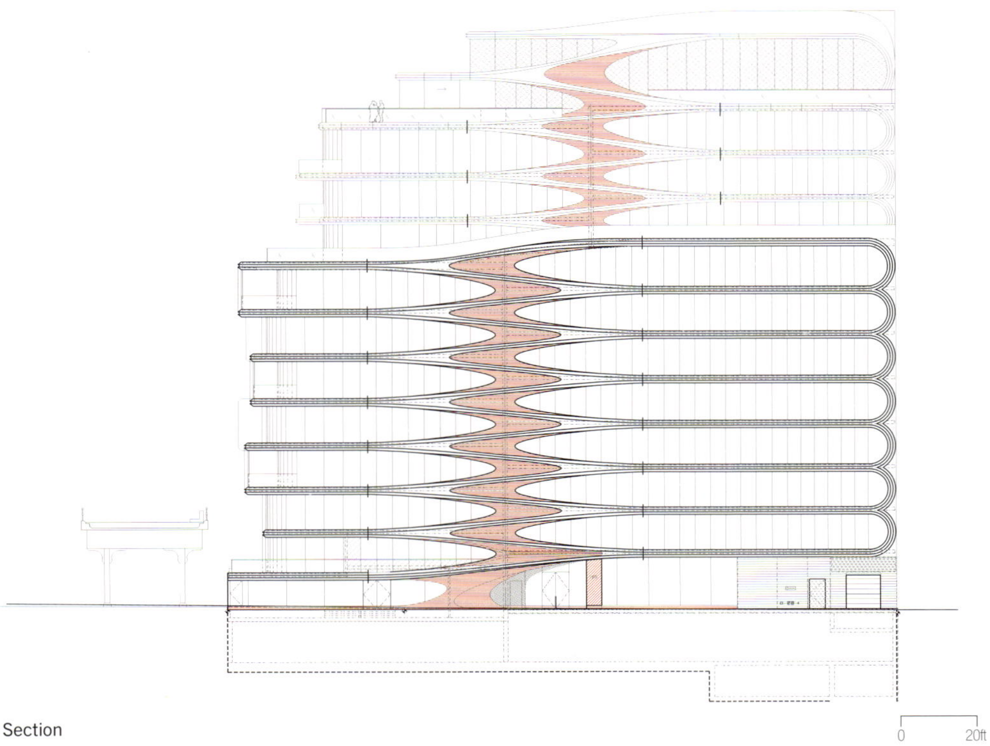

Section

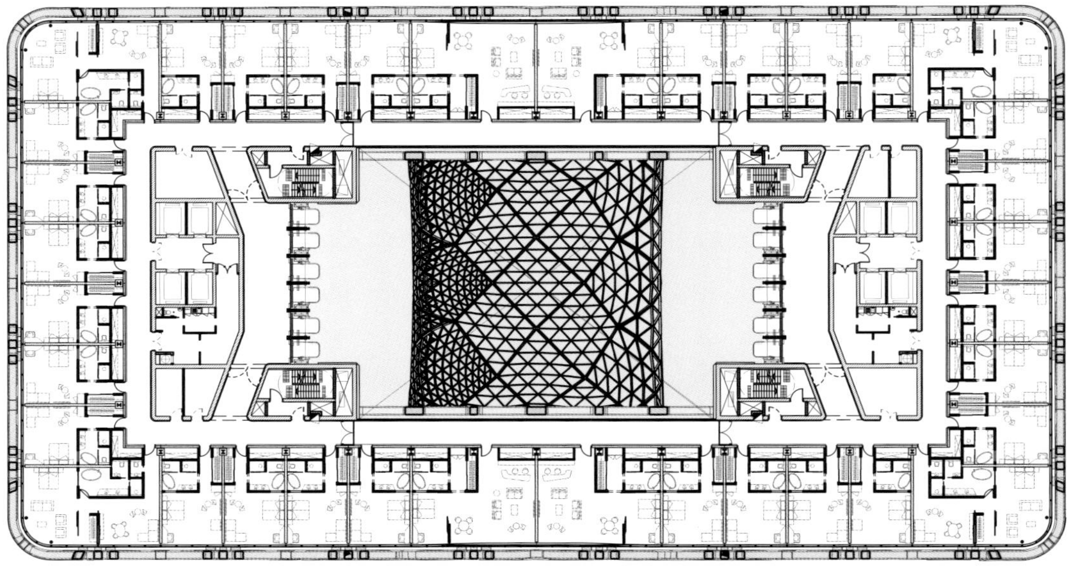

38th-floor plan

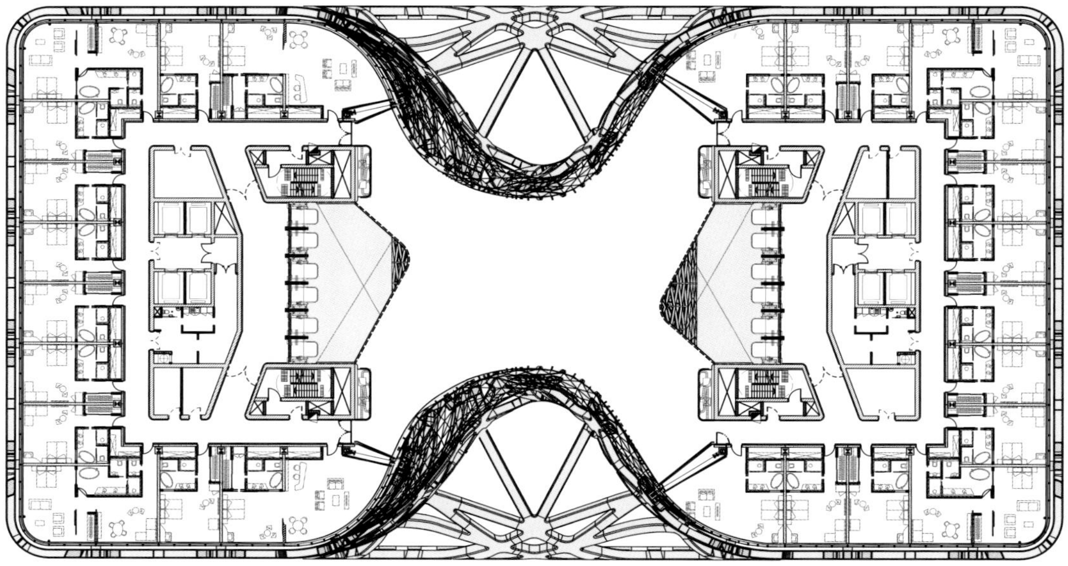

30th-floor plan

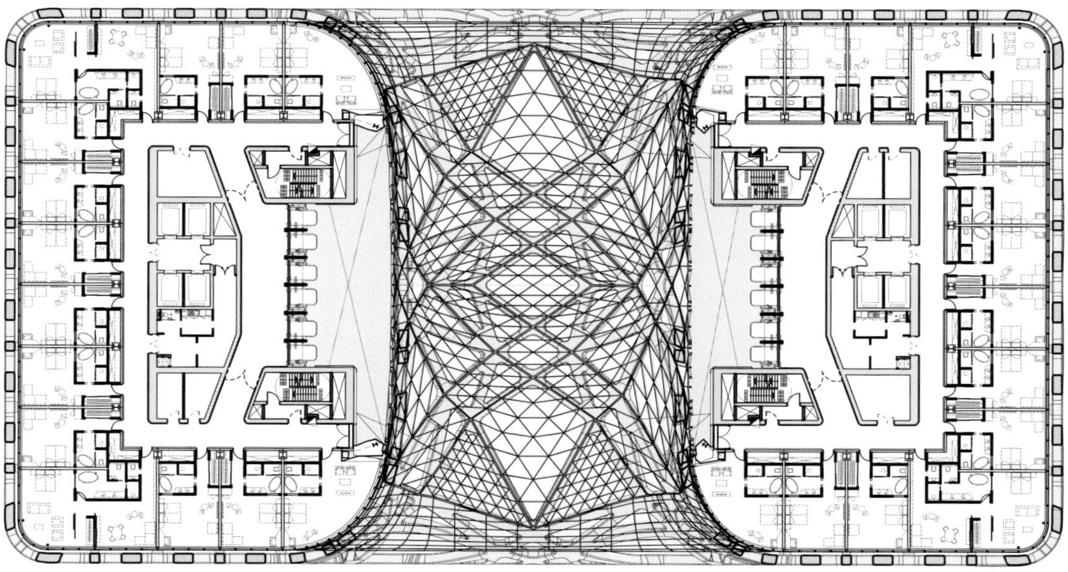

10th-floor plan

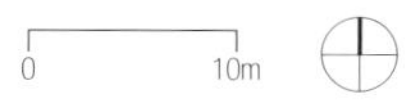

MORPHEUS

With 40 floors and a gross floor area of 150,000 square metres (1,614,587 square feet), Morpheus houses approximately 780 guest rooms, suites and sky villas. The hotel also includes a variety of meeting and event facilities, gaming rooms, lobby atrium, restaurants, spa, and sky pool. Including extensive back-of-house areas and supporting ancillary facilities, the tower's design resolves the many complex programs for the hotel within a single cohesive envelope.

The design combines dramatic public spaces and generous guest rooms with innovative engineering and formal cohesion. The rectangular outline of the site is extruded as a monolithic block with a series of voids, which carve through the centre of the tower, merging traditional architectural elements of roof, wall and ceiling to create a sculptural form that defines many of the hotel's internal public spaces.

The tower's exposed exoskeleton reinforces the dynamism of the design. Expressive and powerful, this external structure optimises the interior layouts and envelops the building, further defining its formal composition and establishing relationships with the new Cotai strip.

Location Cotai, Macau
Client Melco Crown Entertainment Limited
Area 150,000 m^2 (1,614,587 ft^2)
Date 2013–2017

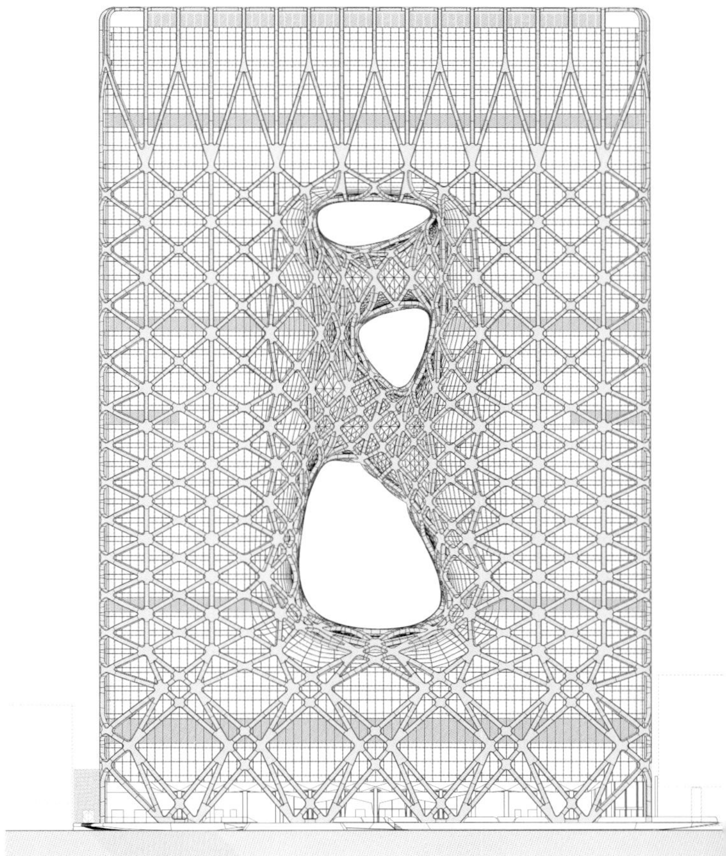

North elevation

0 20m

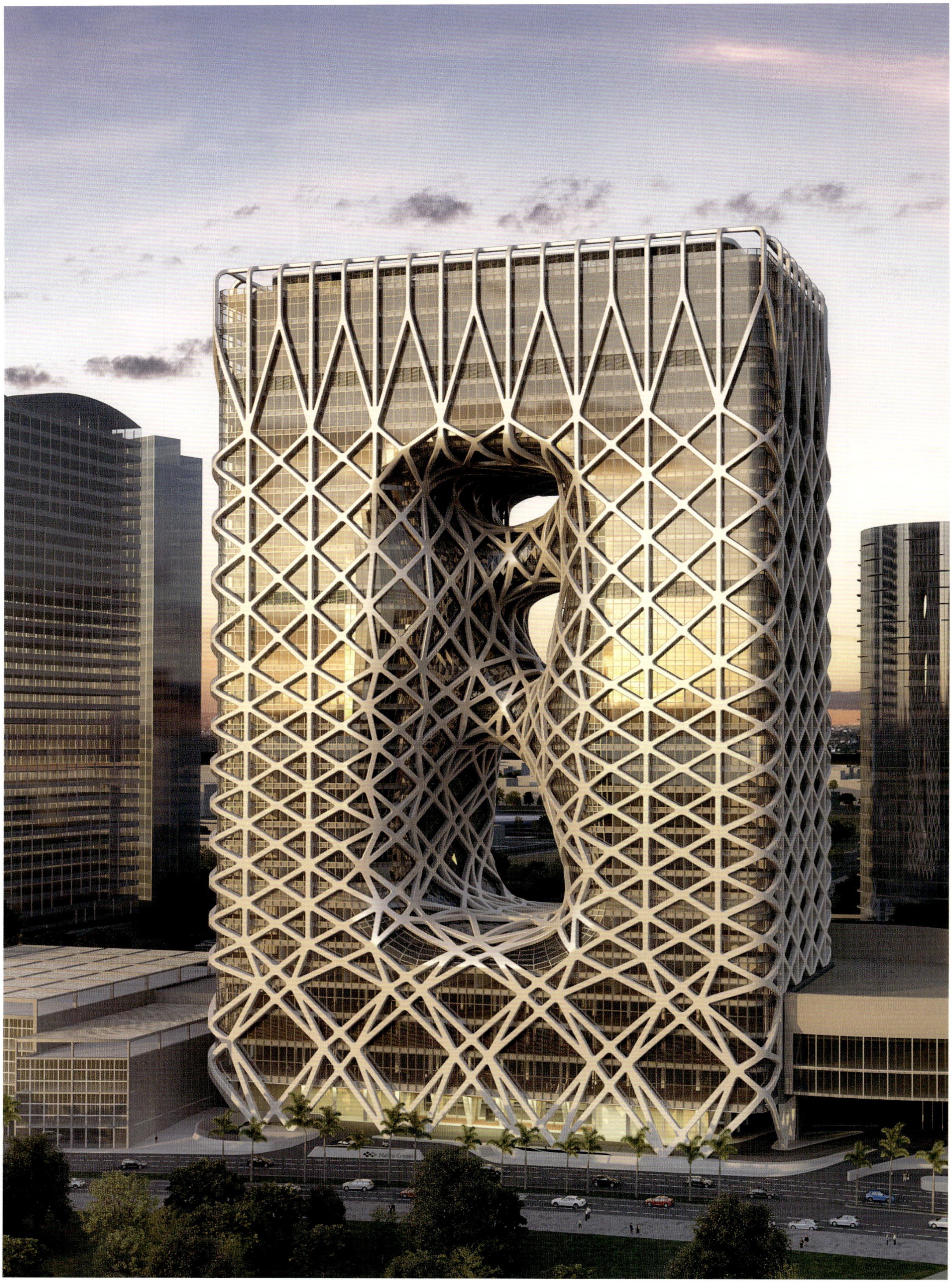

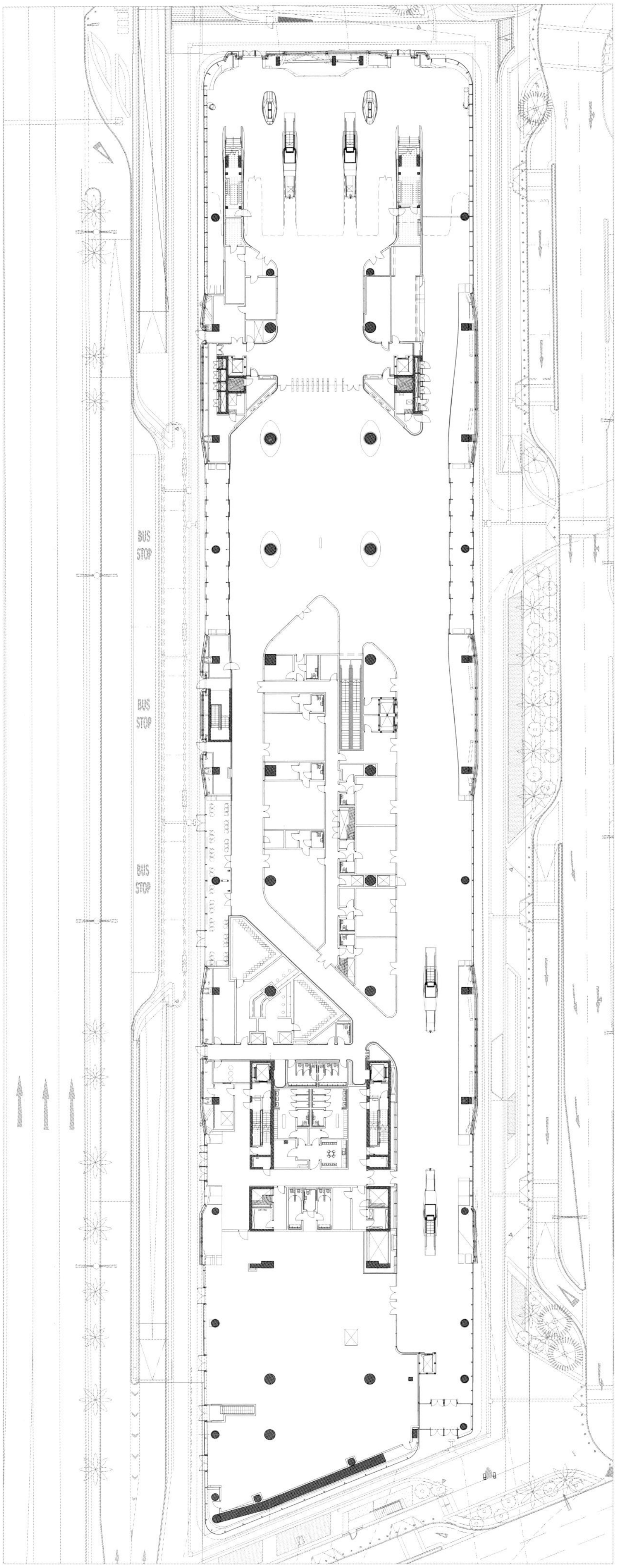

Ground- floor plan

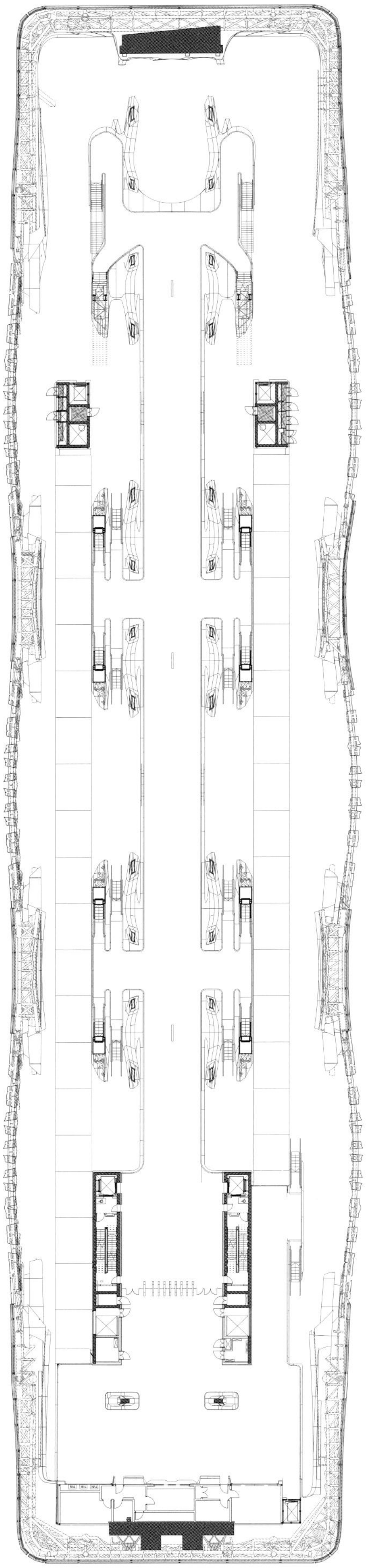
Level two concourse floor plan

KING ABDULLAH FINANCIAL DISTRICT METRO STATION

The King Abdullah Financial District (KAFD) Metro Station will serve as a key interchange on the new Riyadh Metro network for Line 1, as well as the terminus of Line 4 (for passengers to the airport) and Line 6. The local monorail can also be accessed from the station via a sky bridge. With six platforms over four public floors and two levels of underground car parking, the KAFD Metro Station will be integrated within the urban context of the financial district, responding to the functional requirements of a multimodal transport centre and the district's future vision. The project extends beyond the simple station typology to emphasise the building's importance as a dynamic, multi-functional public space; not only an intermediate place perceived through quick transitions, but also a dramatic public space for the city.

Location Riyadh, Kingdom of Saudi Arabia
Client Arriyadh Development Authority
Area 20,434 m^2 (219,950 ft^2)
Date 2012–2017

The design places the station at the centre of a network of pathways, sky bridges and metro lines envisaged by the KAFD master plan. Connectivity diagrams and traffic across the site have been mapped and structured to clearly delineate the pedestrian routes within the building, optimise internal circulation, and avoid congestion. The resulting configuration is a three-dimensional lattice defined by a sequence of movement (generated from the repetition and frequency variation of station's daily traffic flows), which acts as the spine for the building's circulation.

The façade patterning reduces solar gain while its geometric perforations contextualise the station within its cultural environment. The overall composition resembles patterns generated by desert winds in sand dunes, where multiple frequencies and repetition generate complex natural formations.

The King Abdullah Financial District Metro Station applies a discrete subset of elements, which are correlated through repetition, symmetry, and scaling, optimising the design while simplifying technical challenges without compromising spatial quality or design ambition.

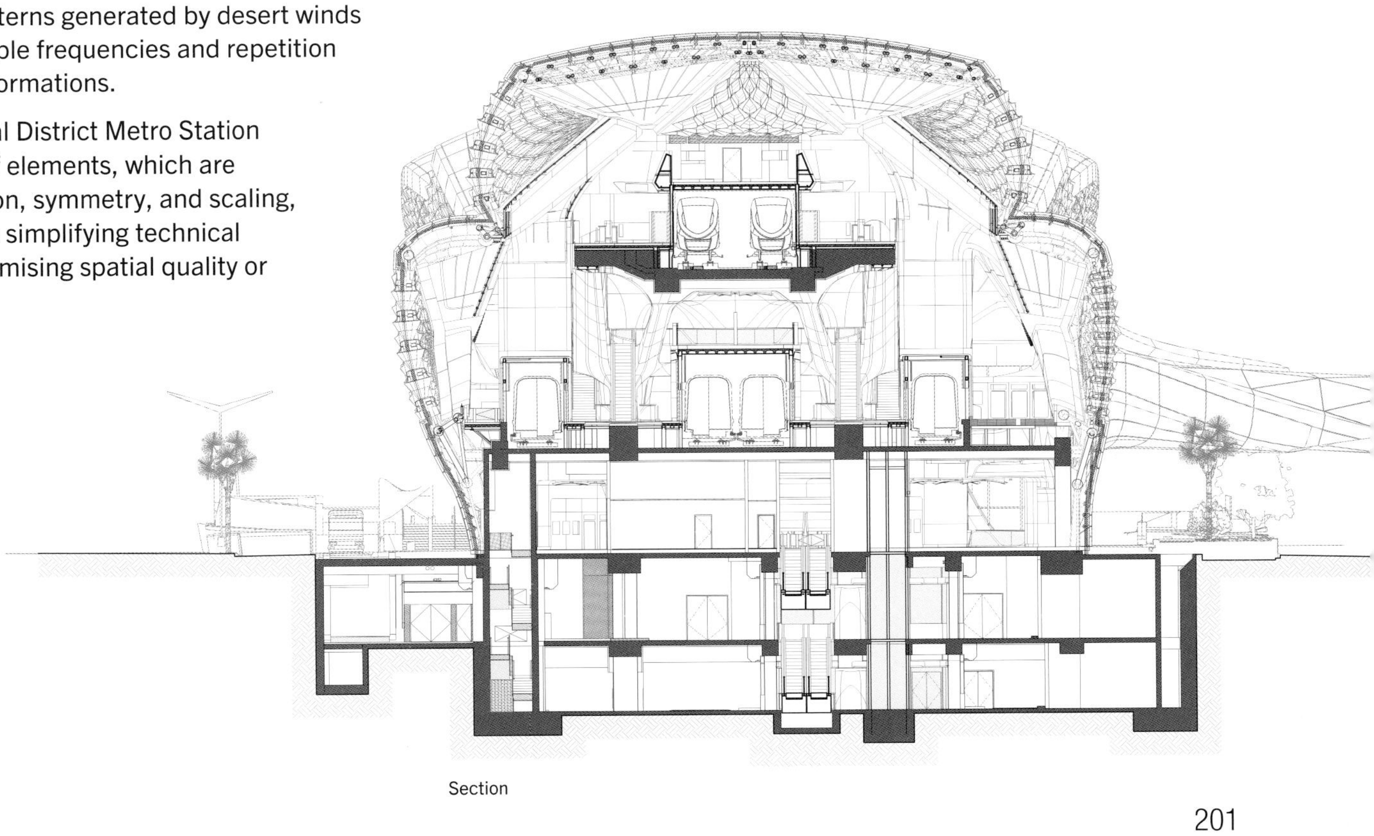

Section

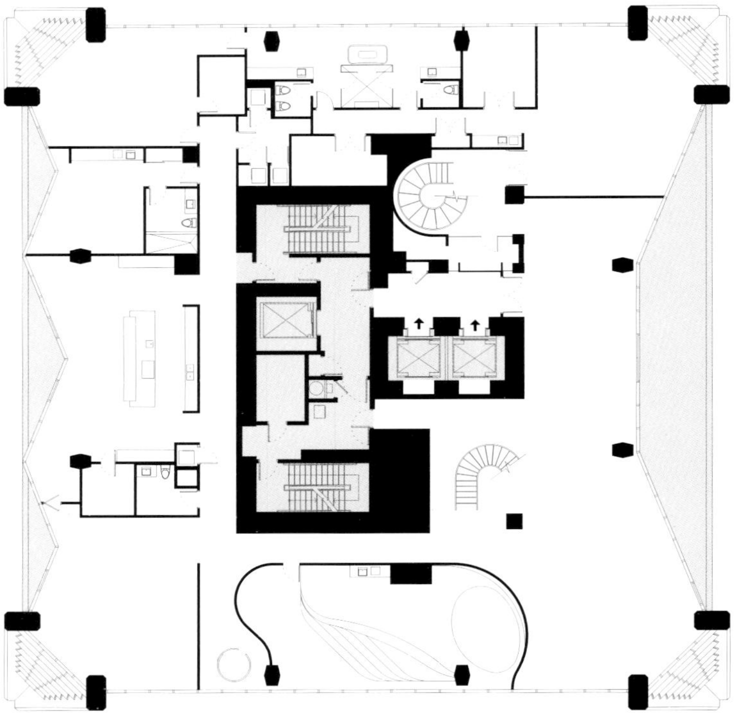

Floor plan, duplex penthouse (Level 58/59), lower level

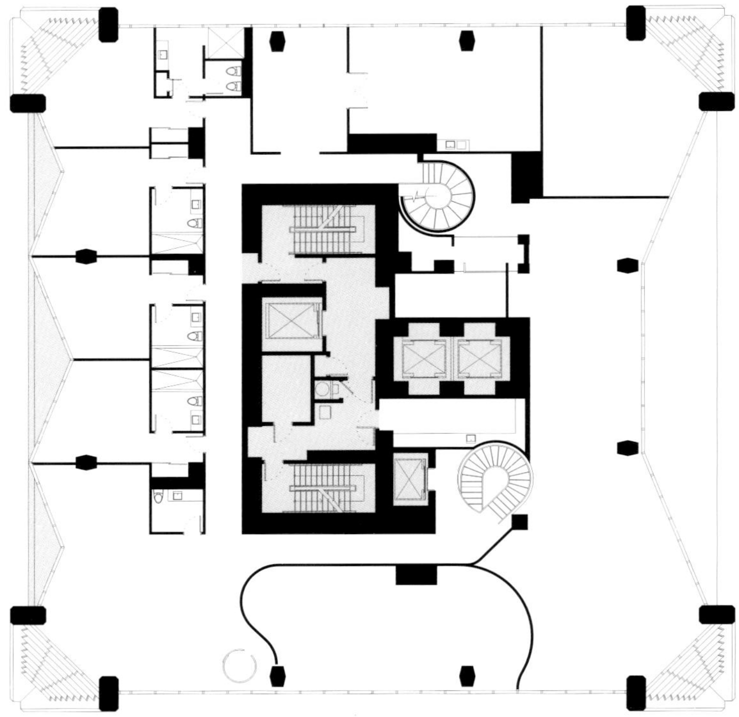

Floor plan, duplex penthouse (Level 58/59), upper level

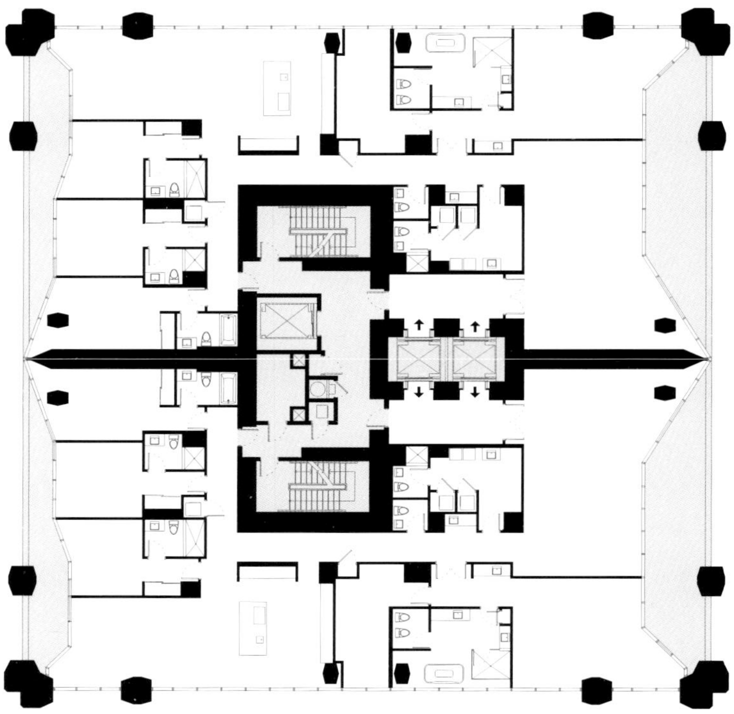

Floor plan, half-floor residences, Zone 3 (Level 45)

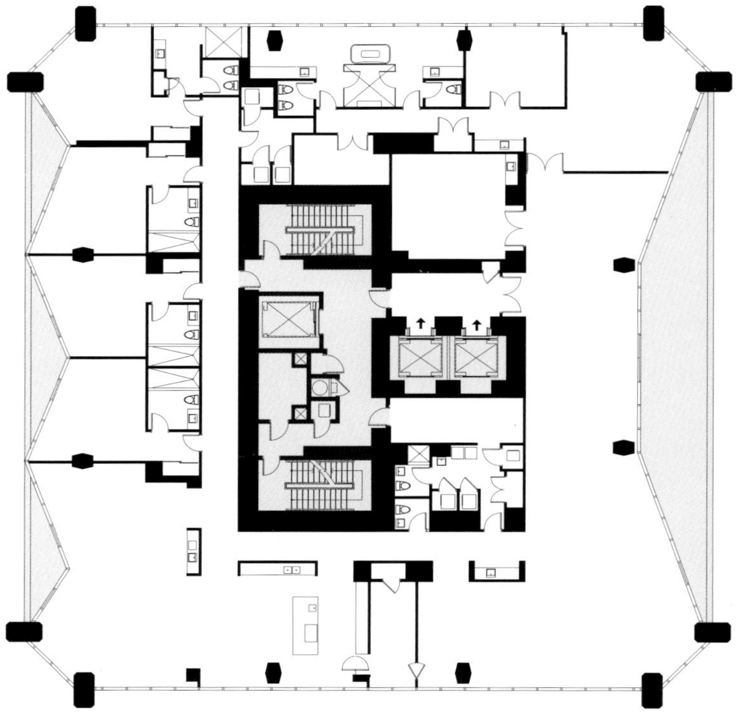

Floor plan, full-floor residences—Zone 4, Levels 50–57

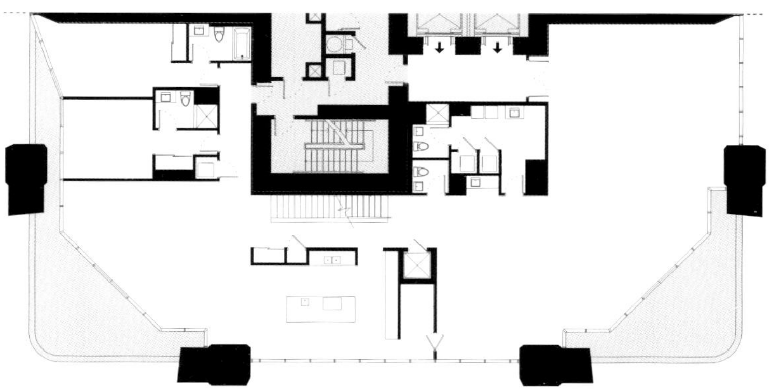

Floor plan, townhouse residences 1201 (Levels 12–14), lower level

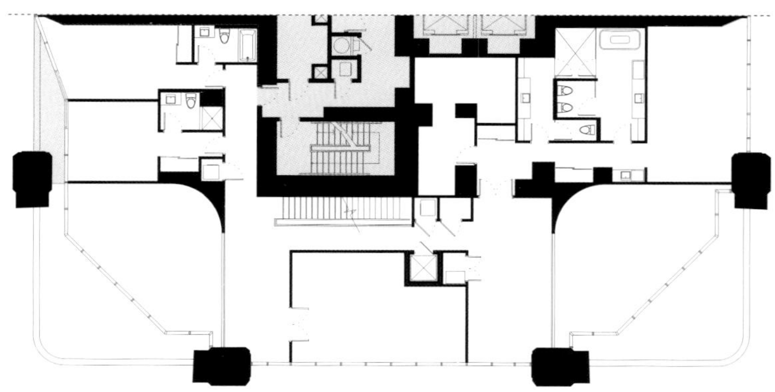

Floor plan, townhouse residences 1201 (Levels 12–14), upper level

1000 MUSEUM

The One Thousand Museum is a 66-storey, 83-unit, super-luxury condominium tower on Biscayne Boulevard in Miami, opposite Museum Park, with views across Biscayne Bay to Miami Beach.

A duplex penthouse occupies the last two residential floors. The final floor features an aquatic centre, leisure area, and event space. There is commercial space at the base, along with several stories of parking. At grade, the tower is ringed by pools and gardens.

A concrete exoskeleton structures the perimeter of the tower in a web of flowing lines that integrates lateral bracing within the lines of structural support. Columnar lines near the base splay out to meet at the corners, forming a rigid tube highly resistant to Miami's demanding wind loads.

With structure at the perimeter, the interior floor plates are almost column-free, allowing maximum variation in floor plans. The bottom two-thirds of the tower has two units per floor, while the upper third boasts units that occupy the entire floor. The moving, curving lines of the exoskeleton mean that each succeeding floor plan is slightly different from the last. On the lower floors, terraces occupy the corners; on the upper floors, the terraces are tucked in from the edges.

Behind the exoskeleton, the architects have created a folded, faceted, crystal-like façade to contrast with the solidity of the exoskeleton. The dependable Miami sun will create plays of light on the glass within the structural frame.

Instead of simply cladding a steel frame, the architects designed expressive form-work, which can be reused as construction progresses up the tower. The concrete will be painted to create a finished architectural surface.

Location Miami Beach, United States
Client 1000 Biscayne Tower, LLC
Area 84,637 m^2 (911,027 ft^2)
Date 2012–2018

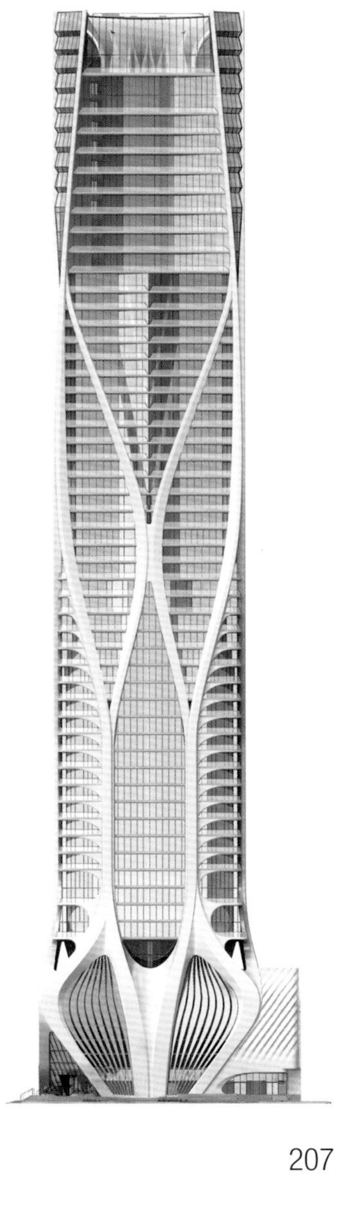

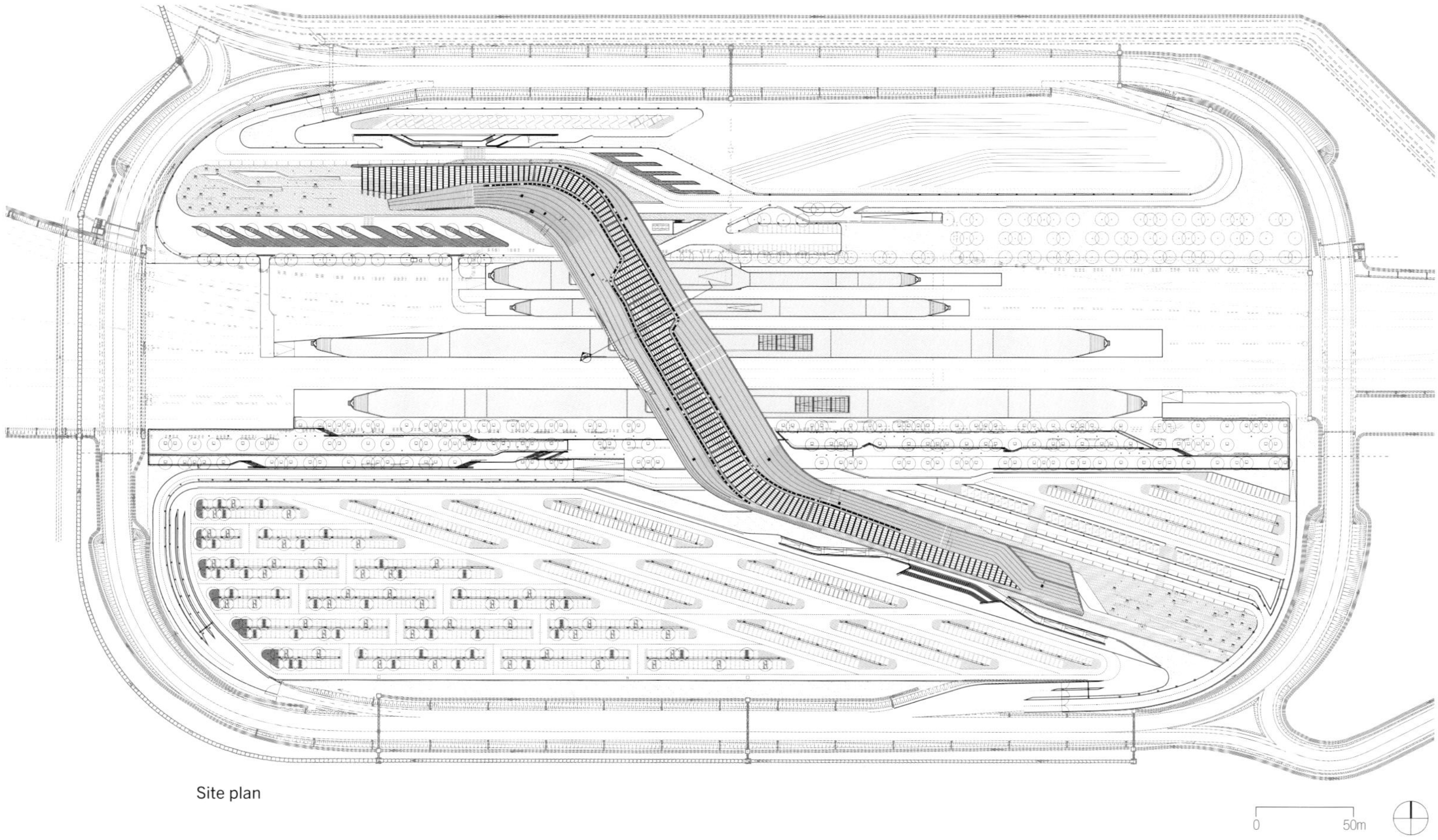

Site plan

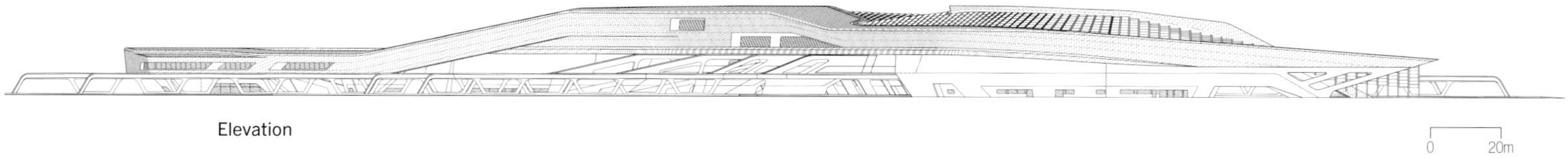

Elevation

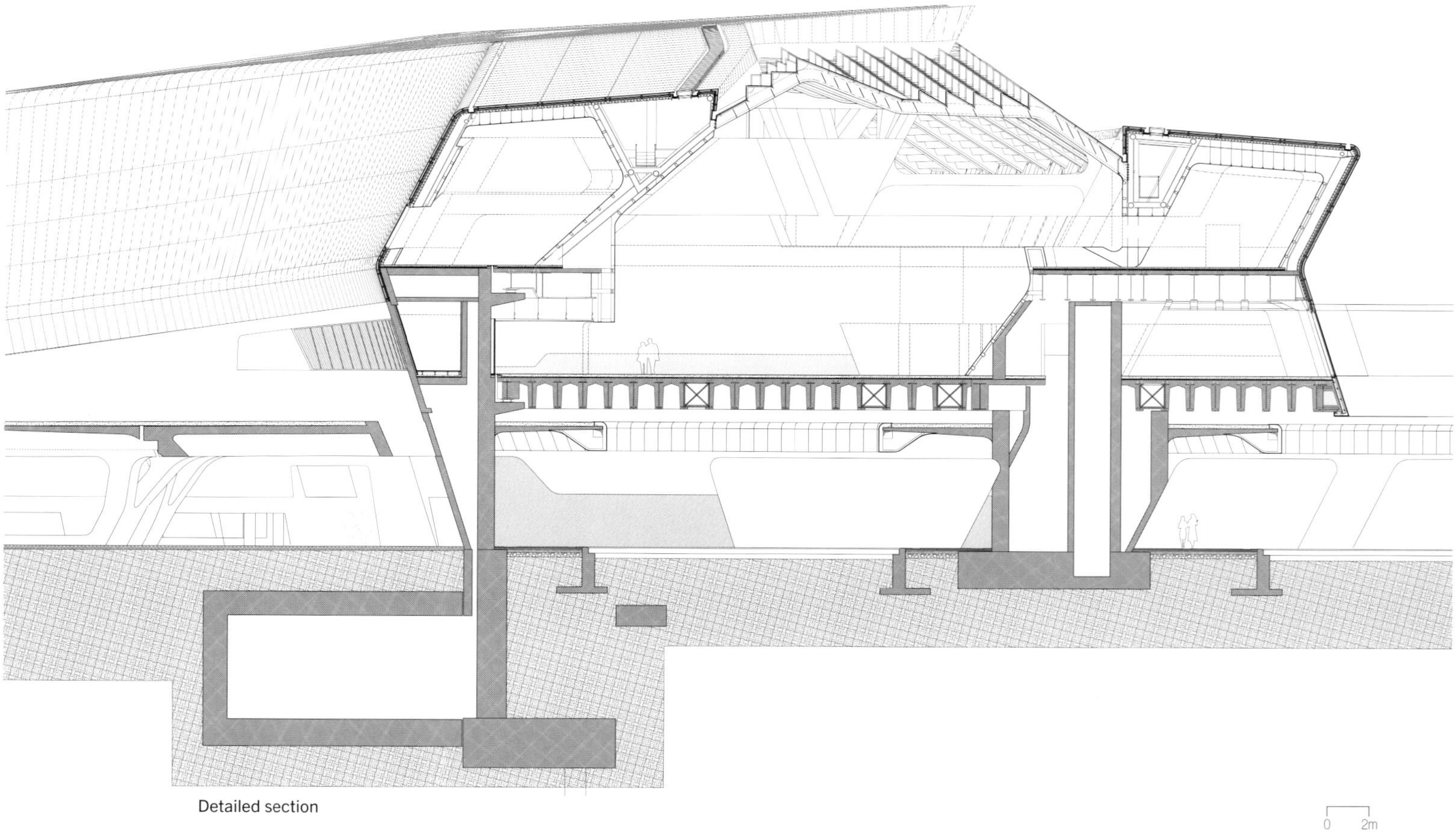

Detailed section

HIGH-SPEED TRAIN STATION, NAPOLI-AFRAGOLA

The new High-Speed Train Station, Napoli-Afragola is a bridge above the tracks. The key challenge of the architectural scheme is to create a well-organised transport interchange that can simultaneously serve as a new landmark to announce the approach to Naples—thus a new gateway to the city. The concept of the bridge comes from the idea of enlarging the overhead concourse, which is used to access the various platforms, to such a degree that it can become the main passenger concourse itself.

Providing an urbanised public link across the tracks, the challenge was to give expression to the imposition of a new through-station that could also act as the nucleus of a new proposed business park linking the various surrounding towns. The bridge concept further allows two strips of parkland to extend through the site alongside the tracks, opening and connecting the site to the surrounding landscape and business park.

The architectural language proposed, geared towards the articulation of movement, is pursued further within the interior of the building, where the trajectory of the travellers determines the geometry of the space.

Location Naples, Italy
Client Rfi S.P.A
Area 30,000 m^2 (322,917 ft^2)
Date 2003–2017

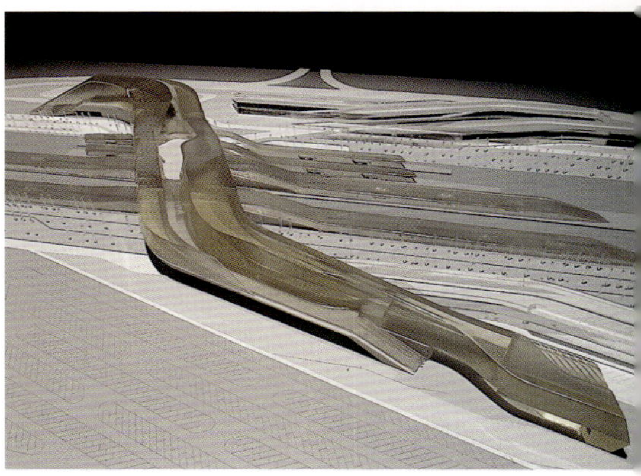

Model

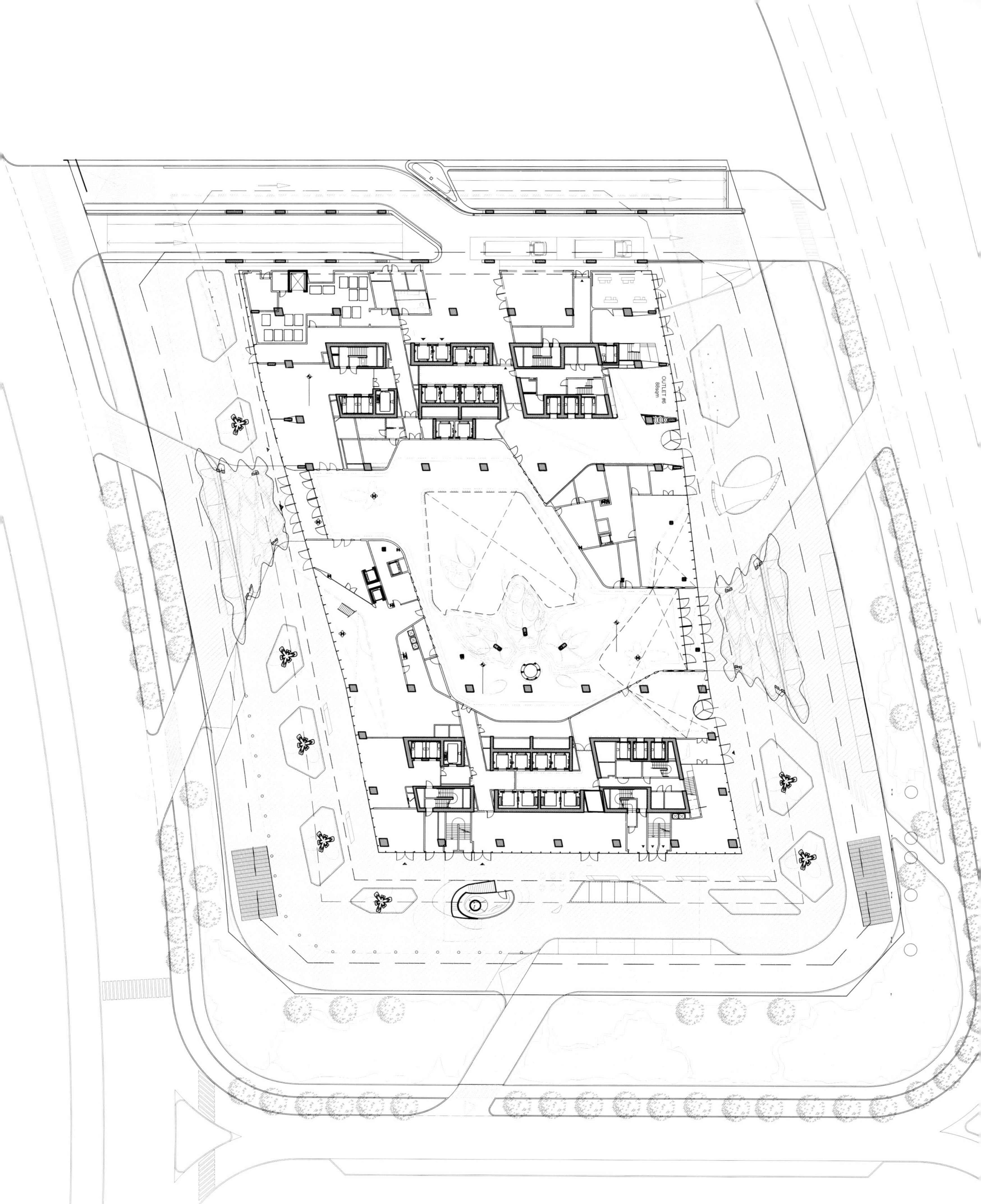

Site plan

OPUS

The Opus is located in prominent location in the Business Bay master plan. The two plots are interlinked by a continuous low-level podium structure that essentially unites the project and provides the unique possibility to interpret the project as one mass.

These two buildings are conceived as a united mass taking the form of a cube hovering off the ground. The cube is carved or eroded by a free-form void—essentially the setback space between the two tower envelopes. The cube is structured by a conventional system of slabs stacked, vertically serviced by central cores, allowing for the areas near the façade to be occupied on all eight sides. The void, which is treated as a volume in its own right, being the space inside the build-mass, is free form and fluid and cuts through the edges of the cube, appearing as if it extends beyond the immediate boundaries of the cube. The interior of the void is clad in tinted double-glazing allowing for views into the void. The external plateaus within the void will be accessible to provide areas for recreation and rest.

Fritting patterns in the form of pixelated striations are applied on to the glass façade to provide a degree of reflectivity and materiality to the cube while assisting the reduction of the solar gains inside the building. These striations dematerialise the building mass, while the surface appears to capture images of both the outside and inside worlds.

The interchange of perception of the tower at night-time is an important factor to this proposal. While the cube appears full in the daytime and the void as empty, the night-time perception would be one of opposites, where the cube appears dark and dematerialised, while the void could be activated with light, visible from a great distance.

Location Dubai, United Arab Emirates
Client Omniyat Properties
Area 84,345 m^2 (907,882 ft^2)
Date 2012–TBC

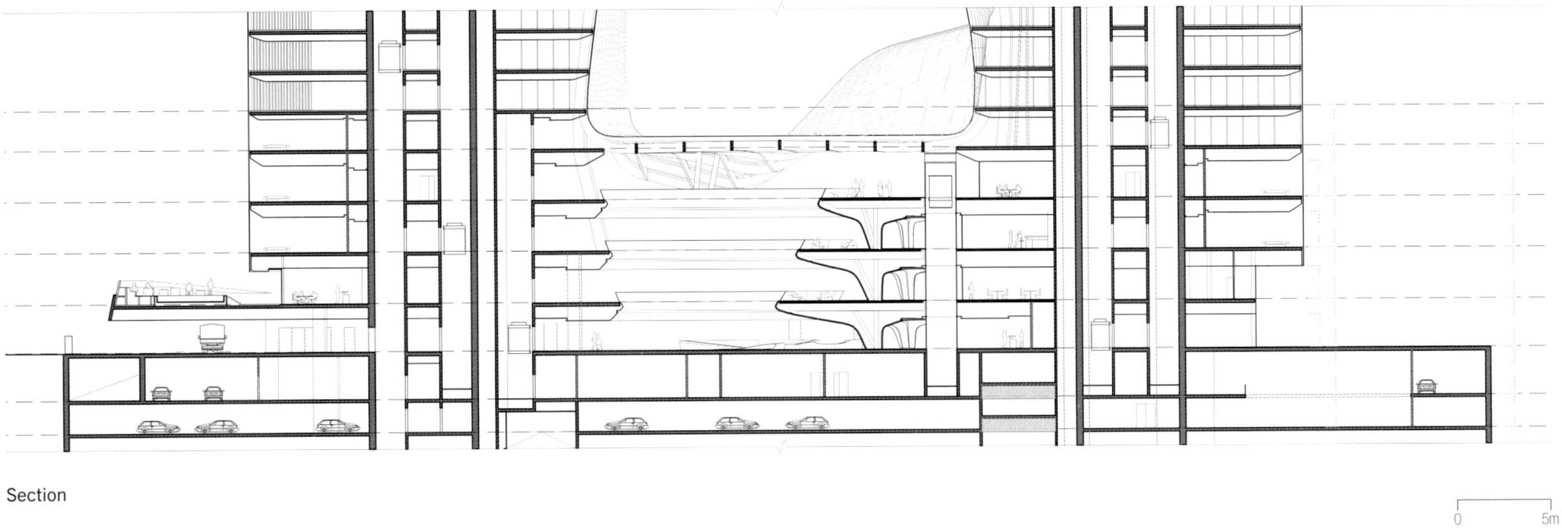

Section

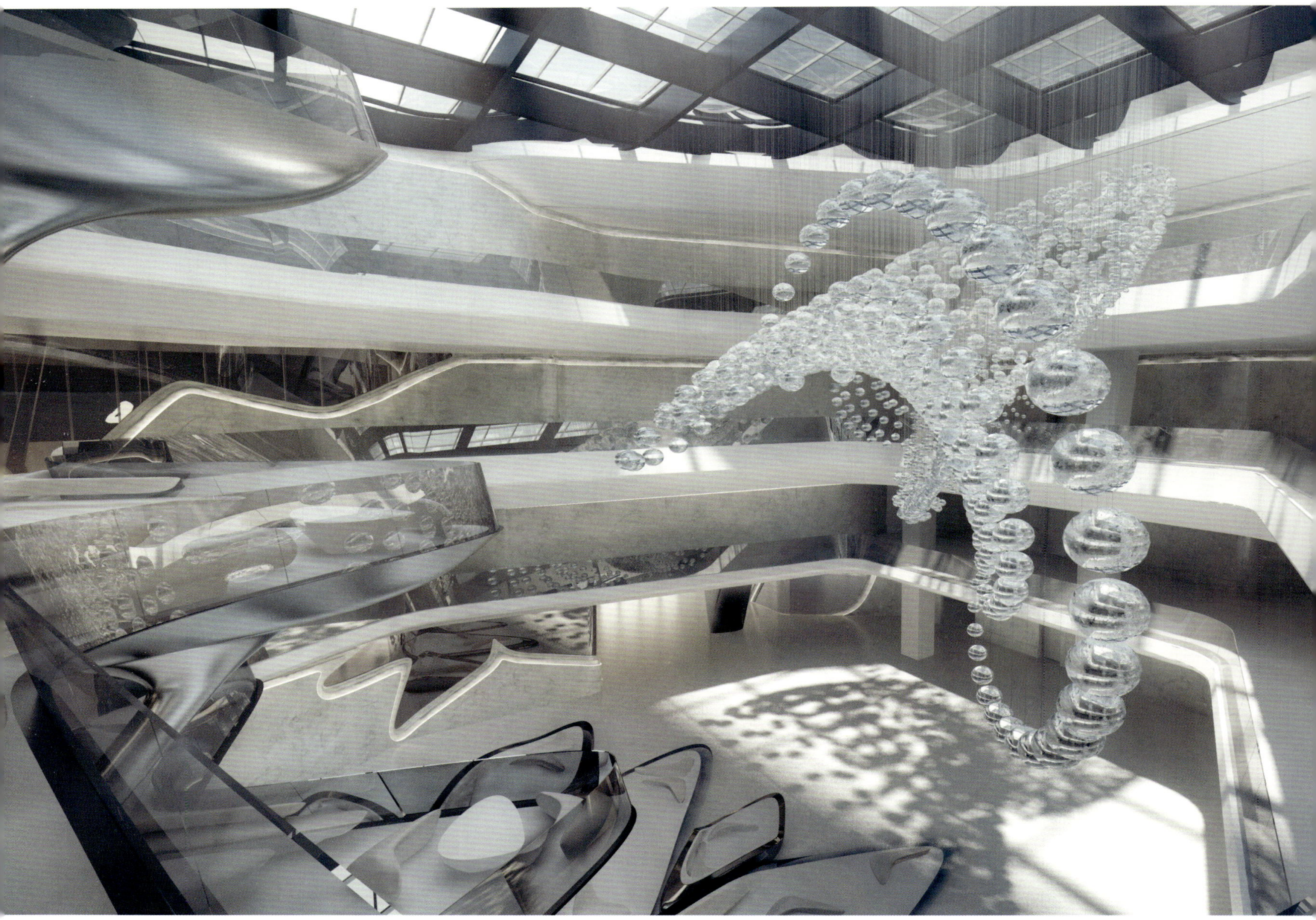

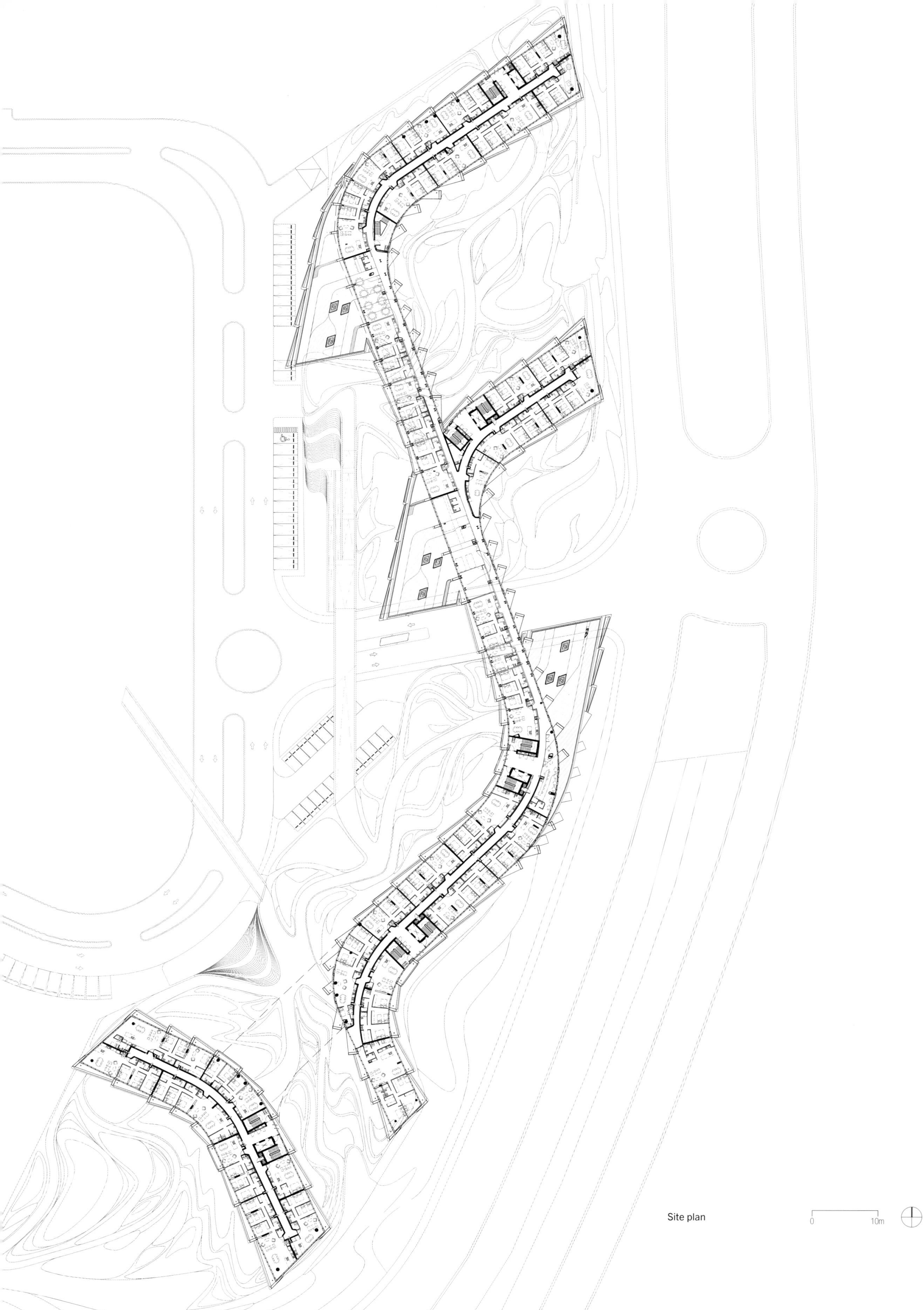

Site plan

ESFERA CITY CENTER, MONTERREY

Zaha Hadid Architects has designed a community-oriented design comprising a low-rise, high-density residential building of 981 apartments. Each side of the building has been shaped to optimise its environmental orientation, creating a sequence of interconnected internal and external courtyards, gardens, and public spaces. By gradually fragmenting the overall volume of the design, its relationship with its context is customised to become solid in some areas and permeable in others. This transition reflects the extreme contrasts that characterise the surrounding urban fabric: from the noisy commercial side with its eight-lane motorway, to the quiet, low-density suburban developments that spread to the base of the mountains in the distance.

The building's envelope references the local architectural language and Mexican tradition of interlocking lattice geometries to provide shading and describe the outdoor space of each residence. These lattice geometries have been used widely throughout pre-Columbian, colonial and contemporary Mexican architecture to give protection from the sun and generate varied and dynamic displays of light and shadow. By considering their solar orientation, internal program, spatial requirements, and adjacencies, each balcony's form has been developed to provide solar protection, privacy, and generous exterior space for the apartments, defining a varied and coherent architectural language that unites the project.

The building's layout responds to the ideal solar orientation for the apartments and aims to channel the site's wind patterns, allowing residents to enjoy the outdoor spaces and natural ventilation offered by the fresher microclimate of the Huajuco Canyon. With façade orientation, ground-level shading, and optimisation of natural ventilation, the ambient temperature is reduced to provide greater comfort. The materials of all external areas have been selected with consideration of their permeability, high reflectivity, and low thermal mass to reduce the mean radiant temperature, together with their ability to drain rainwater into the soil.

Location Monterrey, Mexico
Client Citelis, Organización Ramírez
Area 136,000 m^2 (1,463,892 ft^2)
Date Phase I scheduled for completion in 2018

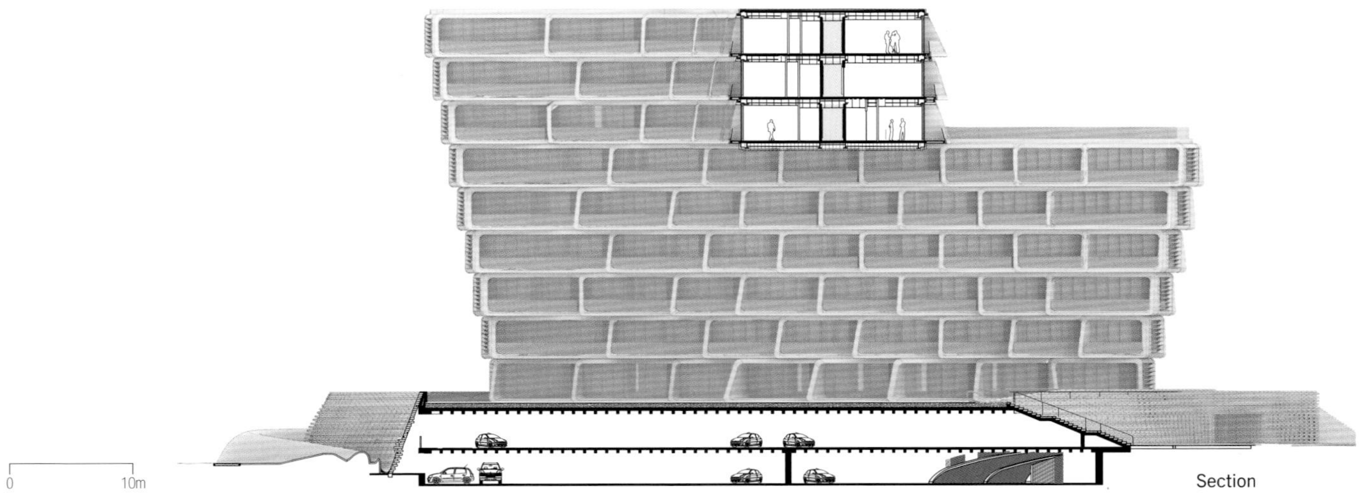

Section

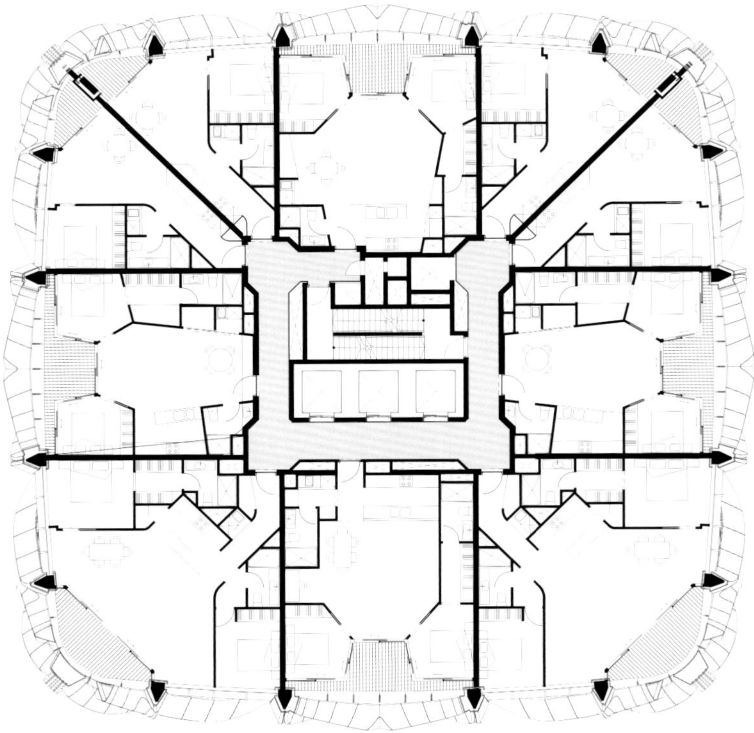

Floor plan, Tower 1

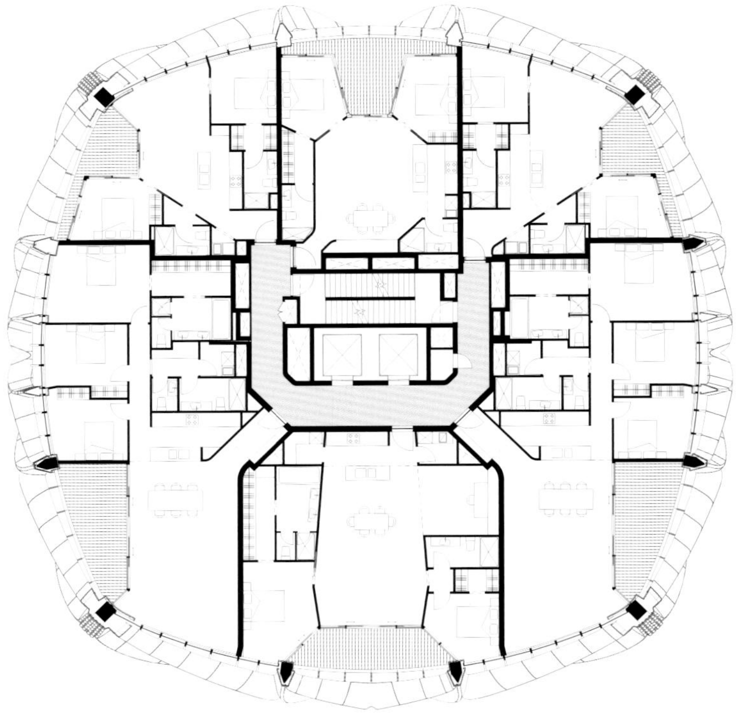

Floor plan, Tower 2

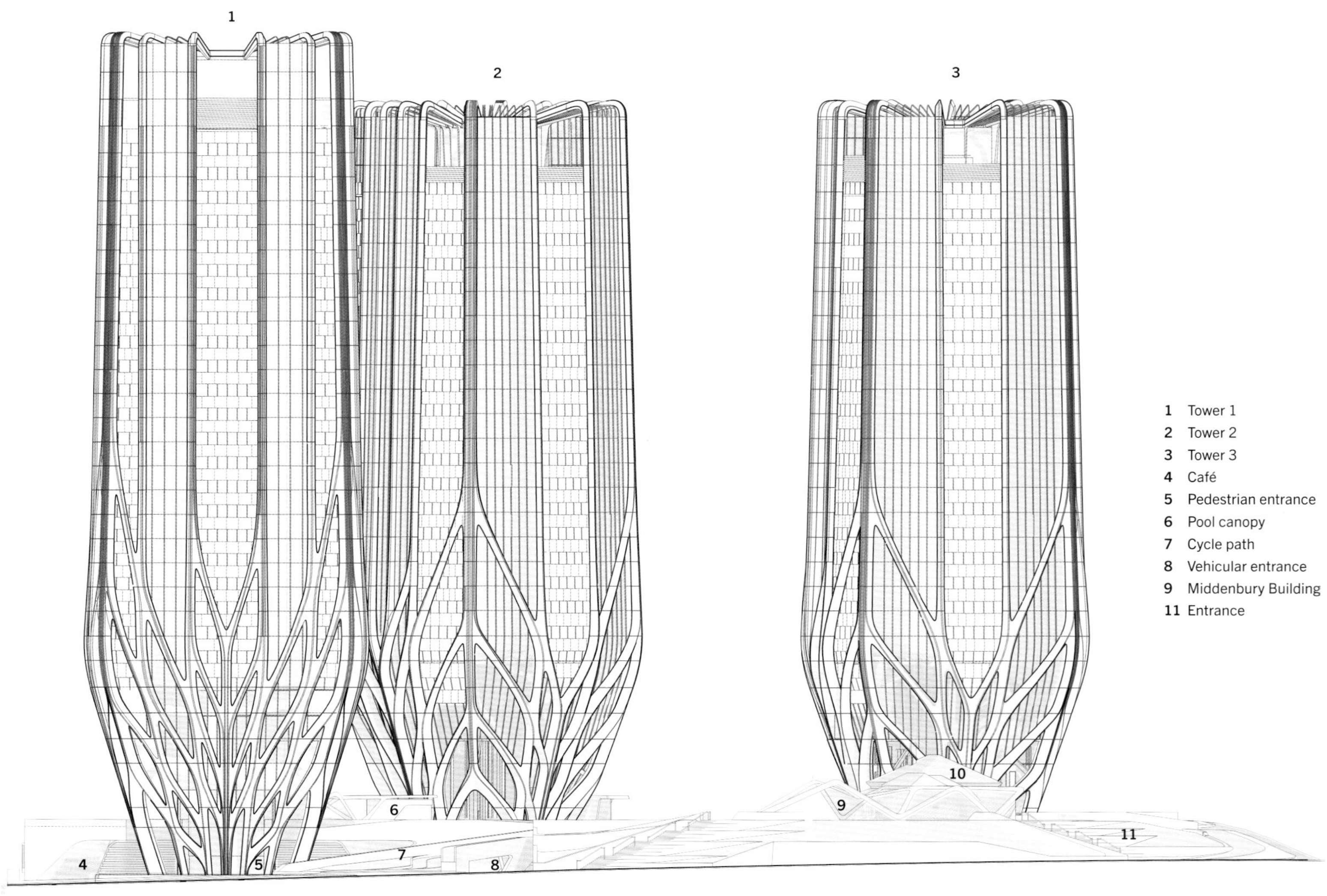

Northwest elevation

GRACE ON CORONATION

The proposal for the subject site was to create an urban park within a site that is unique to the city of Brisbane. Its direct access to the river and the presence of a heritage building require community-orientated planning to create the riverside park.

The above considerations lead to a design of three towers, with a unique tapering feature at ground level to minimise tower footprints, to the advantage of the public realm and to enhance visual permeability and pedestrian circulation. Entry points to the site lead directly to the basement car park to minimise vehicular flow within the site. An improved pedestrian and bicycle route is provided off Coronation Drive, resolving the current narrow path along the main road, gently sloping through the new park. The site is specifically arranged to offer different experiences and amenities to residents and visitors, and provide a large area of public access to the riverfront. The facilities dedicated to the towers are located discretely within the tower podium, while Middenbury House will be refurbished and renovated with an extension to benefit the greater community and enhance the site.

The towers are defined by a simple and elegant form, which gently taper towards the top. The shape is derived from the need to maintain the unique views across the site as well as the internal layouts within each tower. The façade is characterised by a series of slim exoskeleton elements, which respond to the balcony position and interior unit distribution. The new towers emerge as sculptural elements and establish a new local point of reference and identity in Brisbane. The layout is oriented to maximise the views toward the riverfront and the city of Brisbane, with a focus on maximising external spaces and the use of balconies to encourage outdoor living and enjoyment of the local climate.

Location Brisbane, Australia
Client Sunland Group
Area 45,000 m^2 (484,376 ft^2)
Date TBC

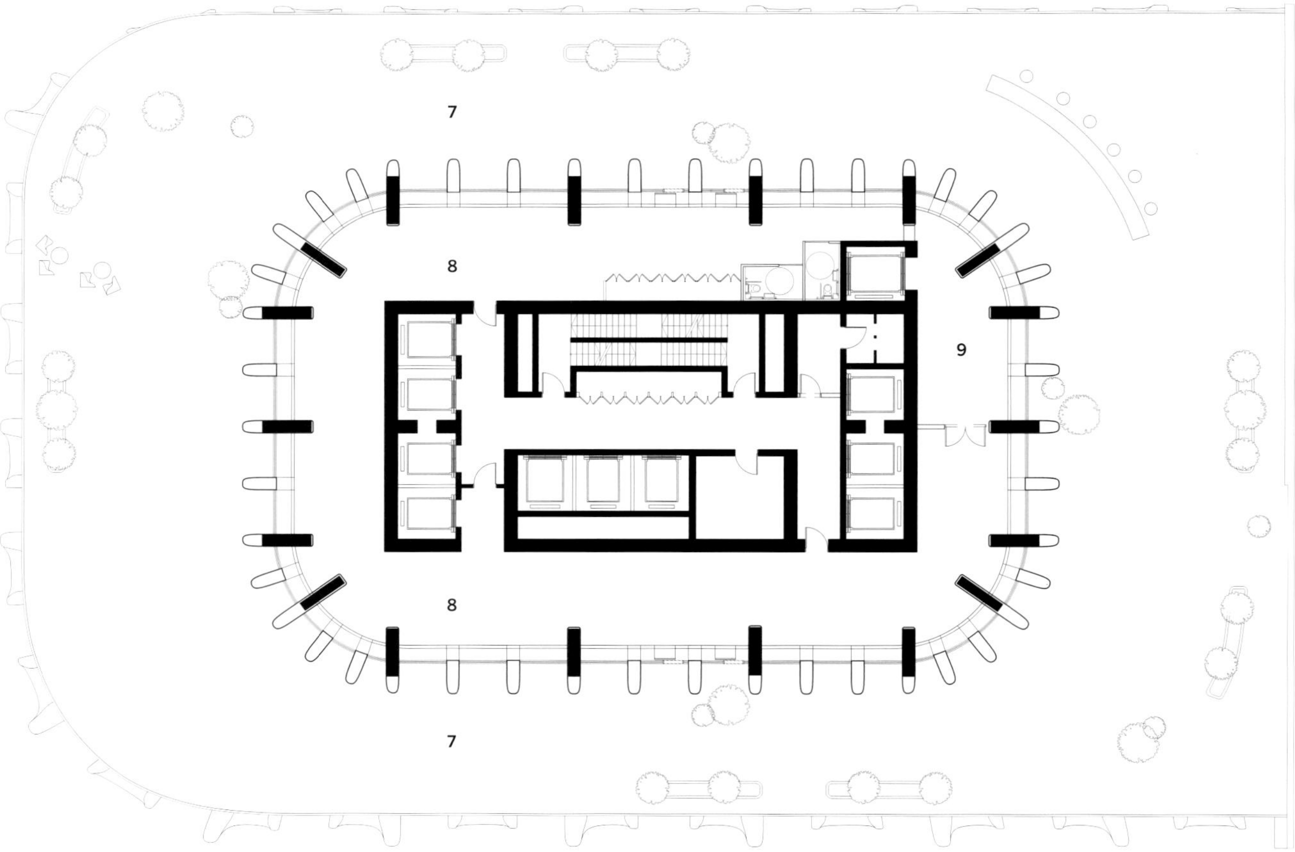

Deck-floor plan

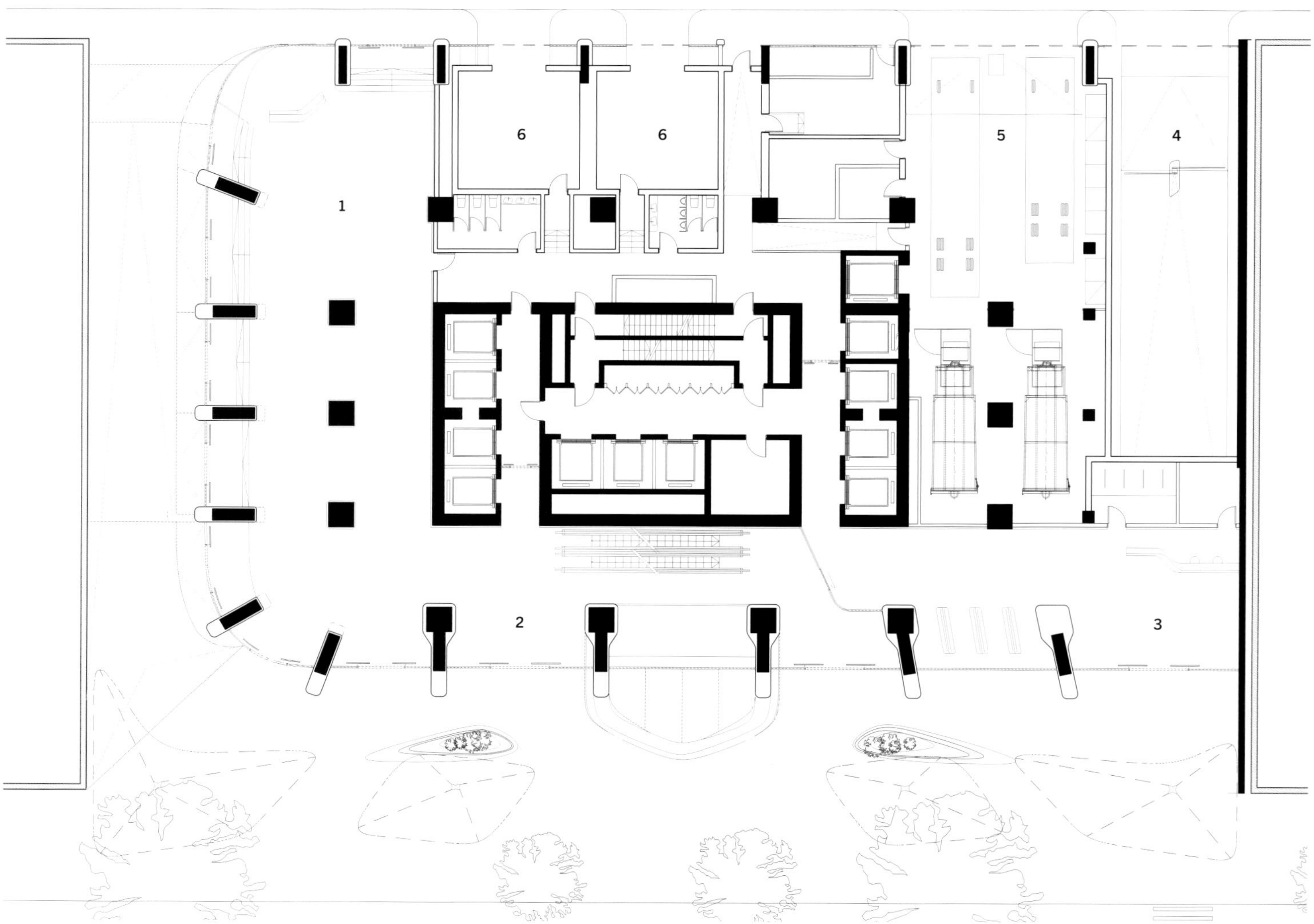

Ground-floor plan

1 Art gallery
2 Retail entrance
3 Residential entrance
4 Visitor parking ramp
5 Service
6 Residential parking lift
7 Exterior terrace
8 Food and beverage
9 Food prep

0 5m

582–606 COLLINS STREET

Located at the western boundary of Melbourne's Central Business District (CBD), adjacent to the city's transport network and Southern Cross Station, the site is within an area of the city that is transforming from transit zone to a new district within Melbourne with the potential to enrich the city's urban fabric for residents, visitors and all who work in the CBD. Melbourne's unique character has developed into one of the world's most cosmopolitan and livable cities with a growing urban population who enjoy the convenience of accessing the city's renowned cultural, civic, academic, and business institutions—as well as the city's many leisure and entertainment venues—without the long commute in from the suburbs.

The design opens a new pedestrian route connecting Collins Street with Francis Street, easing the existing congestion at that junction by creating a shortcut to Southern Cross Station from the CBD. This new pedestrian route will be enhanced with a café and civic space.

The arrangement of the tower takes inspiration from its mixed-use program, diluting the building's overall volume into a series of smaller stacked 'vases.' Each vase houses a different programmatic element. At street level, a new public exhibition space will serve Melbourne's acclaimed artistic community. Restaurants are also located on the ground floor, with offices and additional dining areas at the top of the lower vase to give direct access to the public terrace on the 9th level. A variety of residential units, from generous apartments with one bedroom plus study to two- and three-bedroom units are housed in the vases above this public level. Each vase gently tapers inwards to offer additional civic open space at its base.

The Collins Street façade comprises an elegant colonnade of sculptural, curved columns that support the building's unique façade system. This façade includes solid elements inspired by the finest examples of historic architecture within the CBD where details within the masonry give a strong architectural rhythm to the buildings' exteriors. This remarkable detailing is reinterpreted at 582–606 Collins Street in a contemporary solution defined by the building's structural integrity and the logical division of its overall volume, introducing delicate filigree that gently envelops the building.

582–606 Collins Street has been designed to use 50 percent less energy than a conventional mixed-use tower. Its filigreed façade contributes to reducing the direct solar gain of the building, and emissions. The building's high-performance glazing, central cooling, and lighting systems, and greywater reuse system reduce consumption of resources and lower emissions; 350 bicycle parking spaces and bays for electric vehicles and shared car clubs are included within the design.

Location Melbourne, Australia
Client Landream, Australia
Area 70,075 m^2 (754,281 ft^2)
Date 2020

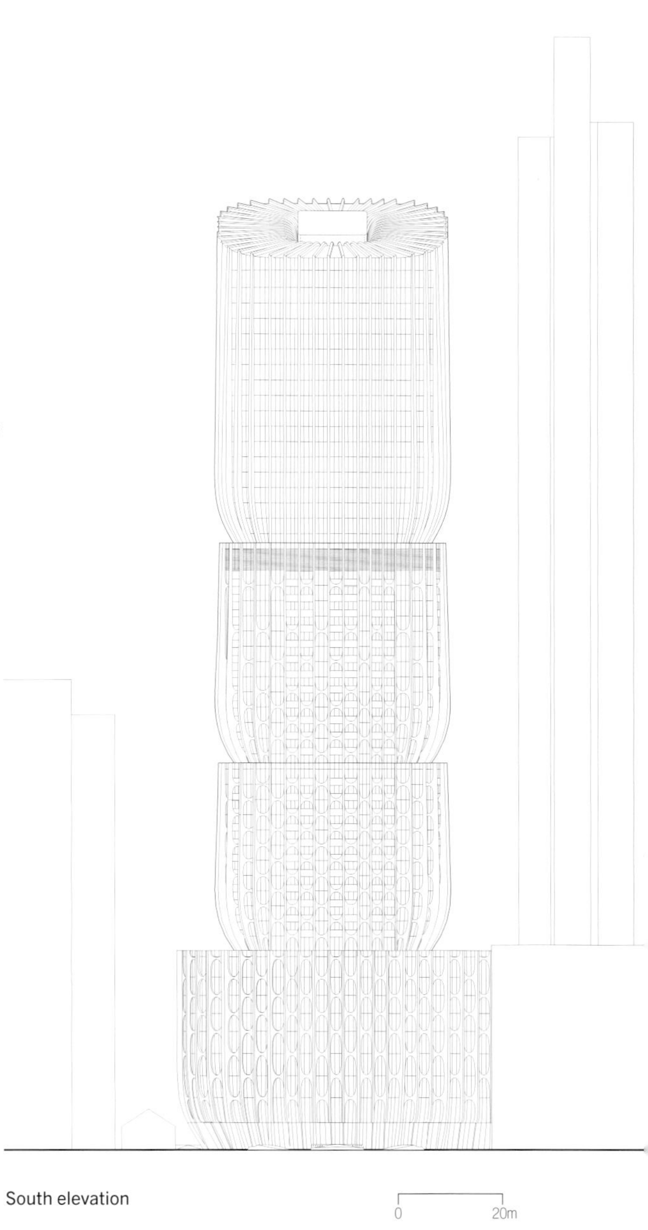

South elevation

Batman's Hil

BEIJING NEW AIRPORT TERMINAL BUILDING

ADP Ingeniérie (ADPI) and Zaha Hadid Architects have completed the concept design for the world's largest airport passenger terminal—the Beijing New Airport Terminal Building—in Daxing, Beijing, under the leadership of the Beijing New Airport Headquarters (BNAH), based on the bid-winning planning scheme by ADPI.

With Beijing's existing Capital Airport already exceeding its planned capacity, the new airport will serve the world's fastest growing aviation sector and enable further connections between Beijing and cultural, economic, and civic centres around the globe. Initially accommodating 45 million passengers per year, the new terminal will be adaptable and sustainable, operating in many different configurations dependant on varying aircraft and passenger traffic throughout each day. With an integrated multimodal transport centre featuring direct links to local and national rail services, including the Gaotie high-speed rail, the new Daxing airport will be a key hub within Beijing's growing transport network and a catalyst for the region's economic development, including the city of Tianjin and Hebei Province.

ZHA's projects include some of the world's most popular, user-focused and adaptable civic architecture that prioritises the public realm and user experience. This expertise, together with ADPI's history and knowledge of airport planning and development, will ensure the new terminal at Daxing to be the world's most convenient, sustainable and future-proof airport. Following the completion of the concept design stage, the project is now being led by the Local Design Institute team under the continued leadership of BNAH.

Location Daxing, Beijing, China
Client Beijing New Airport Headquarters (BNAH)
Area 880,000 m^2 (9,472,241 ft^2)
Date 2011–2019

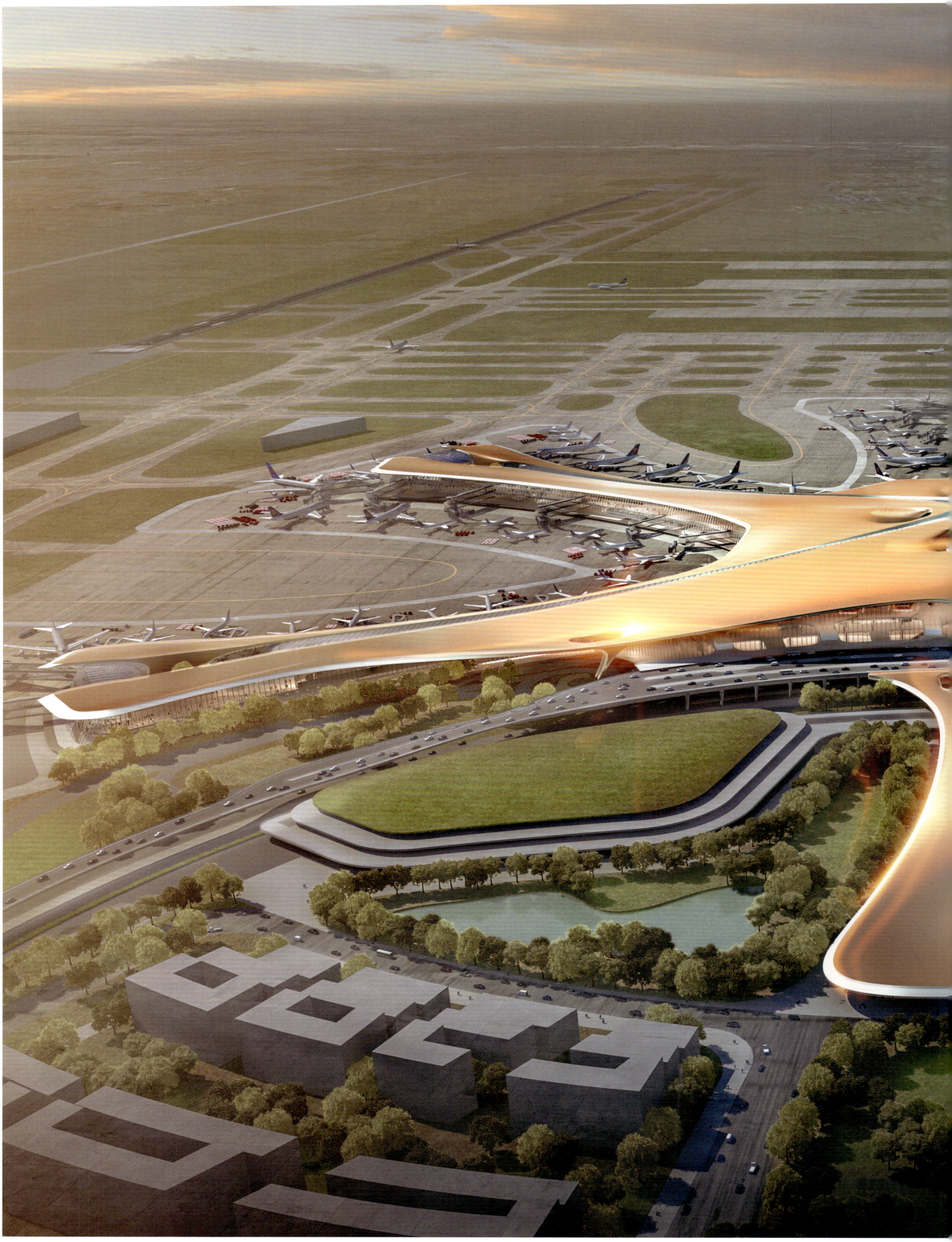

H
G
F
E

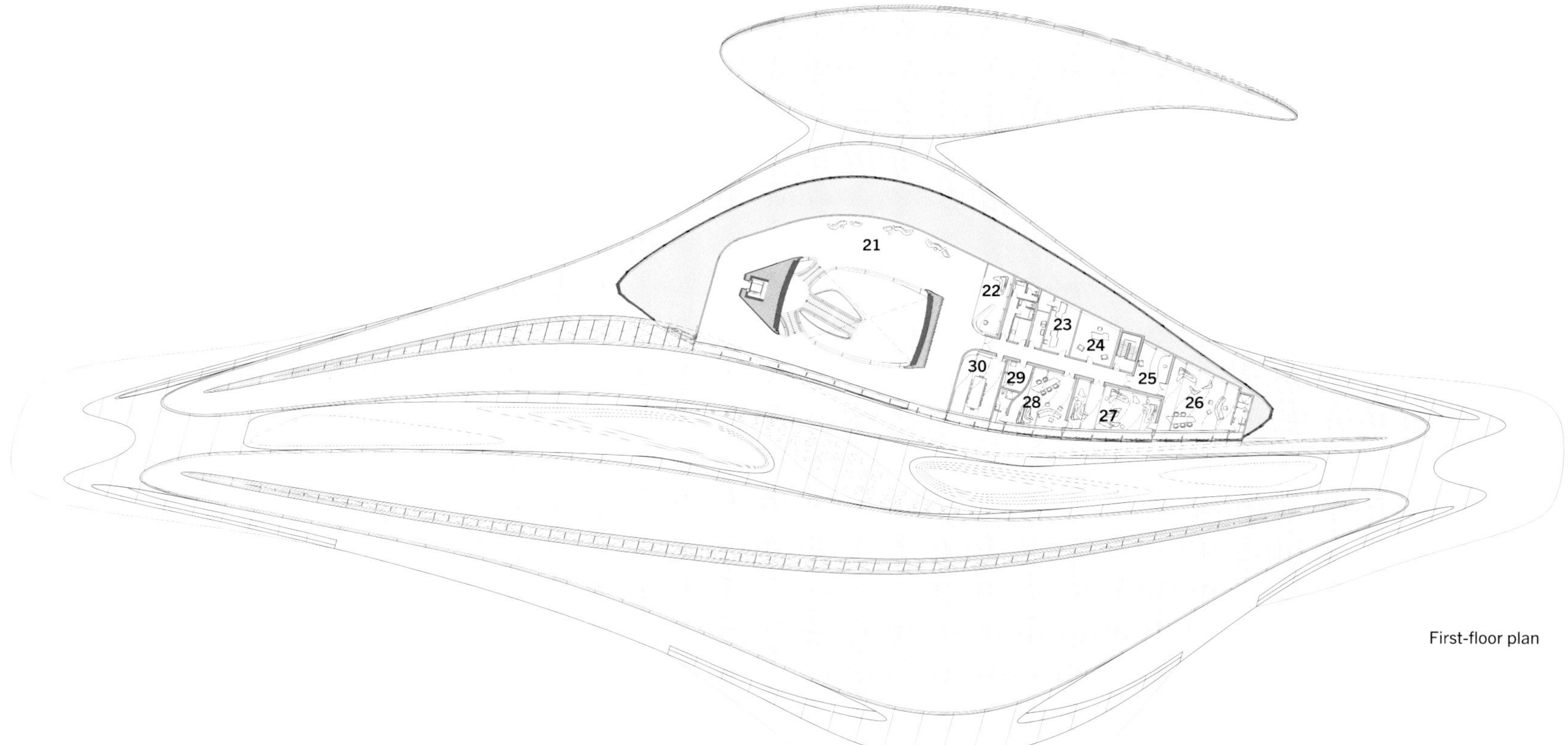

First-floor plan

1 Visitor centre
2 Command Centre
3 Call centre
4 Plant room
5 Drop-off
6 Reception and Foyer
7 Lounge
8 Auditorium
9 Male prayer room
10 Offices
11 Electrical room
12 Departamental offices
13 Cafe/bar
14 Staff entrance
15 Recycling and Waste
16 I.T. department
17 Meeting rooms
18 Female prayer room
19 Research lab
20 Courtyard
21 Gallery
22 Management reception
23 Staff offices
24 Director's office
25 Chairman's secretary
26 Chairman's office
27 Majilis
28 CEO's office
29 CEO's secretary
30 Boardroom

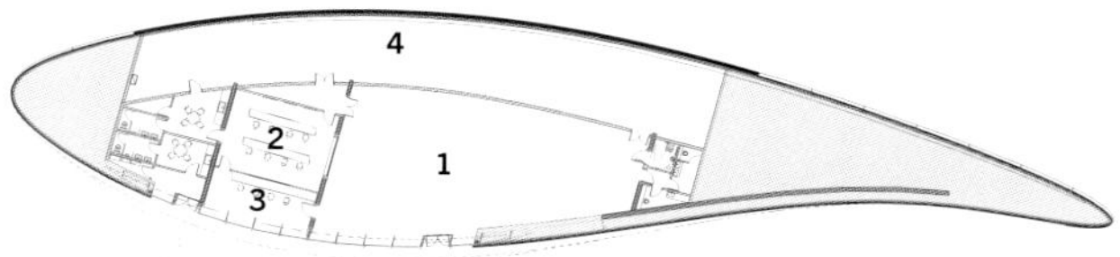

4

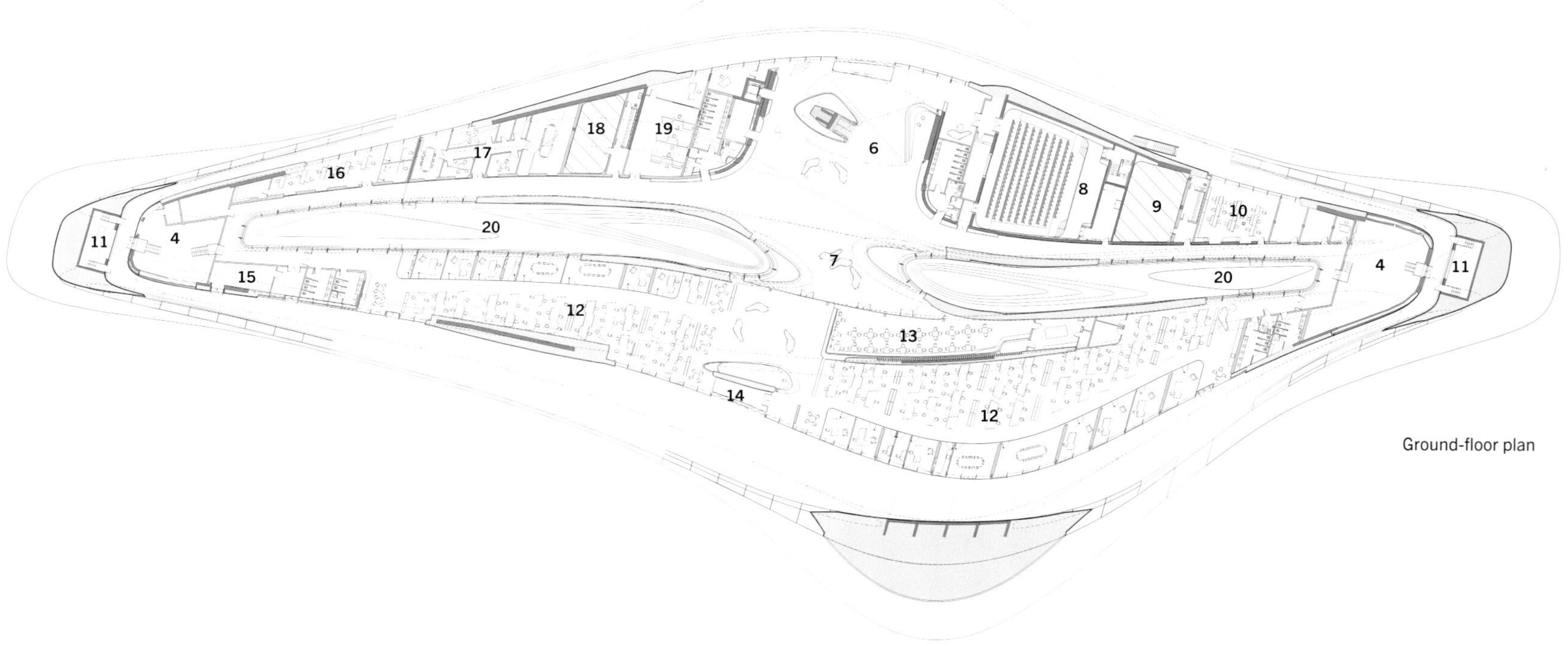

Ground-floor plan

0 10m

BEE'AH HEADQUARTERS

Bee'ah Headquarters was designed to provide comfort alongside minimising energy and resource consumption. The composition of the building has been informed by its desert context as a series of intersecting dunes orientated to accommodate the prevailing Shamal winds, and developed to ensure the internal spaces are provided with ample daylight and views while limiting exposure to the harsh sun.

The large site enabled the development of the design as an array of dunes within its desert landscape leading to the two central dunes of the Headquarters. These two central dunes house the public and management section (entrance lobby, auditorium, visitors education centre and gallery, and management offices), and the administrative section (departmental offices and staff café). The two dunes connect via a central courtyard that forms an 'oasis' inside the building, enhancing the natural ventilation and maximising indirect sunlight to the spaces within.

The building systems have been developed to minimise the energy required for cooling and the need for potable water. In milder months, the façade allows natural ventilation, minimising the need to provide cooling. When air-conditioning is required, it is optimised for energy conservation via the use of ventilation energy recovery, allowing fresh air into the spaces with reduced energy impact.

The exterior finishes of the building have been selected to reflect sunlight and help reduce energy consumption by providing a local heat profile that is akin to the natural desert environment rather than the high heat profiles associated with conventional roofing systems. The building's structure has been developed to minimise material consumption through architectural and structural integration. Individual elements of the building's structure and skin are of standard orthogonal dimensions, enabling significant portions to be constructed from materials recovered from the local construction and demolition waste streams managed by Bee'ah, minimising demand for new materials.

Location Sharjah, United Arab Emirates
Client Bee'ah
Area 7000 m^2 (75,347 ft^2)
Date 2014–TBC

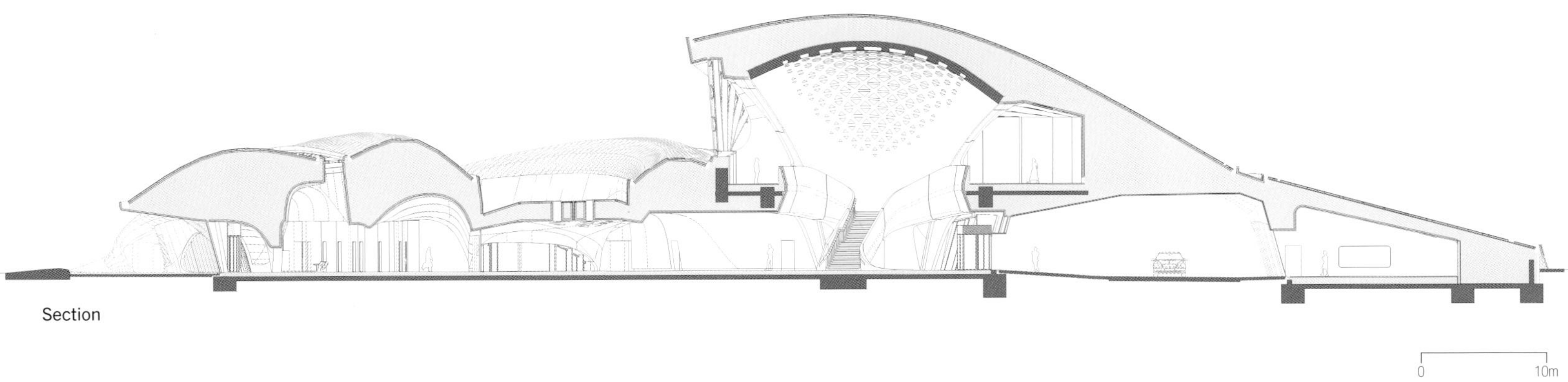

Section

SLEUK RITH INSTITUTE

The institute's design is organised as five wooden structures that are separate volumes at ground level, but interweave and link together as they rise upwards, connecting the different departments, visitors, students and staff into a singular whole. The structures range between three to eight stories. Visitors approach the building on causeways above reflecting catchment pools that mirror the building's form and bring light deep into the internal spaces.

The design connects the museum, library, school, and institute at various levels, allowing users to interact and collaborate, enhancing their understanding and experience. Yet each of the institute's functions is also able to operate independently when required.

Constructed from sustainably sourced timber, the primary structure, exterior shading, and interior partitions give natural scale, warmth and materiality. The more complex forms have been designed to be assembled from economical straight and single-curved timber sections. To accommodate Cambodia's tropical climate, the narrower lower levels of the institute are shaded by the building's form, while louvers on the upper levels keep out strong sunshine. The institute's buildings will be built on raised terraces, to protect from Phnom Penh's seasonal flooding.

The building's design, including measures to reduce energy and water consumption while increasing system efficiencies, and the installation of renewable energy sources, will increase its ecological performance. The institute's form minimises solar gain, and the external shading system will be varied on each elevation to reduce solar gain while maintaining sufficient daylight levels.

The horizontal roof of the building houses renewable energy sources that are extremely effective in Phnom Penh's climate: photovoltaic cells for power and a solar thermal array for hot water generation. Plant and air-system heat exchangers will also be located on the roof, maximising the area within the building for the institute's commemorative, educational, cultural, and community programs.

Location Phnom Penh, Cambodia
Client Sleuk Rith Institute, Document Center of Cambodia
Area 8000 m^2 (86,111 ft^2)
Date TBC

COMPANY PROFILE

Zaha Hadid founded Zaha Hadid Architects (ZHA) in 1979 and completed her first building, the Vitra Fire Station, Germany, in 1993. Zaha Hadid passed away on the 31st of March 2016, but her legacy endures within the DNA of the design studio she created.

Her working methods and principles continue to drive and inspire us every day, and we work on as she taught us—with curiosity, integrity, passion and determination. Through research, experimentation and collaboration we make the discoveries we did not think were possible, working on new ideas, pushing them into the mainstream to raise standards and benefit all. Marrying concepts of integration and connectivity with tremendous advancements in design technologies, ecologically sound materials and construction practices, we do not look at the disparate parts, but work to understand them as a whole to find solutions to the defining challenges of our era.

Zaha Hadid Architects continues as one of the most innovative and successful architectural practices worldwide. The principal, Patrik Schumacher, worked with Zaha for nearly 30 years and our Board of Directors, as well as the Associate Directors and Senior Associates, are amongst the most experienced architects in the industry.

The MAXXI: Italian National Museum of XXI Century Arts in Rome, the London Aquatics Centre for the 2012 Olympic Games and the Heydar Aliyev Centre in Baku are built manifestos of ZHA's quest for complex, fluid space. Previous seminal buildings such as the Guangzhou Opera House and Contemporary Arts Centre in Cincinnati have also been hailed as architecture that transforms our ideas of the future with visionary spatial concepts defined by advanced design, material and construction processes.

The practice recently completed the Oxford University's Middle East Centre at St Antony's College and is currently working on a diversity of projects worldwide, including the new Beijing Airport Terminal Building in Daxing, China, the Sleuk Rith Institute in Phnom Penh, Cambodia, residential projects in the United States, as well as in Australia. Zaha Hadid Architects' portfolio also includes cultural, corporate, academic, sporting and infrastructure projects across Asia, the Middle East, Europe and the Americas, in addition to national institutions such as the Central Bank of Iraq and the Grand Theatre de Rabat.

Now 400 strong, based in London and with offices in Beijing, New York, Hong Kong, Mexico City, and Dubai, Zaha Hadid Architects has created a unique aesthetic that is at once unclassifiable and yet instantly recognisable for its clarity of vision.

The practice is driven to provide clients and members of the community with schemes that surpass their expectations for what is achievable within their site, brief, and budget; our track record of highly satisfied clients attests to the success of our methodology in designing and building truly transformational projects.

ZAHA HADID | FOUNDER

Born in Baghdad, Iraq, Zaha Hadid (1950–2016) studied mathematics at the American University of Beirut before moving to London in 1972 to attend the Architectural Association (AA) School where she was awarded the Diploma Prize in 1977. She then became a partner of the Office for Metropolitan Architecture, taught at the AA with OMA collaborators Rem Koolhaas and Elia Zenghelis, and later led her own studio at the AA until 1987. Having founded Zaha Hadid Architects in 1979 she completed her first building, the Vitra Fire Station, Germany, in 1993.

Since 1987 Zaha held numerous chairs and guest professorships at universities around the world, including at Columbia, Harvard, and Yale; University of Illinois in Chicago; Hochschule für Bildende Künste in Hamburg; the Knowlton School of Architecture in Ohio; and University of Applied Arts in Vienna. Most recently she was the Eero Saarinen Visiting Professor of Architectural Design at Yale.

In addition, she was made Honorary Member of the American Academy of Arts and Letters, Fellow of the American Institute of Architecture, Commander of the British Empire, 2002 and Dame Commander of the Order of the British Empire in 2012. Zaha was also awarded the Pritzker Architecture Prize (considered the Nobel Prize of architecture) in 2004.

She was internationally known for her built, theoretical, and academic work. Each of her projects built on more than 30 years of exploration and research in the interrelated fields of urbanism, architecture, and design.

Working with senior office partner, Patrik Schumacher, Zaha's interests lay in the rigorous interface between architecture, urbanism, landscape, and geology, as her practice integrated natural topography, and human-made systems, leading to innovation with new technologies.

Zaha's work of the past 30 years was the subject of critically acclaimed exhibitions at New York's Solomon R. Guggenheim Museum in 2006, London's Design Museum in 2007, the Palazzo della Ragione, Padua, Italy, in 2009, the Philadelphia Museum of Art in 2011, the DAC Copenhagen in 2013, and the State Hermitage Museum in Saint Petersburg in 2015.

Zaha's outstanding contribution to the architectural profession has been acknowledged by the world's most respected institutions, including the Forbes List of the 'World's Most Powerful Women' in 2008, and the Japan Art Association presenting her with the 'Praemium Imperiale' in 2009. In 2010 and 2011 the Royal Institute of British Architects awarded her designs the Stirling Prize, one of architecture's highest accolades. Other awards include UNESCO naming Zaha as an 'Artist for Peace'; the Republic of France honouring Zaha with the 'Commandeur de l'Ordre des Arts et des Lettres'; and *TIME* magazine included her in their list of the '100 Most Influential People in the World.' In 2012 Queen Elizabeth II made Zaha a Dame Commander of the Order of the British Empire; and in September 2015, the Royal Institute of British Architects announced Zaha Hadid as the recipient of the 2016 Royal Gold Medal.

PATRIK SCHUMACHER | PRINCIPAL

Patrik Schumacher has been a designer at Zaha Hadid Architects since 1988. He is a company director and senior designer of the practice, as well as a co-author and project partner on seminal projects, such as the MAXXI: National Museum of XXI Century Arts in Rome, the BMW Central Building in Leipzig, and the Guangzhou Opera House in China. He is registered with the Architect's Registration Board, and is a member of the Royal Institute of British Architects.

Patrik studied architecture at the University of Stuttgart and at the Southbank University in London. He completed his architectural diploma and received his degree from Stuttgart University in 1990, and also studied philosophy at both Bonn and London Universities. In 1999, he received his doctoral degree from the Institute for Cultural Sciences at the University of Klagenfurt.

Since 1992, Patrik has been teaching at architectural schools in Britain, continental Europe and the USA. He is a co-director of the Design Research Laboratory (DRL) at the Architectural Association School of Architecture. He has co-taught a series of postgraduate option studios with Zaha Hadid at the University of Illinois—Chicago, Yale, Columbia, and the Graduate School of Design at Harvard University, in addition to having been tenured Professor at the Institute for Experimental Architecture, Innsbruck University.

His contribution to the discourse of contemporary architecture is also evident in his published works and interviews. In 2010 and 2012 he published the two volumes of his theoretical opus magnum *The Autopoiesis of Architecture*.

JIM HEVERIN | DIRECTOR

Jim joined Zaha Hadid Architects in 1997. He has worked on a variety of completed projects from pavilions to offices, museums and sports venues. He became an Associate in 2006, Associate Director in 2008 and Director in 2013, and currently is responsible for the overall management and delivery of key projects. Jim was project director of the London Aquatics Centre, as well as of the Investcorp Building in Oxford.

Jim has a Bachelor's degree in Architecture from Scott Sutherland School of Architecture, Aberdeen (1995) and a Diploma of Architecture from University of North London (1997). He has been registered with the ARB since 1999.

GIANLUCA RACANA | DIRECTOR

Gianluca joined Zaha Hadid Architects in 2000 after working in practices in Paris, Rome and New York. He became a Director in 2013. He studied architecture at the ETSAB in Barcelona, at Columbia University in New York, at the University 'La Sapienza' in Rome, and at the Architectural Association in London.

Gianluca was instrumental in the design and delivery of MAXXI: National Museum of XXI Century Arts, in Rome, which he led from the earliest competition stages through to the project's completion in 2009 (it opened to the public in 2010). Currently, he is project director for the City Life project in Milan, alongside the King Abdullah Financial District Metro Station and a high-speed railway station in Naples, as well as overseeing the practice's work in Australia and Singapore.

CHARLES WALKER | DIRECTOR

Charles Walker joined Zaha Hadid Architects in early 2007 and was made a Director in 2014. He studied architecture at the University of Waterloo in Ontario, Canada, and structural engineering at the Imperial College of Science Technology, and Medicine in London. Before joining Zaha Hadid Architects, Charles worked at some of the United Kingdom's best-known engineering firms, including Richard Horden Associates, Ron Arad Associates, and Atelier One. He co-founded Ove Arup and Partners' Advanced Geometry Unit in 2000, where he was instrumental in building the unit's reputation for innovative design and engineering.

Charles is both a registered architect and a chartered structural engineer, bringing a unique perspective to Zaha Hadid Architects' work. He also has an extensive pedigree as a teacher, leading a unit at the Architectural Association from 2003 to 2013 and serving as Head of Architecture at the Royal College of Art in London. Currently, Charles oversees much of the practice's work in China, as well as acting as project director for the Danjiang Bridge in Taiwan and government buildings in Algeria and Iraq.

MOUZHAN MAJIDI | DIRECTOR (CHIEF EXECUTIVE)

Mouzhan Majidi joined Zaha Hadid Architects in 2015 following a distinguished 27-year career with Foster and Partners. He studied architecture at Strathclyde University, graduating in 1987 with first-class honours, and receiving numerous awards, including the RIBA Silver Medal for Best National Diploma Project in 1987. On graduation, Mouzhan joined Foster and Partners, where he held a number of increasingly senior roles within the practice, culminating with his appointment as Chief Executive Officer in May 2007 after his leadership of the management buyout funded by 3i. Recognized as an outstanding designer and architect, Mouzhan has overseen a diverse range of acclaimed cultural, commercial, educational, infrastructure, leisure, residential, and transport projects around the world. At Zaha Hadid Architects he combines close day-to-day involvement in design with the strategic direction of the practice, in collaboration with Patrik Schumacher, and the Directors.

SATOSHI OHASHI | DIRECTOR (HEAD OF REGION/FAR EAST)

Born in Japan and raised in America, Satoshi Ohashi has worked globally in New York, London, Paris and Tokyo. He has worked and collaborated closely with Zaha Hadid since 1987. He is based in Beijing as Zaha Hadid Architects' Head of Region in the Far East. Satoshi is continuously pursuing the possibilities of architecture and design from large-scale urban design to smaller-scale furniture and product design.

He has received numerous awards including 2005 IIDA International Lighting Award, NTT DoCoMo Kansai Telecommunications Tower and 2009 CIID China International Interior Design Awards.

Satoshi graduated from the College of Architecture & Urban Planning at the University of Michigan, where he obtained a B.S. Arch in 1984. He subsequently studied as a postgraduate at the University of Illinois Chicago and in Versailles, France. He has taught and lectured at many universities around the world. In 2004 he held a position as a visiting critic at Yale University Graduate School of Architecture. He addressed the 2005 World Expo in Aichi, Japan, and participated in the exhibition. He was also a Selection Committee Juror and visiting critic at China Central Academy of Fine Arts. From 1988 to 1993, he was the director and project architect for Zaha Hadid Architects' Tokyo office working on the design of the practice's early works, including the first major interior project Moonsoon restaurant.

In recent years he has delivered several large-scale projects, including three SOHO projects in China: Galaxy SOHO, Wangjing SOHO, and Sky SOHO. His current projects include hotel and service apartments, as well as a design museum, both in China.

TIAGO CORREIA | DIRECTOR (HEAD OF REGION/UNITED STATES)

Tiago first joined Zaha Hadid Architects in 2000, working on a wide range of projects including the One North master plan in Singapore, the Ordrupgaard Museum extension in Denmark, and the BMW Central Building in Leipzig, Germany. He was also involved in the practice's major exhibitions, including a retrospective at the Guggenheim Museum in New York and the Venice Biennale, before leaving the practice in 2012 to continue his studies. He re-joined Zaha Hadid Architects in 2015 to lead its New York office, with a focus on United States–based projects and expanding the practice's presence in North America. Currently, Tiago is working on several mixed-use high-rise and transportation schemes in the United States.

Tiago studied architecture at the University of Lisbon's School of Architecture, graduating with honours in 2001. He is a registered architect in both Portugal and the United Kingdom. Tiago also holds an MBA with honours from the Wharton School at the University of Pennsylvania, where he double majored in Real Estate and Finance. After completing his MBA, Tiago worked for Tishman Speyer in New York, including rotations in their Debt Finance, Equity Capital Markets, and Development groups as part of the firm's Leadership Development Program.

PAOLA CATTARIN | ASSOCIATE DIRECTOR

Paola joined the Zaha Hadid Architects team as a Designer in 1999, became an Associate in 2006 and an Associate Director in 2016. She has been involved in a wide range of project designs, including the Maritime Terminal Salerno in Italy, and project management assignments. Paola is a registered architect in Italy and the United Kingdom. Paola studied architecture at the ETSAB in Barcelona and at the University of Rome, 'La Sapienza', where she received her Diploma of Architecture in 1996.

CRISTIANO CECCATO | ASSOCIATE DIRECTOR

Since joining the company in 2008, Cristiano's work has spanned a range of management, design and technology leadership responsibilities. He previously worked for Gehry Partners and was Director of Research & Consulting for Gehry Technologies. Cristiano received a Diploma of Architecture from the Architectural Association in 1996 and a Master's Degree in Computer Science from the Imperial College of Science and Technology, London in 1997. He became an elected Fellow of the Royal Society of Arts in 2004. Cristiano has lectured widely on the subject of computational rule-based design systems and parametric form-finding in digital building processes. He has also held academic faculty positions in London, Milan, Hong Kong, Los Angeles and Australia.

NILS FISCHER | ASSOCIATE DIRECTOR

Nils joined Zaha Hadid Architects in 2004 and has developed a large design portfolio spanning Europe, the Middle East and Asia, with a focus on cultural facilities, such as performing arts facilities and museums, as well as projects involving novel design, engineering and manufacturing solutions. Nils also leads the Computational Design Research Group (CODE), developing next-generation technologies for form-finding and rationalisation. Previously, he worked for ABB Architekten and Bernhard Franken Architekten in Frankfurt on award-winning projects for BMW—and as a freelance engineering consultant on projects by Massimiliano Fuksas, among others. Nils has an academic background in experimental computational geometry. He studied in Germany and Italy and graduated from the Technische Universitat Darmstadt, Germany with a degree in architecture in 2002.

MANUELA GATTO | ASSOCIATE DIRECTOR

Manuela joined Zaha Hadid Architects in 2002. She has worked as Project Architect on a number of our projects in Europe and China. As an Associate Director, she's involved in all aspects of project organisation, including design and technical team management along with contract administration. Manuela has an architecture degree with honours from the Istituto Universitario di Architettura di Venezia (1998) and a Master's of Architecture with distinction from the Design Research Laboratory of the Architectural Association, London (2002). She is co-author of the book *Negotiate My Boundary!: Mass-Customization and Responsive Environments*, published by the Architectural Association Publications and re-issued by Birkhaeuser Verlag. Manuela was joint Unit Master at the Architectural Association and has held an academic faculty position at the University of Venice. She has lectured widely in Europe about mass customisation and innovative fabrication techniques.

JOHANNES HOFFMANN | ASSOCIATE DIRECTOR

Johannes joined Zaha Hadid Architects in 2005 to work on the competitions for the Riverside Museum of Transport in Glasgow, United Kingdom, and has since then been involved in a variety of cultural, as well as sport, projects. Johannes has a Degree of Architecture from Technische Universitaet Muenchen (1991–1994), a Professional Diploma from the University of North London (1995–1997) and a Certificate in Professional Practice in Management in Architecture from The Bartlett School of Architecture (2000–2001).

FILIPPO INNOCENTI | ASSOCIATE DIRECTOR

Filippo joined the company in 2002. He spent a number of years in Rome to oversee the firm's Italian projects before relocating to London. Filippo is currently the project director for the new high-speed train station for Naples–Afragola, as well as of the King Abdullah Financial District Metro Station in Riyadh. Filippo brings a wealth of experience to the team. Filippo holds a Master's in Design Research from the Architectural Association in London, and he teaches at both Florence University of Architecture and the Milan Polytechnic.

SARA KLOMPS | ASSOCIATE DIRECTOR

Sara Klomps first joined Zaha Hadid Architects as an intern in 1998–1999, when she worked on several competitions. After completing her studies in Germany, she returned to the practice in 2000 as a qualified architect. An Associate since 2007 and Associate Director since 2014, Sara is involved in both the design and delivery of a range of the practice's projects, including museums, sports facilities and civic buildings. Sara is a registered architect in both Germany and the United Kingdom.

Sara studied in Germany at the Universität Dortmund and at the Universität Karlsruhe, graduating with a Diploma of Architecture in 2000. She has a particular interest in construction methodology and concrete design, and lectures on the subject regularly at architecture schools and industry events. Sara has worked on a number of the practice's seminal projects, including the Rosenthal Center for Contemporary Art in Cincinnati; the RIBA Stirling Prize–winning MAXXI: National Museum of XXI Century Arts in Rome; the Car Park and Terminus Hoenheim-Nord in Strasbourg, France; and the 800-metre-long (2625-foot-long) Sheikh Zayed Bridge in Abu Dhabi. She was also the project architect for the multi-award-winning Phaeno Science Center in Wolfsburg, Germany, leading the project team from the initial concept design through construction to the completion of the project. Alongside project director Jim Heverin, Sara was one of two project architects for the London Aquatics Centre for the 2012 Olympic and Paralympic Games. Sara led the project team from the beginning of the concept phase through to the completion of the project for both the Olympic and Legacy stages of the project, with a focus on the project's successful delivery. Her most recent projects include the new 90,000-square-meter (968,751-square-foot) high-rise headquarters for the Central Bank of Iraq, and a residential development on a technically demanding site in New York.

CHRIS LÉPINE | ASSOCIATE DIRECTOR

A member of the firm since 2006, Chris Lépine has experience in large-scale international projects and the use of advanced digital technology to resolve complex design challenges. Chris is currently the project director of 1000 Museum, a residential tower in Miami, United States. Chris was formerly an associate at Foster and Partners where he had many leadership roles on completed international projects, including lead designer and project architect for a prestigious winery in Spain. He also worked with Foster and Partners' exclusive Specialist Modelling Group.

Chris obtained a Master's degree at Clemson University in South Carolina, where he received both the top graduate prize and the Best Thesis Project award. He also holds a degree in finance from the University of South Carolina's Honours College. Chris' continued interest in the relationship between architectural form and drawing techniques has led to lectures presented at the Architectural Association in London.

VIVIANA MUSCETTOLA | ASSOCIATE DIRECTOR

Viviana joined Zaha Hadid Architects in 2004, having worked for a number of different practices in China, the Netherlands and Italy. An Associate since 2009, a Senior Associate since 2014, and an Associate Director since 2016, Viviana has worked on a wide range of projects and competitions in Malaysia, China, Egypt, Singapore, France and the United Kingdom. Viviana worked on winning competitions for the Glasgow Riverside Museum of Transport, the CMA CGM Tower in Marseille and the Architecture Foundation, London. She has since worked as project architect and project director on a number of international projects.

Viviana began her architecture studies at the University of Naples, receiving her degree in architecture in 2001 and winning the prize for Best Thesis Project. She continued her studies at the Architectural Association's Design Research Laboratory, receiving her Master's degree in 2004. She has also done research into key urban quarters in Paris and Los Angeles. She is a registered architect in both the United Kingdom and Italy.

As project director, Viviana has led a number of major projects for the practice, including the d'Leedon residential development in Singapore, which was completed in 2014, a master plan for the Cairo Expo City's exhibition and conference centre in Egypt (unbuilt), and a mixed-use development in Beijing featuring a luxury department store, entertainment complex and apartments (currently on site). She has contributed to the design of a number of the firm's product and furniture pieces, such as the Moon System Sofa for B&B Italia, Dune Formations shelving and the Zaha Hadid Exhibition in Padua, Italy. Currently, Viviana is the project director of the Morpheus hotel tower project in Macau.

MICHELE PASCA DI MAGLIANO | ASSOCIATE DIRECTOR

Within two months of joining the team in 2004, Michele worked on winning competitions for the Riverside Transport Museum, Glasgow, CMA CGM Tower, Marseille, and Architecture Foundation, London. He has since worked as project architect and project director on a number of projects, including d'Leedon, a large residential project in Singapore. Michele studied architecture at the University of Naples and has a Master's of Architecture from the Architectural Association in London. He is registered as an architect in London and Italy.

CHRISTOS PASSAS | ASSOCIATE DIRECTOR

Christos has worked with Zaha Hadid Architects as a Senior Designer since February 1998 and has subsequently operated as project director on numerous projects and winning competitions. Christos gained his B Arch (Hons) degree as a Fulbright Scholar at the Pratt Institute's School of Architecture in Brooklyn, New York, in 1995. He received his Graduate Design Diploma in 1998 in Advanced Architectural Design at the Architectural Association, London. Christos teaches Parametric Design and Urbanism at the Architectural Association in London and is Guest DAAD Professor in the Dessau Institute of Architecture (HA) at Bauhaus, Dessau. He is at the forefront of design research and often participates in design juries at universities around the United Kingdom.

WOODY YAO | ASSOCIATE DIRECTOR

Since joining the team in 1994, Woody has successfully managed and designed a number of key projects, including the Jockey Club Innovation Tower at the Hong Kong Polytechnic, and has curated major exhibitions, including Zaha Hadid Retrospective at MAK (Vienna), Guggenheim Museum (New York), Design Museum (London) and the State Hermitage Museum (St Petersburg). Woody also has considerable experience in interiors and product design and he is a Director of Zaha Hadid Design. As a senior member, he continues to direct his team from competition to construction. Woody was project director of the Jockey Club Innovation Tower at Hong Kong Polytechnic.

Woody studied in Hong Kong and Merchiston Castle, Edinburgh, before graduating from the Architectural Association School of Architecture, in London. During his time at the AA, Woody completed a number of private commissions, and contributed to large-scale projects with YRM London.

TARIQ KHAYYAT | SENIOR ASSOCIATE (HEAD OF REGION/MIDDLE EAST)

Tariq has worked as architect and project designer since first joining the firm in 2005. He is based in Dubai to oversee all Zaha Hadid Architects' projects in the Middle East, as well as North Africa. Among many other projects, Tariq is the project director of the Bee'ah Headquarters in Sharjah, United Arab Emirates. Tariq has a Master's degree in Architecture and Urbanism from the Design Research Laboratory of the Architectural Association, London.

JUAN IGNACIO ARANGUREN | SENIOR ASSOCIATE (HEAD OF REGION/SOUTH AMERICA)

Juan joined Zaha Hadid Architects in 2003, having previously worked in other valued practices in London and Caracas. In 2004 he led the winning competition for the new EuskoTren Headquarters Development in Durango. Juan is Head of Region/South America and is currently the project director of the Esfera City Center in Monterrey, Mexico, as well as of other projects in the region. Juan received his Diploma of Architecture from the Universidad Central de Venezuela, (Caracas, 1996) before completing postgraduate studies at the Architectural Association leading to a Master's degree in Architecture and Urbanism (London, 2000).

CHRONOLOGY OF WORKS

BUILT PROJECTS

1990 Moonsoon Restaurant (Interior) (Sapporo, Japan)

1993 Vitra Fire Station (Weil am Rhein, Germany)
IBA Housing (Berlin, Germany)

1995 Blueprint Pavilion, Interbuild 95 (Birmingham, England)

1999 Land Formation One / Landesgartenschau (Weil am Rhein, Germany)
Mind Zone (London, England)

2001 Car Park and Terminus Hoenheim-Nord (Strasbourg, France)

2003 Lois & Richard Rosenthal Center for Contemporary Art (Cincinnati, Ohio, United States)

2005 BMW Central Building (Leipzig, Germany)
Phaeno Science Center (Wolfsburg, Germany)
Hotel Puerta America (Interior) (Madrid, Spain)
Ordrupgaard Museum Extension (Copenhagen, Denmark)

2006 Spittelau Viaducts Housing (Vienna, Austria)
BMW Showroom Spittel (Leipzig, Germany)
Maggie's Fife Cancer Care Centre (Kircaldy, Scotland)
R Lopez de Heredia Wine Pavilion (Haro, Spain)

2007 Nordpark Cable Railway Stations (Innsbruck, Austria)

2008 Mobile Art Chanel Contemporary Art Container (Hong Kong, China) (p. 34)
Zaragoza Bridge Pavilion (Zaragoza, Spain)
Neil Barrett Flagship Store (Tokyo, Japan)
Home House Club (Interior) (London, England)

2009 JS Bach Chamber Music Hall (Manchester, England)
Burnham Pavilion (Chicago, United States)

2010 MAXXI: National Museum of XXI Century Arts (Rome, Italy)
Shanghai Expo 2010 Egypt Pavilion (Shanghai, China)
Evelyn Grace Academy (London, England)
Sheikh Zayed Bridge (Abu Dhabi, United Arab Emirates)
Guangzhou Opera House (Guangzhou, China)

2011 Glasgow Riverside Museum of Transport (Glasgow, Scotland)
London Aquatics Centre (London, England) (p. 16)
Roca London Gallery (London, England)
CMA CGM Tower (Marseille, France) (p.27)

2012 Pierresvives Archive & Library (Montpellier, France)
Eli & Edythe Broad Art Museum (East Lansing, Michigan, United States) (p. 44)
Galaxy Soho (Beijing, China) (p. 54)
Heydar Aliyev Center (Baku, Azerbaijan) (p. 64)

2013 Stuart Weitzman Flagship Store (Milan, Italy) (p. 88)
The Serpentine Sackler Gallery (London, England) (p. 80)
Library and Learning Centre—University of Economics Vienna (Vienna, Austria) (p. 74)

2014 Jockey Club Innovation Tower, Hong Kong Polytechnic University (Hong Kong, China) (p. 139)
Dongdaemun Design Plaza (Seoul, Korea) (p. 132)
Stuart Weitzman Boutique (Rome, Italy)
Stuart Weitzman Boutique (Hong Kong, China)
City Life Milano Residencial Complex (Milan, Italy) (p. 102)
Nuremberg Messe (Nuremberg, Germany)
Issam Fares Institute for Public Policy & International Affairs, American University of Beirut (Beirut, Lebanon) (p. 94)
Wangjing Soho (Beijing, China) (p. 116)
d'Leedon Apartments (Singapore) (p. 108)
Sky Soho (Shanghai, China) (p. 122)

2015 Investcorp Building for Oxford University at St Antony's College (Oxford, England) (p. 144)
Messner Mountain Museum Corones (South Tyrol, Italy) (p. 158)
Dominion Office Building (Moscow, Russia) (p. 152)

2016 Maritime Terminal Salerno (Salerno, Italy) (p. 166)
Port House Headquarters (Antwerp, Belgium) (p. 172)
King Abdullah Petroleum Research Centre (Riyadh, Kingdom of Saudi Arabia)
Mathematics: The Winton Gallery at the Science Museum (London, England) (p. 180)

PROJECTS IN PROGRESS
[UNDER CONSTRUCTION (U/C) / DETAILED DESIGN STAGE (D/D)]

520 West 28th Street (New York City, United States) (u/c) (p. 188)
Al Wakrah Stadium 2022 (Al Wakrah, Qatar) (u/c)
Changsha Meishihu International Cultural Centre (Changsha, China) (u/c)
Eleftheria Square (Nicosia, Cyprus) (u/c)
Grand Theatre de Rabat (Rabat, Morocco) (u/c)
High-Speed Train Station, Napoli-Afragola (Naples, Italy) (u/c) (p. 212)
Opus (Dubai, United Arab Emirates) (u/c) (p. 218)
TSG Beirut Department Store (Beirut, Lebanon) (u/c)
Argos Residences Graz Austria u/c
Zorrozaure Masterplan (Bilbao, Spain) u/c
Nuremberg Messe, Phase II (Nuremberg, Germany) u/c
Leeza Soho (Beijing, China) u/c
Capital Hill Residence (Moscow, Russia) u/c
CityLife Tower (Milan, Italy) u/c
Nanjing Culture and Conference Centre (Nanjing, China)
Morpheus (Macau, China) (p. 194)
1000 Museum Residential Tower (Miami, Florida, United States) (p. 206)
Esfera City Center, Monterrey (Monterrey, Mexico) (p. 224)
Beijing New Airport Terminal Building (Beijing, China) (p. 242)
King Abdullah Financial District Metro Station (Riyadh, Kingdom of Saudi Arabia) (p. 200)
Sberbank Technopark (Moscow, Russia)
Masaryk Railway Station Central Business District (Prague, Czech Republic)
Hotel and Residences for Lusail City (Lusail, Qatar)
One-North Masterplan (Singapore)
220 11th Avenue (New York City, United States) d/d
Bee'ah Headquarters (Sharjah, United Arab Emirates) d/d (p. 248)
Casa Atlantica (Rio de Janeiro, Brazil) d/d
Central Bank of Iraq (Baghdad, Iraq) d/d
Culenova City Centre (Bratislava, Slovakia) d/d
Danjiang Bridge (Taipei, Taiwan) d/d
582–606 Collins Street (Melbourne, Australia) d/d (p. 236)
Grace on Coronation (Brisbane, Australia) d/d (p. 230)
Jesolo Magica (Jesolo, Italy) d/d
National Parliament of Iraq (Baghdad, Iraq) d/d
Pavilion Gardens (Bournemouth, United Kingdom) d/d
Sleuk Rith Institute (Phnom Penh, Cambodia) d/d (p. 254)
Urban Heritage Administration Centre (Diriyah, Kingdom of Saudi Arabia) d/d
Forest Green Rovers stadium (Stroud, United Kingdom) d/d

AWARDS AND RECOGNITION

Zaha Hadid's work has been recognized internationally with significant commendations, memberships, medals, and prizes. Her paintings, drawings, installation pieces and other works have always been an important testing field, and a medium for the exploration of her design.

AWARDS

1982 59 Eaton Place, London—Gold Medal Architectural Design, British Architecture

1998 Honourable Member of the Bund Deutscher Architekten

2000 Honourable Member of the American Academy of Arts and Letters

Honorary Fellowship of the American Institute of Architects

Mind Zone, Millennium Dome, London—RIBA Awards

2001 Car Park and Terminus Hoenheim North, Strasbourg—Equerre d'Argent special mention

2002 Car Park and Terminus Hoenheim North, Strasbourg—AIA UK Chapter Award

One-north Master Plan, Singapore—AIA UK Chapter Honourable Mention

Car Park and Terminus Hoenheim North, Strasbourg—Red Dot Award

Bergisel Ski-Jump, Innsbruck—Austrian State Architecture Prize

Bergisel Ski-Jump, Innsbruck—Tyrolean Architecture Award

Commander of the British Empire, CBE

2003 Car Park and Terminus Hoenheim North, Strasbourg—Mies van der Rohe Award

2004 Architect of the Year—Blueprint Award

Rosenthal Centre for Contemporary Art, Cincinnati—RIBA Worldwide Award

Zaha Hadid, Laureate of the Pritzker Architecture Prize

London Architect of the year, London Architectural Biennale

2005 Honorary Fellow of Columbia University, New York City, 2005 Member of the Royal Academy of Arts, London

RIBA Medal, European Commercial Building of the Year (BMW Central Building)

Deutsche Architektur Prize, Building of the Year (BMW Central Building)

Finalist for the RIBA Stirling Prize (BMW Central Building)

Gold Medal for Design, International Olympic Committee (Bergisel Ski Jump)

Austrian Decoration of Science and Art, Commissions of Science and Art, Austria

Designer of the Year, Design 05 Art Basel Miami

2006 AIA UK Chapter Award (Phaeno Science Center)

Honorary Doctorate, Yale University, United States

RIBA Medal, European Cultural Building of the Year (Phaeno Science Center)

Honorary Doctorate, American University of Beirut

Finalist for the RIBA Stirling Prize (Phaeno Science Center)

RIBA Jencks Award

Academician, The International Academy of Architecture

Leading European Architects Forum (LEAF) Award (Phaeno Science Center)

2007 AIA UK Chapter Award for Excellence (Maggie's Centre Fife)

Finalist for the Mies van der Rohe Award for European Architecture (Phaeno Science Center)

Thomas Jefferson Foundation Medal in Architecture, United States

Scottish Design Awards, Best Public Building Award (Maggie's Centre, Fife)

London Design Medal, Outstanding Contribution for Design

Travel & Leisure Award, United States (Nordpark Cable Railway)

2008 Maison & Objet Designer of the Year

Dedalo Minosse International Prize for Commissioning a Building (BMW Central Building)

Honorary Degree from The Pratt Institute, New York City

Spirit of Achievement Award, New York City

Cityscape Architectural Award, Dubai (Signature Towers)

Chicago Athenaeum Award, Chicago (Maggie's Centre, Fife)

RIBA European Award, UK (Nordpark Cable Railway)

Architektur und Tirol, Austria (Nordpark Cable Railway)

World Architecture Festival Transport Category, Barcelona, (Nordpark Cable Railway)

RIBA Stirling Prize Nomination (Nordpark Cable Railway)

Forbes' list of 'The 100 Most Powerful Women'

2009 Conde' Nast Innovation&Design Award, London (Zaragoza Bridge Pavilion)

Architectural Digest Spain Editor's Award, Madrid

Praemium Imperiale, The Japanese Art Association, Tokyo

DDI Awards 'Neil Barrett Flagship Store, Tokyo'

The Sunday Times Fast-track 100

The Times '50 People of the Decade'

2010 TIME magazine 'The World's100 Most Influential People'

UNESCO Artist for Peace, Paris

RIBA Stirling Prize (MAXXI, National Museum of XXI Century Arts)

Structural Steel Design Awards, Glasgow Riverside Museum of Transport

Structural Steel Design Awards, London Aquatics Centre

Best Small Project Award, SEAOI, Burnham Pavilion

The Sunday Times '100 Top International Companies'

Innovation & Design Awards, Conde Nast, MAXXI Museum

The New Statesman '50 People Who Matter', Zaha Hadid

Woman of the Year Outstanding Achievement Award

Commandeur de l'Ordre des Arts et des Lettres, Republic of France

WAF World Building of the Year (MAXXI, National Museum of XXI Century Arts)

Visionary of the Year, Harper's Bazaar

Conde' Nast Innovation & Design Award, London (MAXXI, National Museum of XXI Century Arts)

2011 American Institute of Architects UK Chapter Award, (Guangzhou Opera House)

RIBA European Award 2011 (Evelyn Grace Academy)

RIBA Stirling Prize 2011 (Evelyn Grace Academy)

RIBA Award 2011 (Guangzhou Opera House)

Philadelphia Museum of Art, Collab Design Excellence Award 2011: Zaha Hadid

Honourary Doctorate from the University of the Arts, London: Zaha Hadid

Foreign Policy magazine 'Top 100 Global Thinkers of 2011:' Zaha Hadid

Arabian Business magazine 'The World's 50 Most Powerful Arabs:' Zaha Hadid

Newsweek magazine '150 Women Who Shake The World': Zaha Hadid

Huffington Post Game Changer 2011: Zaha Hadid

First Prize, Outstanding Engineering Design Excellence in China (Guangzhou Opera House)

2012 International Road Federation, Global Road Achievement Award for Design (Sheikh Zayed Bridge)

Travel & Leisure Award, Berlin (Sheikh Zayed Bridge)

Jane Drew Prize 'Outstanding contribution to the status of women in architecture'

The Sunday Times 'Makers & Shakers 1962–2012'

Gulf Business magazine, 'World's Most Influential Arabs for 2012'

European Museum Academy Micheletti Award (Riverside Museum)

The Design Week Awards (Roca London Gallery)

Dame Commander of the Order of the British Empire (DBE) (Zaha Hadid)

Architectural Record China Award, Best Public Project (Guangzhou Opera House) Women of the Year, Glamour magazine (Zaha Hadid)

Honorary President of the FT/Citi Ingenuity Awards Urban Ideas in Action program judging committee (Zaha Hadid)

Best Retail Space, FX International Interior Design Awards (Roca London Gallery)

Best of Year Awards, Interior Design 'Beauty / Spa / Fitness' (London Aquatics Centre)

2013 DLD2013 'The Aenne Burda Award for Creative Leadership' (Zaha Hadid)

Veuve Clicquot 'Businesswoman of the Year' (Zaha Hadid)

European Museum of the Year (Riverside Museum) BBC Women's Hour 'Power 100' (Zaha Hadid)

Arabian Business '100 Most Powerful Arab Women 2013' (Zaha Hadid ranked number 4) Best European Plant, (BMW Leipzig)

Issam M. Fares Award for Excellence (Zaha Hadid)

Architizer A+ Award (Heydar Aliyev Center, Baku)

Arison Award by The National Young Arts Foundation (Zaha Hadid)

2014 Innovative Design in Engineering & Architecture with Structural Steel (Broad Art Museum) Structural Excellence Awards HK, Commendation of Merit (Jockey Club Innovation Tower)

McKim Medal American Academy in Rome (Zaha Hadid) RIBA National Award (London Aquatics Centre)

RIBA EU Award (Library & Learning Centre, Vienna)

CTBUH 2014 Best Tall Buildings Awards Finalist (JCIT & Wangjing Soho)

Design Museum: Design of the Year Award (Heyder Aliyev Center)

New London Award (London Aquatics Centre)

Restaurant & Bar Designs Award (The Magazine Restaurant)

British Construction Industry Award (London Aquatics Centre)

Honorary Degree of Doctor of Literature of the University of London (Zaha Hadid)

ACADIA Lifetime Achievement Award (Zaha Hadid)

Elle Decoration British Design 2014 Award (Serpentine Sackler Gallery)

Mies van der Rohe Award Nomination (London Aquatics Centre) Mies van der Rohe Award Nomination (Library & Learning Centre, Vienna)

Best Public Space Award CIDA (China) (Galaxy SOHO, Beijing) Architectural Society of China CASC Silver Award (Galaxy SOHO, Beijing) Honorary Key to the City of Miami by Mayor Tomas Regalado (Zaha Hadid)

2015 London Building Excellence Award (Serpentine Sackler Gallery)

AJ 120 International Practice of the Year (Zaha Hadid Architects)

Österreich (Gold Medal of Honour for Services to the Republic of Austria) (Zaha Hadid)

IOC/IAKS Award for Exemplary Sports and Leisure Facilities, Silver Medal, (London Aquatics Centre)

The 2015 WIRED 100 (59/100) (Zaha Hadid)

Louise Blouin Foundation Award (Zaha Hadid)

Announced as RIBA 2016 Royal Gold Medal winner (Zaha Hadid)

Oxford Preservation Trust Award (Investcorp Building)

Joint-winner of the Wood Awards: Bespoke Furniture category (Ves-el)

LUX Award (Investcorp Building)

FIABCI Singapore Property Award, Residential (High-Rise) Category (d'Leedon)

2016 RIBA Award for International Excellence (Jockey Club Innovation Tower)

Finalist for the RIBA International Prize (Heydar Aliyev Center)

PUBLICATIONS

1983 *Zaha Hadid: Planetary Architecture* Two (No. 11)

1986 'Zaha Hadid', *GA Architect* (No. 5, Japan)

1986 'Zaha Hadid', *AA Files* (No. 5)

1991 'Zaha Hadid 1983–1991', *El Croquis* (No. 52, Madrid, Spain)

1995 'Zaha M Hadid', *GA Document Extra*, (No. 3, Japan)

'Zaha Hadid 1992–1995', *El Croquis* (No. 73, Madrid, Spain)

1998 *Zaha Hadid: The Complete Buildings and Projects* (Thames & Hudson)

1999 *Zaha Hadid-LF One* (Birkhäuser)

2000 *Architecture of Zaha Hadid in Photographs*, by Helene Binet (Lars Muller Publishers)

2001 'Zaha Hadid 1996–2001', *El Croquis* (No. 103, Madrid, Spain)

2002 'Zaha Hadid', *Opere e Progetti* (Italy)

2003 'Zaha Hadid Architektur', (MAK, Vienna, Austria)

GA Document (Nos. 65 and 66 (Japan)

2004 *Zaha Hadid Space for Art* (Lars Muller Publishers)

'Zaha Hadid 1983–2004', *El Croquis* (Madrid, Spain)

Digital Hadid (Birkhauser)

Car Park and Terminus Strasbourg (Lars Muller Publishers)

Zaha Hadid: Complete Works (Thames & Hudson)

2006 *BMW Central Building* (Princeton Architectural Press)

Zaha Hadid, catalogue for the Solomon R. Guggenheim Museum)

2007 'Zaha Hadid', *GA Document, Special Issue* (No. 99, Japan)

Zaha Hadid (Motta Architettura)

2008 *Total Fluidity*, catalogue for Seoul Design Olympiad Exhibition

2009 *Zaha Hadid: Complete Works* (Thames & Hudson)

Hadid: Complete Works 1979–2009 (Taschen)

2010 *MAXXI: Zaha Hadid Architects* (Skira/Rizzoli)

'Zaha Hadid', *GA Document, Special Issue* (Japan)

2011 'Being Zaha Hadid', *Abitare*, special issue (Italy)

2012 *Hadid* (Taschen)

2014 'Zaha Hadid', *GA exhibition catalogue* (Japan)

EXHIBITIONS, INSTALLATIONS AND SET DESIGNS

1983 'Retrospective,' Architectural Association (London, England)

1985 'Zaha Hadid' at the GA Gallery (Tokyo, Japan)

1988 'Deconstructivist Architecture,' MoMA (New York, United States)

1992 'The Great Utopia,' Guggenheim Museum (New York, United States)

1995 'Blueprint Pavilion,' Interbuild 95 (Birmingham, England)
'Zaha Hadid,' Grand Central Station (New York, United States)

1996 'Wishmachine: World Invention,' Kunsthalle (Vienna, Austria)

1998 'Addressing the Century: 100 Years of Art and Fashion,' Hayward Gallery (London, England)

1999 'Mind Zone,' Millennium Dome (London, England)
'Pet Shop Boys World Tour' (London, England)

2000 'City Visionaries,' Venice Architecture Biennale, UK Pavilion (Venice, Italy)
'Zaha Hadid,' Jewellery Exhibition (Zurich, Switzerland)
'Summer Pavilion,' Serpentine Gallery (London, England)
'Meshworks,' Villa Medici (Rome, Italy)
'Metapolis' for Charleroi Dance Production Company (Charleroi, Belgium)

2002 'Zaha Hadid: Opere e Progetti,' centro Nazionale Arti Contemporanee (Rome, Italy)
'City of Towers,' Venice Biennale, (Venice, Italy)
'Zaha Hadid Laboratory,' Yale (New Haven, United States)
'Zaha Hadid' National Building Museum (Washington D.C., United States)

2003 'Ice Storm,' MAK (Vienna, Austria)
'Latent Utopias,' Graz Festival (Graz, Austria)
'Beat Furrer's Opera 'Desire' commissioned by Steirischer Herbst (Graz, Austria)

2004 'Snow Show' (Lapland, Finland)
'Zaha Hadid Paintings,' Somerset House (London, England)

2005 '25 Years of Art,' Deutsche Guggenheim (Berlin, Germany)
'Elastika' for Design '05 / Art Basel Miami (Miami, United States)
'Silver Paintings' Rove Gallery (London, England)

2006 'Tokyo Blossons,' Hara Museum (Tokyo, Japan)
'Zaha Hadid,' Guggenheim Museum (New York, United States)
'25 Years of Art,' Singapore Museum (Singapore, Singapore)
'Global Edit,' Wallpaper (Milan, Italy)

2007 'Ideal House,' IMM (Cologne, Germany)
'Airs de Paris,' Pompidou Centre (Paris, France)
'Urban Voids,' Lisbon Architecture Triennale (Lisbon, Portugal)
'Global Cities,' Tate Modern (London, England)
'Zaha Hadid: Architecture & Design,' Design Museum (London, England)
'Lilas,' Serpentine Gallery (London, England)
'Urban Nebula,' London Design Festival (London, England)

2008 'Designer of the year exhibition' Maison & Objet (Paris, France)
'Designers of the Year,' Design Museum (London, England)
'Wirl,' City Art Square (Hong Kong, China)
'Silver Paintings,' Art Cologne (Cologne, Germany)
'Lotus,' 11th International Architecture Biennale (Venice, Italy)
'Total Fluidity,' Seoul Design Olympiad (Seoul, Korea)
'Zaha Hadid,' Sonnabend Gallery (New York, United States)
'Henry Moore—Ideas for Sculpture' Table for Hauser & Wirth (London, England)

2009 'Super Contemporary,' Design Museum (London, England)
'Summer Show,' Royal Academy (London, England)
'Zaha Hadid,' Architecture Biennale Barbara Cappochin (Padova, Italy)
'RSA Annual Exhibition 2009,' Royal Scottish Academy (Edinburgh, Scotland)
'First Works,' Architecture Association (London, England)

2010 'Zaha Hadid—Fluidity & Design,' Bin Matar House (Muharraq, Bahrain)
'Zaha Hadid and Suprematism,' Galerie Gmurzynska (Zurich, Switzerland)

2011 'Zaha Hadid, Une Architecture,' Mobile Art Pavilion (Paris, France)
'Zaha Hadid: Form in Motion' at Philadelphia Museum of Art (Philadelphia, United States)

2012 'Parametric Tower Research' AIT ArchitekturSalon (Cologne, Germany)
'Zaha Hadid,' Buchmann Galerie (Berlin, Germany)
'Zaha Hadid Design Gallery' (London, England)
'Arum Installation and Exhibition,' Venice Architecture Biennale (Venice, Italy)
'Zaha Hadid, Beyond Boundaries, Art and Design' Ivorypress Space (Madrid, Spain)
Zaha Hadid Design Gallery and Fudge Pop-up Salon (London, England)

2013 'Zaha Hadid; World Architecture,'Danish Architecture Centre (Copenhagen, Denmark)
'Multiplicities' Fonderia Napoleonica Eugenia (Milan, Italy)

2014 'Zaha Hadid 360,' Dongdaemun Design Plaza (Seoul, Korea)
'Cosi Fan Tutte' set Design, L.A Philharmonic (Los Angeles, United States)
'Zaha Hadid,' Tokyo Opera City Art Gallery (Tokyo, Japan)
'Crest,' V&A Museum for London Design Festival (London, England)
'Women, Fashion, Power,' Design Museum (London, England)

2015 'Zaha Hadid,' State Hermitage Museum (Saint Petersburg, Russia)

2017 International tour of works (Serpentine Sackler Gallery, London, United Kingdom; MAXXI, Rome, Italy)

PRODUCTS AND FURNITURE

1985 Bitar Furniture for Edra S.p.A (Perignano, Italy)

1997 Tea & Coffee Set for Sawaya Moroni (Milan, Italy)

2002 Z-Scape Furniture for Sawaya Moroni (Milan, Italy)

2003 Vortexx Chandelier for Sawaya Moroni / Zumtobel (Milan, Italy)
Bench Aluminium for Max Protetch (New York, United States)
Tea and Coffee Set for Alessi (Milan, Italy)

2004 Crevasse Vase for Alessi (Milan, Italy)

2005 Z. Car for Kenny Schachter at ROVE (London, England)
Aqua Table for Established & Sons (London, England)
The Crystal Chairs for Sawaya Moroni (Milan, Italy)

2006 Z Island for DuPont Corian (Milan, Italy)
Flow Vase for Serralunga (Milan, Italy)
Icone Bag for Louis Vuitton (Paris, France)
Swarm Chandelier for Established & Sons (London, England)
Seamless Collection for Established & Sons (London, England)

2007 Cutlery for WMF (Geislinger Steige, Germany)
Silver Bowl for Sawaya Moroni (Milan, Italy)
Moon System Sofa for B&B Italia (Milan, Italy)
Mesa Table for Vitra (Basel, Switzerland)
Crater for David Gill Galleries (London, England)
Belu for Kenny Schachter at ROVE (London, England)
Doorhandles for Valli & Valli (Renate, Italy)
Dune Formations for David Gill Galleries (Venice, Italy)

2008 Rug for Arzu (London, England)
Zaha Hadid Chandelier for Swarovski (Milan, Italy)
Scoop Sofa for Sawaya Moroni & ROVE (Milan, Italy)
Cirrus with the Contemporary Arts Center / Formica Corporation (Cincinnati, United States)
Gold Plates; Crevasse Vase for Alessi (London, England)
Z-Stream, Sudeley Castle (Gloucestershire, England)
Neckpiece for Swarovski Rocks (London, England)
Aura, Villa Foscari La Malcontenta (Venice, Italy)
Kloris, Chatsworth House (Derbyshire, England)
Seoul Desk & Table for NY Project (Seoul, Korea)
Melissa Shoes (London, England)
Zaha Hadid Footwear for Lacoste (London, England)
Orchis for Kenny Schachter at ROVE (New York, United States)

2009 Avilion Triflow Taps (London, England)
Genesy Lamp for Artemide (Milan, Italy)

2010 Glace Collection for Swarovski (London, England)
Art Borders Wallpaper (Kirchhain, Germany)
Parador Flooring (London, England)

2011 Tide Shelving for Magis (Milan, Italy)
Z-Chair for Sawaya & Moroni (Milan, Italy)

2012 Citco Marble Reliefs (Milan, Italy)
Liquid Glacial Dining & Coffee Tables (London, England)

2013 Serac Bench for LAB23 (Milan, Italy)
Array Auditorium Seat for Poltrona Frau Contract (Milan, Italy)
Zephyr Sofa by Cassina Contract (Milan, Italy)
Mercuric Marble Tables Collection for Citco (Milan, Italy)
Avia and Aria for Slamp (Milan, Italy)
Kuki Chair for Sawaya&Moroni (Milan, Italy)
Nova Shoe (Amsterdam, the Netherlands)
Skein Jewellery Collection for Caspita (Geneva, Switzerland)
ICON Hill Wine Bottle for Leo Hillinger (Vienna, Austria)
Unique Circle Yachts for Blohm + Voss (Hamburg, Germany)

2014 Crystal Architecture Vases for Lalique (Paris, France)
Manta Ray Duo seating for Sawaya & Moroni (Milan, Italy)
Peekaboo Bag for Fendi (Paris, France)
Liquid Skyline for Faberge Big Egg Hunt (New York, United States)
Tela Shelving for Citco (Milan, Italy)
Calla Fireplace for Citco (Milan, Italy)
Luna Table for Citco (Milan, Italy)
Zaha Hadid Homeware Collection (London, England)
Silene Cuff (Beirut, Lebanon)
Loa & Vesu Silver Vases for Vienna Silver (Vienna, Austria)
Paddington Bear for NSPCC (London, England)
Bobbi Bear for AIDS Life (New York, United States)

2015 Quad Tables for Citco (Milan, Italy)
Tau Vases for Citco (Milan, Italy)
Chevron Door-handle for Olivari (Milan, Italy)
Bulgari Serpenti Installation (Milan, Italy)
Avia Lamp Trasparente for SLAMP (Milan, Italy)
Liquid Glacial Collection for David Gill Gallery (London, England)
Adidas Superstar Supershell in collaboration with Pharrell Williams (Herzogenaurach, Germany)
Fritz Hansen Series 7™ chair (Copenhagen, Denmark)

2016 Designer, BRIT Awards trophy 2017

PROJECT CREDITS

BUILT PROJECTS

LONDON AQUATICS CENTRE (P. 16)

Design Zaha Hadid, Patrik Schumacher | **Project director** Jim Heverin | **Project architect** Glenn Moorley Sara Klomps | **Project team** Alex Bilton, Alex Marcoulides, Barbara Bochnak, Carlos Garijo, Clay Shorthall, Ertu Erbay, George King, Giorgia Cannici, Hannes Schafelner, Hee Seung Lee, Kasia Townend, Nannette Jackowski, Nicolas Gdalewitch, Seth Handley, Thomas Soo, Tom Locke Torsten Broeder, Tristan Job, Yamac Korfali, Yeena Yoon | **Project team (competition)** Saffet Kaya Bekiroglu (Project Architect), Agnes Koltay, Feng Chen, Gemma Douglas, Kakakrai Suthadarat, Karim Muallem, Marco Vanucci ,Mariana Ibanez, Sujit Nair | **Sports architect** S+P Architects (London, United Kingdom)| **Structural engineer** Ove Arup & Partners (London/Newcastle, United Kingdom) | **Services** Ove Arup & Partners (London, United Kingdom) | **Fire safety** Arup Fire (London, United Kingdom) | **Acoustics** Arup Acoustics (London, United Kingdom) | **Façade engineer** Robert-Jan Van Santen Associates (Lille) | **Lighting design** Arup Lighting (London, United Kingdom) | **Kitchen design** Winton Nightingale (London, United Kingdom) | **Maintenance access** Reef (London, United Kingdom) | **Temporary construction** Edwin Shirley Staging (London, United Kingdom) | **Security consultant** Arup Security (London, United Kingdom) | **AV + IT consultant** Mark Johnson Consultants (London, United Kingdom) | **Access consultant** Access = Design (London, United Kingdom) | **CDM coordinator** Total CDM Solutions (Cardigan) | **BREEAM consultant** Southfacing (London, United Kingdom) | **Quantity surveyor & project manager** CLM | **Contractor** *Main contractor* Balfour Beatty (United Kingdom); *Timber sub-contractor* Finnforest Merk GmbH; *Concrete sub-contractor* Morrisroe

CMA CGM TOWER (P. 26)

Design Zaha Hadid Architects | **Project director** Jim Heverin | **Project architect** Stephane Vallotton | **Project team** Karim Muallem, Simone Contasta, Leonie Heinrich, Alvin Triestanto, Muriel Boselli, Eugene Leung, Bhushan Mantri, Jerome Michel, Nerea Feliz, Prashanth Sridharan, Birgit Eistert, Evelyn Gono, Marian Ripoll, Andres Flores, Pedja Pantovic | **Competition team** Jim Heverin, Simon Kim, Michele Pasca, Di Magliano, Viviana Muscettola | **Local architect** SRA (Paris) with RTA (Marseille, France) | **Local Engineer** Coplan Provence (Nice, France) | **Structural engineer** Ove Arup & Partners (London, United Kingdom) | **Services** Ove Arup & Partners (London, United Kingdom) | **Façade engineer** Ove Arup & Partners (London, United Kingdom) Robert-Jan Van Santen Associates (Lille, France) | **Cost consultant** R2M (Marseille, France) | **Engineer** Arup (London, United Kingdom) | **Façade consultant** Robert-Jan Van Santen (Lille, France) | **Acoustician** Albarique Rouche | **Contractor** *Structure* GTM Sud (Marseille, France) | **Façade** Epitekh (Italy)

MOBILE ART CHANEL CONTEMPORARY ART CONTAINER (P. 34)

Design Zaha Hadid, Patrik Schumacher | **Project architect** Thomas Vietzke, Jens Borstelmann | **Project team** Helen Lee, Claudia Wulf, Erhan Patat, Tetsuya Yamasaki, Daniel Fiser | **Engineer** Arup (London, United Kingdom) | **Cost consultant** Davis Langdon (London, United Kingdom) | **Main contractor/tour operator** ES Projects | **FRP manufacturer** Stage One Creative Services Ltd

ELI & EDYTHE BROAD ART MUSEUM (P. 44)

Design Zaha Hadid, Patrik Schumacher | **Project director** Craig Kiner | **Project architect** Alberto Barba | **Project team** Michael Hargens Edgar Payan Pacheco Sophia Razzaque Arturo, Revilla Charles Walker | **Project director (competition)** Nils-Peter Fischer | **Project architect (competition)** Britta Knobel Fulvio Wirz | **Competition team** Melike Altinisik, Rojia Forouhar, Mariagrazia Lanza, Daniel Widrig | **Consultant** *Structural* Adams Kara Taylor (London, United Kingdom), SDI (Michigan, United States), *Environmental/ M&E* Max Fordham (London, United Kingdom), Peter Basso (Michigan, United States)

GALAXY SOHO (P. 54)

Design Zaha Hadid, Patrik Schumacher | **Architect** Zaha Hadid Architects | **Project director, associate** Satoshi Ohashi | **Associate** Cristiano Ceccato | **Project architect** Yoshi Uchiyama | **Project team** Kelly Lee Rita Lee, Eugene Leung, Lillie Liu, Rolando Rodriguez-Leal, Seung-ho Yeo; *DD Phase* Dorian Bybee, Michael Grau, Shu Hashimoto, Shao-Wei Huang, Chikara Inamura, Lydia Kim, Christoph Klemmt, Yasuko Kobayashi, Raymond Lau, Wang Lin, Yereem Park, Tao Wen, Stephan Wurster; *SD Phase* Samer Chamoun, Michael Hill, Tom Wuenschmann, Shuojiong Zhang | **Competition team** DaeWha Kang (Lead designer), Monika Bilska, Elizabeth Bishop, Diogo Brito, Brian Dale, Kent Gould, Jwalant Mahadevwala, Michael Powers, Vignesh Ramaraju | **Local design institute** BIAD Beijing Institute of Architecture & Design | **Consultant** *Lighting* LIGHTDESIGN | **Contractor** China Construction First Building (Group) Corporation Ltd

HEYDAR ALIYEV CENTER (P. 64)

Design Zaha Ha did, Pat rik Schumacher, Saffet Kaya Bekiroglu | **Project architect** Saffet Kaya Bekiroglu | **Project team** Sara Sheikh Akbari, Shiqi Li, Phil Soo Kim, Marc Boles, Yelda Gin, Liat Muller, Deniz Manisali, Lillie Liu, Jose Lemos, Simone Fuchs, Jose Ramon, Tramoyeres, Yu Du, Tahmina Parvin, Erhan Patat, Fadi Mansour, Jaime Bartolome, Josef Glas, Michael Grau, Deepti Zachariah, Ceyhun Baskin, Daniel Widrig; *Special thanks* Charles Walker | **Main contractor & architect of record** DiA Holding | **Consultant** *Structure* Tuncel Engineering AKT; *Mechanical* GMD Project; *Electrical* HB Engineering; *Façade* Werner Sobek; *Fire safety* Etik Fire Consultancy; *Acoustics* Mezzo Stüdyo; *Geotechnical* Enar Engineering; *Infrastructure* Sigal; *Lighting* MBLD | **Subcontractor & manufacturer** *Steel*

Space Frame MERO; *Installation of space frame* Bilim Makina; *Formwork* Doka; *External cladding panels* Arabian Profile; *Internal skin cladding* Lindner; *Auditorium wooden cladding* Sanset İkoor; *Auditorium seats* Quinette; *Lighting fixtures* Zumtobel; *Special acoustic ceilings* Baswa; *Installation of ceilings* Astas; *Multipurpose hall façade door* Solarlux; *Polyurethane floor finish* Bolidt; *Installation of elevators* Kone Elevators + Ikma; *Marble cladding works* MM Mühendisler Mermer; *Landscape LED installation* HRN Dizayn; *Escalator* Thyssen Group; *Fire doors & concrete-clad doors* Remak Makina; *Gypsum panel works* Tema; *Structural steel* MIM Mühendislik; *Main building lighting control system* Elekon Enerji Sistemleri; *Epoxy works* NIS Epoksi Kaplama, Sistemleri; *Lighting fixtures* Light Projects Group; *External skin insulations & structure* Limit Insaat; *Procurement* Design-build

LIBRARY AND LEARNING CENTRE—UNIVERSITY OF ECONOMICS VIENNA (P. 74)

Design Zaha Hadid, Patrik Schumacher **Project architect** Cornelius Schlotthauer | **Project team (construction)** Enrico Kleinke, Markus Planteu, Vincenco Cocomero, Peter Irmscher, Katharina Jacobi, Constanze Stinnes, Peter Hornung, Frédéric Beaupère, Mirjam Matthiessen, Marc-Philipp Nieberg, Tom Finke, Kristoph Nowak, Susanne Lettau, Jahann Shah Beyzavi, Florian Goscheff, Daniela Nenadic, Judith Wahle, Rassul Wassa, Julian Breinersdorfer, Nastasja Schlaf, Muhammed Patat, Elisabeth Dirnbacher | **Structural engineer** Vasko und Partner Ingenieure | **M&E** Vasko und Partner Ingenieure | **Façade engineer** Arup Deutschland GmbH | **Lighting engineer** Arup Berlin | **Fire safety** HHP West, Bielefeld | **Site supervision** Ingenos Gobiet ZT GmbH, IC Consulenten Ziviltechniker GmbH | **Project team (competition)** Cornelius Schlotthauer, Marc-Philipp Nieberg, Enrico Kleinke, Kristoph Nowak, Stefan Rinnebach, Romy Heiland, Richard Baumgartner

THE SERPENTINE SACKLER GALLERY (P. 80)

Design Zaha Hadid, Patrik Schumacher | **Project director** Charles Walker | **Project lead** *(Phase 1)* Ceyhun Baskin, Inanc Eray; *(Phase 2)* Thomas Vietzke, Jens Borstelmann; *(Phase 3)* Fabian Hecker | **Project team** *(Phase 2)* Torsten Broeder, Timothy Schreiber, Laymon Thaung, David Campos, Suryansh Chandra, Matthew Hardcastle, Dillon Lin, Marina Duran Sancho, Jianghai Shen *(Phase 3)* Torsten Broeder, Anat Stern, Timothy Schreiber, Marcela Spadaro, Inanc Eray, Ceyhun Baskin, Elke Presser, Claudia Wulf | **Restaurant mise en scene & gift shop** Melodie Leung, Maha Kutay, Claudia Glas-Dorner, Evgeniya Yatsyuk, Kevin Sheppard, Carine Posner, Maria Leni Popovici, Loulwa Bohsali, Karine Yassine, Steve Blaess | **Conservation architects** Liam O'Connor Architects | **Lighting** Isometrix | **Structure** Arup | **Services** Arup | **Fire safety** Arup | **Kitchen** Sefton Horn Winch| **Planning consultant** DP9 | **Project management** Rise **Cost consultant** Gleeds **Contract administrator** Gleeds | **Glazing** OAG Optima | **Seating manufacturer** Alias | **Kitchen/bar manufacturer** Stage One | **Restaurant consultant** Nick Lander

STUART WEITZMAN FLAGSHIP STORE (P. 88)

MILAN

Design Zaha Hadid, Patrik Schumacher | **Project architect** Paola Cattarin | **Design team** Alessio Costantino, Maren Klasing, Jorge Mendes-Caceres, Vincenzo Barilari, Zetta Kotsioni | **Local executive architect** Milano Layout, Marco Claudi, Sara Acconcia | **Structural engineer** Bruni Salesi | **M&E** Studio Planning, Gigi Marazzi | **Lighting project** Illuminazione, Marco Pollice | **Health & safety** Annalisa Calastretti | **General contractor** Tecnolegno Allestimenti, Claudio Radice

HONG KONG

Design Zaha Hadid, Patrik Schumacher | **Project architect** Paoloa Cattarin | **Design team** Alessio Costantino, Maren Klasing, Jorge Mendes-Caceres, Vincenzo Barilari, Zetta Kotsioni, Hinki Kuong | **Local executive architect** CW Tang | **Client project manager** Wong Chi Lap | **M&E** Davy So | **Lighting** Twinsen Ho | **General contractor** Vitus Man

ROME

Design Zaha Hadid, Patrik Schumacher | **Project architect** Paola Cattarin | **Design team** Jorge Mendes-Caceres, Vincenzo Barilari, Zetta Kotsioni, Soungmin Yu, Kyle Dunnington | **Local executive architect** Milano Layout, Marco Claudi, Sara Acconcia | **Structural engineer** Ing. Bruno Zeuli | **M&E** Studio Planning, Gigi Marazzi | **Lighting project** Illuminazione, Marco Pollice | **Craftsmanship** Me Cubo, Marco Marelli | **General contractor** Tecnolegno Allestimenti srl, Claudio Radice | **Executive company** D'Errico Construzioni, Vincenzo D'Errico

ISSAM FARES INSTITUTE FOR PUBLIC POLICY AND INTERNATIONAL AFFAIRS (P. 94)

Design Zaha Hadid, Patrik Schumacher | **Project architect** Saleem A. Jalil | **Project team** Saleem A.Jalil, Christos Passas, Graham Modlen, Human Talebi, Brandon Buck, Miya Ushida | **Competition team** Saleem A. Jalil, Rokhsana Rakhshani, TeakjinKim, Ben Holland, Charbel Chagoury, Anas Younes, Fulvio Wirtz, Mariagrazia Lanza, Renata Dantas | **Local architect** Rafik El Khoury & Partners (Hazar Mansour, Roger Skaff) | **Structural engineer** Rafik El Khoury & Partners (Rafik El Khoury, Georges Sfeir, Maya Charry, Guy Ghosn, Roger Skaff) | **Mechanical engineer** ZEF London (DD stage) Rabih. Rafik El Khoury & Partners (Issam Mourrad) | **Electrical engineer** Rafik El Khoury & Partners (Wassim Sader) | **Acoustic consultant** Rafik El Khoury & Partners (Wassim Sader) | **Contract administrator** Rafik El Khoury & Partners (Roger Skaff, Zeina Bou Mikhael) | **Contractor shop drawings & construction** Kettaneh Construction s.a.r.l.; *Project director* Bahzad Choubassi; *Site manager* Elie Awaad; *Project coordinator* Sabine Choubassi, Assem Soubra; *Mechanical coordinator* Georges Saade | **MEP subcontractor** CLIMTECH | **Structural engineer** *Post-tension* Darweesh Haddad

CITY LIFE MILANO RESIDENTIAL COMPLEX (P. 102)

Design Zaha Hadid Architects | **Project director** Gianluca Racana | **Project architect** Maurizio Meossi | **Design team** Vincenzo Barilari, Cristina Capanna, Giacomo Sanna, Paola Bettinsoli, Gianluca Bilotta, Fabio Ceci, Veronica Erspamer, Arianna Francioni, Stefano Iacopini, Mario Mattia, Serena Pietrantonj, Florindo Ricciuti, Giulia Scaglietta, Giovanna Sylos Labini, Anja Simons, Marta Suarez, Tamara Tancorre, Giuseppe Vultaggio, Massimiliano Piccinini, Samuele Sordi, Alessandra Belia | **Site supervision team** Cristina Capanna, Veronica Erspamer, Stefano Iacopini, Giulia Scaglietta, Florindo Ricciuti | **Competition team** Simon Kim, Yael Brosilovski, Adriano De Gioannis, Graham Modlen, Karim Muallem, Daniel Li, Yang Jingwen, Tiago Correia, Ana Cajiao, Daniel Baerlecken, Judith Reitz | **Consultant** *Structure* MSC Associati, Milan; *M&E* Hilson and Moran Italia, Milan; *Fire safety* Ing. Silvestre Mistretta; *Project specifications* Building Consulting, Naples; *General contractor* City Contractor srl, Milan; *Electrical (construction)* Impes; *Mechanical (construction)* Panzeri; *Façade* Permasteelisa Group

D'LEEDON (P. 108)

Design Zaha Hadid, Patrik Schumacher | **Project director** Michele Pasca di Magliano, Viviana Muscettola | **Design team** Ludovico Lombardi, Clara Martins, Loreto Flores, Stephan Bohne, Amita Kulkarni, Soomeen Hahm, Yung-Chieh Huang Kanop Mangklapruk, Marina Martinez, Andres Moroni, Juan Camilo Mogollon, Michael Rissbacher, Luca Ruggeri, Luis Miguel Samanez, Nupur Shah, Puja Shah, Muhammed Shameel, Shankara Subramaniam, Manya Uppal, Katrina Wong, Paolo Zilli, Andrea Balducci Caste, Kutbuddin Nadiadi, Effie Kuan, Helen Lee, Hee Seung Lee, Annarita Papeschi, Feng Lin, Bianca Cheung, Dominiki Dadatsi, Kelly Lee, Jeonghoon Lee, Hoda Nobakhti, Judith Wahle, Zhong Tian, Akhil Laddha, Naomi Chen, Jee Seon Lim, Line Rahbek, Hala Sheikh, Carlos S. Martinez, Arianna Russo, Peter McCarthy, Sevil Yazici, Sandra Riess, Federico Rossi, Eleni Pavlidou, Federico Dunkelberg, Evan Erlebacher, Gorka Blas, Bozana Komljenovic, Sophie Le Bienvenu, Jose M. Monfa, Selahattin Tuysuz, Edward Calver, Yung-Chieh Huang | **Concept team** Michele Pasca di Magliano, Viviana Muscettola, Ta-Kang Hsu, Emily Chang, Helen Lee, Kelly Lee | **Consultant** *Local architect* RSP, Singapore; *Structure* AECOM, Singapore; *M&E* BECA, Singapore, Max Fordham, London (Concept); *Quantity surveyor* Gardiner & Theobald, London; *Landscape* ICN, Singapore, GROSSMAX, Edinburgh (Concept); *Lighting design* LPA, Tokyo; *Acoustic engineer* Acviron, Singapore

WANGJING SOHO (P. 116)

Design Zaha Hadid, Patrik Schumacher, | **Project director** Satoshi Ohashi | **Project associate** Armando Solano | **Project team** Yang Jingwen, Christoph Klemmt, Shu Hashimoto, Yung-Chieh Huang, Rita Lee, Samson Lee, Feng Lin, Seungho Yeo, Di Ding, Xuexin Duan, Chaoxiong Huang, Ed Gaskin, Bianca Cheung, Chao-Ching Wang, John Klein, Ho-Ping Hsia, Yu Du, Sally Harris, Oliver Malm, Rashiq Muhamadali, Matthew Richardson | **Competition team** Satoshi Ohashi, Cristiano Ceccato, Inanc Eray, Ceyhun Baskin, Chikara Inamura, Michael Grau, Hoda Nobakhati, Yevgeniya Pozigun, Michal Treder| **Consultant** *Structure* Adams Kara Taylor, United Kingdom (competition), CCDI Beijing (SD), (DD), (CD); *Façade* Arup Facade HK (SD), Inhabitat Beijing (DD); *MEP, Vt, fire safety & sustainability* Hoare Lea, United Kingdom (competition), Arup Engineers (SD)

SKY SOHO (P. 122)

Design Zaha Hadid, Patrik Schumacher | **Project director** Manuela Gatto | **Associate consultant** Satoshi Ohashi (site supervision) | **Project architect** Edgar Payan (SD, DD, CD), Yoshi Uchiyama (construction administration) | **Lead façade** Alberto Barba, Maria Rodero (design stages), Kaloyan Erevinov (construction supervision) | **Lead interiors** Claudia Glass Dorner (schematic design stages), Mei-Ling Lin (construction supervision) | **Lead landscape** Samson Lee | **Project team** Arturo Revilla, Muriel Boselli, Chao-Ching Wang, Ai Sato, Michael Harris, Dennis Brezina, Claudia Doner, Mei-Ling Lin, Osbert So, Pierandrea Angius, Diego Perez Espitia, Kaloyan Erevinov, Laurence Dudeney, Albert Ferrer, Leonid Krykhtin, Mu Ren, Kwanphil Cho, Evgeniya Yatsyuk, Lauren Barclay, Henning Hansen, Ben Kikkawa, Nicholette Chan, Michael Grau, Sarah Thurow, Adrian Krezlik, Chiwai Chan, Gordana Jakimovska, Ed Gaskin, Andrea D'imperio, Samson Lee, Shaowen Deng, Will Chen, Joei Kung, Maren Klasking, Carlos Parraga-Botero | **Competition team** Ergin Birinci, Maria Tsiorni, Michael Rissbacher, Seda Zirek, Spyridon Kaprinis, Xiaosheng Li | **Consultant** *Local Design Institute* SIADR (Shanghai Institute of Architectural Design & Research); *Façade* Thornton Tomasetti; *Lighting* Lightdesign; *Structural engineer* SIADR (Shanghai Institute of Architectural Design & Research); *MEP* Parsons Brinckerhoff; *Sustainability* AECOM

JOCKEY CLUB INNOVATION TOWER (P. 132)

Design Zaha Hadid, Patrik Schumacher | **Project director** Woody K.T. Yao | **Project leader** Simon K.M. Yu | **Project team** Hinki Kong, Jinqi Huang, Bianca Cheung, Charles Kwan, Juan Liu, Junkai Jian, Zhenjiang Guo, Uli Blum, Long Jiang, Yang Jingwen, Bessie Tam, Koren Sin, Xu Hui, Tian Zhong | **Competition team** Hinki Kwong, Melodie Leung, Long Jiang, Zhenjiang Guo, Yang Jingwen, Miron Mutyaba, Pavlos Xanthopoulus, Margarita Yordanova Valova | **Consultant** *Local architect* AGC Design Ltd (Hong Kong), AD+RG (competion stage); *Geotechnical, structure, MEP, façade engineer* Ove Arup & Partners, Hong Kong Ltd; *Landscape* Team 73 Hong Kong Ltd; *Acoustic* Westwood Hong & Associates Ltd; *Quantity surveyor* Rider Levett Bucknall Ltd | **Construction** *General contractor* Shui On Construction Company Ltd, Hong Kong; *Façade contractor* YKK AP Facade Hong Kong Ltd /Beijing Jangho, Curtain Wall Co. Ltd

DONGDAEMUN DESIGN PLAZA (P. 138)

Design Zaha Hadid, Patrik Schumacher | **Project leader** Eddie Can Chiu-Fai | **Project manager** Craig Kiner Charles Walker | **Project team** Kaloyan Erevinov, Martin Self, Hooman Talebi, Carlos S. Martinez, Camiel Weijenberg, Florian Goscheff, Maaike Hawinkels, Aditya Chandra, Andy Chang, Arianna Russo, Ayat Fadaifard, Josias Hamid, Shuojiong Zhang, Natalie Koerner, Jae Yoon Lee, Federico Rossi, John Klein, Chikara Inamura, Alan Lu | **Competition team** Kaloyan Erevinov, Paloma Gormley, Hee Seung Lee, Kelly Lee, Andres Madrid, Deniz Manisali, Kevin McClellan, Claus Voigtmann, Maurits Fennis | **Consultant** *Structural engineer* Arup; *MEPF services engineer* Arup; *Lighting* Arup; *Acoustics* Arup; *Landscape architect* Gross Max; *Façade* Group 5F; *Geometry* Evolute; *Quantity surveyor* Davis Langdon & Everest | **Local architect** Samoo Architects | **Local consultant** *Structural* Postech; *Mechanical* Samoo Mechanical Consulting (SMC); *Electrical & telecommunications* Samoo TEC; *Façade* M&C; *Civil* Saegil; Engineering & Consulting; *Landscape* Dong Sim Won; *Fire safety* Korean Fire Protection

INVESTCORP BUILDING (P. 144)

Design Zaha Hadid | **Project director** Jim Heverin | **Project associate** Johannes Hoffmann, Ken Bostock | **Project architect** Alex Bilton | **Project team** Sara Klomps, Goswin Rothenthal, Andy Summers, George King, Luke Bowler, Barbara Bochnak, Yeena Yoon, Saleem A Jalil, Theodora Ntatsopoulou, Mireira Sala Font, Amita Kulkarni | **Structural engineer** AKTII | **Mechanical, electrical, acoustic engineer** Max Fordham | **Client's M&E consultant** Elementa | **Façade supplier** Frener + Reifer | **Façade consultant** Arup Façade Engineering | **Client's façade consultant** Eckersley O'Callaghan | **Contractor** BAM | **Project manager** Bidwells | **Lighting design** Arup Lighting | **Cost consultant** Sense Cost Ltd| **Fire safety** Arup Fire | **Planning supervision** Jppc Oxford | **Forestry & arboriculture consultant** Sarah Venner | **Access** David Bonnet | **Landscape design** Gross Max | **CDM** Andrew Goddard Associates | **Visualization** Cityscape

DOMINION OFFICE BUILDING (P. 152)

Design Zaha Hadid, Patrik Schumacher | **Concept design stage 2004/2009** *Design director* Christos Passas; *Project architect* Yevgeniy Beylkin; *Interior design team* Juan Ignacio, Aranguren C., Yevgeniy Beylkin, Simon Kim, Agnes Koltay, Larisa Henke, Tetsuya Yamazaki | **Construction stage 2012** *Design director* Christos Passas; *Project architect* Veronika Ilinskaya, Kwanphil Cho; *Interior design team* Emily Rohrer, Raul Forsoni, Veronika Ilinskaya, Kwanphil Cho; *Art installation* Bruno Pereira; *Contributors* Hussam Chakouf, Reza Esmaeeli, Thomas Frings | **Local architect** AB Elis Ltd | **Façade consultant** Ove Arup London, United Kingdom | **Structural engineer** Mosproject | **Concrete engineer** PSK Stroiltel Promstroicontract | **MEP & general contractor** Stroigroup | **Electrical MEP** Novie Energiticheskie Reshenia | **Façade contractor** StroyBit | **Façade contractor** Prostie reshenia/ ALUCOBOND™ | **Glazing contractor** MBK Stroi Interior contractor LCC Contractcity | **GRC** Architectura Blagopoluchie/Façade Light | **Lighting consultant** FisTechenergo | **Furniture contractor** M Factor

MESSNER MOUNTAIN MUSEUM CORONES (P. 158)

Design Zaha Hadid, Patrik Schumacher | **Project architect** Cornelius Schlotthauer | **Design team** Cornelius Schlotthauer, Peter Irmscher | **Execution team** Peter Irmscher, Markus Planteu, Claudia Wulf | **Consultants** *Structural engineer* IPM; *Mechanical engineer & fire safety* Jud & Partner; *Electrical engineer* Studio GM; *Lighting design* Zumtobel; | **Contractor** *Concrete* Kargruber und Stoll; *Façade* Pichler Stahlbau; *Façade panels* B&T Bau& Technologie

MARITIME TERMINAL SALERNO (P. 166)

Design Zaha Hadid Architects | **Project architect** Paola Cattarin | **Design team** Andrea Parenti, Giovanna Sylos Labini, Cedric Libert, Filippo Innocenti, Paolo Zilli, Eric Tong | **Competition Team** Paola Cattarin, Sonia Villaseca, Chris Dopheide | **Local firm** Interplan Seconda (Naples, Italy), Alessandro Gubitosi | **Structural engineer** Ingeco (Rome, Italy), Francesco Sylos Labini, Ove Arup and Partners (preliminary design), Sophie Le Bourva | **M&E** Macchiaroli and Partners (Naples, Italy) Roberto Macchiaroli, Itaca (Naples, Italy), Felice Marotta | **Maritime/transport engineer** Ove Arup and Partners (London, United Kingdom), Greg Heigh | **Lighting** Equation Lighting Design (London, United Kingdom), Mark Hensmann, Paolo Giovane | **Building consulting** Pasquale Miele (Naples, Italy)

PORT HOUSE (P. 172)

Design Zaha Hadid, Patrik Schumacher | **Project director** Joris Pauwels | **Project architect** Jinmi Lee | **Project team** Florian Goscheff, Monica Noguero, Kristof Crolla, Naomi Fritz, Sandra Riess, Muriel Boselli, Susanne Lettau | **Competition team** Kristof Crolla, Sebastien Delagrange, Paulo Flores, Jimena Araiza, Sofia Daniilidou, Andres Schenker, Evan Erlebacher, Lulu Aldihani | **Consultants** *Executive architect* Bureau Bouwtechniek; *Structural engineer* Studieburo Mouton Bvba; *Services engineer* Ingenium Nv; *Acoustic engineer* Daidalos Peutz; *Restoration* Origin; *Fire safety* Fpc

MATHEMATICS: THE WINTON GALLERY (P. 180)

Design Zaha Hadid, Patrik Schumacher | **Director** Charles Walker | **Project senior associate** Bidisha Sinha | **Project associate** Shajay Bhooshan | **Project team** Vishu Bhooshan, Henry Louth, David Reeves, Nhan Vo, Mattia Santi, Sai Prateik Bhasgi, Karthikeyan Arunachalam, Tommaso Casucci, Marko Margeta, Filippo Nassetti, Mostafa El Sayed, Suryansh Chandra, Ming Cheong, Carlos Parraga-Botero, Ilya Pereyaslavtsev, Ramon Weber | **Consultants** *Structure* Arup; *MEP* Arup; *Lighting* Arup Lighting; *Project manager* Lendlease; CDM Gardiner & Theobald; Cost Gardiner & Theobald | **Construction team** *Main contractor* Paragon; *Bench fabricator* ODICO; *Flooring* Bolidt; *Showcases* Reier

PROJECTS IN PROGRESS

520 WEST 28TH STREET (P. 188)

Design Zaha Hadid, Patrik Schumacher | **Project director** (Schematic Design) Cristiano Ceccato | **Project Manager** Hannes Schafelner | **Project architect** Alberto Barba | **Local architect** Ismael Leyva Architects | **Package architects** Filipe Pereira, Aurora Santana, Stella Dourtme, Natacha Viveiros, Michael Sims | **Project team** Natacha Viveiros, Jakub Klaska, Michael Sims Jr., Niran Buyukkoz, Sharan Sundar, Jamie Mann, Kevin Sheppard, Nicola Berkowski, Manpreet Singh, Elizabeth Bishop | **Schematic design team** Cristiano Ceccato, Johannes Schafelner, Alberto Barba, Jakub Klaska, Natacha Viveiros, Sharan Sundar, Kevin Sheppard, Manpreet Singh, Yung Zhang, Elisabeth Bishop

MORPHEUS (P. 194)

Design Zaha Hadid, Patrik Schumacher| **Project director** Viviana Muscettola, Michele Pasca di Magliano | **Façade director** Paolo Matteuzzi | **Project architect** Maria Loreto Flores, Clara Martins, Michele Salvi | **Project team** Pierandrea Angius, Luis Miguel Samanez, Massimo Napoleoni, Bianca Cheung, Miron Mutyaba, Milind Khade, Stefano Iacopini Davide, Del Giudice Luciano, Letteriello Cyril Manyara, Alvin Triestanto, Muhammed Shameel, Goswin Rothenthal, Santiago Fernandez-Achury, Vahid Eshraghi, Melika Aljukic | **Concept team** Viviana Muscettola, Tiago Correia, Clara Martins, Loreto Flores, Victor Orive, Danilo Arsic, Ines Fontoura, Fabiano Costinanza, Rafael Gonzalez, Muhammed Shameel | **Consultants** *Executive architect* L&O (Hong Kong); *Local Architect* CAA (Macau); *Structural engineer* Buro Happold (London/Hong Kong); *M&E* JRP (Hong Kong), Buro Happold (concept; London, United Kingdom); *Façade engineer* Buro Happold (Hong Kong); *Interior design* Remedios Studio (Long Beach, California, United States); *Gaming design* Friedmutter Group (Las Vegas, Nevada, United States); *Quantity surveyor* WTP (Hong Kong); *Lighting design* Isometrix (London/Hong Kong); *Fire safety* Ove Arup (Hong Kong); *Acoustic* Shen Milson & Wilke (Hong Kong); *Traffic engineer* MVA (Hong Kong); *Building contractor* Dragages (Hong Kong)

KING ABDULLAH FINANCIAL DISTRICT METRO STATION (P. 200)

Design Zaha Hadid, Patrik Schumacher | **Project principal** Gianluca Racana | **Project director** Filippo Innocenti | **Project associate** Fulvio Wirz | **Project architect** Gian Luca Barone | **Project team** Abdel Halim Chehab, Alexandros Kallegias, Alexandre Kuroda, Arian Hakimi Nejad, Carine Posner, David Wolthers, Domenico Di Francesco, Izis Salvador Pinto, Jamie Mann, Manuele Gaioni, Marco Amoroso, Mario Mattia, Massimo Napoleoni, Mohammadali Mirzaei, Niki Okala, Nima Shoja, Roberto Vangeli, Sohith Perera, Stefano Iacopini | **Competition team** Alexandre Kuroda, Fei Wang, Lisa Kinnerud, Jorge Mendez-Caceres | **Consultants** *Structural engineer* Buro Happold; *Services* Buro Happold; *Transportation and civil engineer* Buro Happold; *Fire safety* Buro Happold; *Façade* NewTecnic; *Cost* AECOM

1000 MUSEUM (P. 206)

Design Zaha Hadid, Patrik Schumacher | **Project director** Chris Lépine | **Project team** Alessio Constantino, Martin Pfleger, Oliver Bray, Theodor Wender, Irena Predalic ,Celina Auterio, Carlota boyer | **Competiton Team** Sam Saffarian, Eva Tiedemann, Brandon Gehrke, Cynthia Du, Grace Chung, Aurora Santan, Olga Yatsyuk | **Consultants** *Local architect* O'Donnell Dannwolf Partners; *Structural* DeSimone; *MEP* HNGS Consulting Engineers; *Civil* Terra Civil Engineering; *Landscape* Enea Garden Design; *Fire safety* SLS Consulting Inc; *Vertical transportation* Lerch Bates Inc; *Wind tunnel* RWDI

HIGH-SPEED TRAIN STATION, NAPOLI-AFRAGOLA (P. 212)

Design Zaha Hadid, Patrik Schumacher | **Project director** Filippo Innocenti | **Project leader** Paola Cattarin (first phase), Roberto Vangeli | **Design team** Michele Salvi, Federico Bistolfi, Cesare Griffa, Paolo Zilli, Mario Mattia, Tobais Hegemann, Chiara Baccarini, Alessandra Bellia, Serena Pietrantonj, Roberto Cavallaro, Karim Muallem, Luciano Letteriello-Di Francesco, Marco Guardincerri, Davide Del Giudice | **Competition team** Fernando Perez Vera, Ergian Alberg, Hon Kong Chee, Cesare Griffa, Karim Muallem, Steven Hatzellis, Thomas Vietzke, Jens Borstelmann, Robert Neumayr, Elena Perez, Adriano De Gioannis, Simon Kim, Selim Mimita | **Consultants** *Structural & geotechnics* AKT (Hanif Kara, Paul Scott), Interprogetti (Giampiero Martuscelli); *Environmental engineering, M&E* Max Fordham (Henry Luker, Neil Smith), Studio Reale (Francesco Reale, Vittorio Criscuolo Gaito); *Building regulation, coordination (local team)* Interplan 2 srl (Alessandro Gubitosi); *Costing* Building Consulting (Pasquale Miele); *Fire safety* Macchiaroli & Partners srl (Roberto Macchiaroli); *Landscape design* Gross Max (Eelco Hooftman); *Transport engineering* JMP (Max Matteis); *Acoustic design* Paul Guilleron Acustics (Paul Guilleron)

OPUS (P. 218)

Design Zaha Hadid Architects | **Project director** Christos Passas| **Competition team** Christos Passas (Project architect), Daniel Baerlecken, Gemma Douglas, Alvin Huang, Paul Peyrer-Heimstaett, Saleem Al-Jalil | **Base built design team** Vincent Nowak (Project architect, development phase), Dimitris Akritopoulos, Chiara Ferrari, Thomas Frings, Jesus Garate, Sylvia Georgiadou, Javier Ernesto-Lebie, Wenyuan Peng, Paul Peyrer-Heimstaett, Phivos Skroumbelos, Marilena Sophocleous | **Supervision team** Fabian Hecker (Project associate), Barbara Bochnak (Lead architect), Dimitris Kolonis (Senior architect), Tomasz Starczewski, Kwanphil Cho, Bruno Pereira | **Hotel interior design team** Reza Esmaeeli (Project architect), Eider Fernandez Eibar (Design coordination), Laura Micalizzi (Senior interior designer), Emily Rohrer (Senior interior designer), Stella Nikolakaki, Alexandra Fischer, Raul Forsoni, Chrysi Fradellou, Sofia Papageorgiou, Christos Sazos, Kwanphil Cho, Andri Shalou, Eleni Mente (Senior landscape designer | **Luxury apartments design team** Spyridon Kaprinis (Project architect), Thomas Frings, Chrysi Fradellou, Sofia Papageorgiou, Carlos Luna | **Consultants (design stage)** *Project manager* Gleeds (London, United Kingdom); *Local architect* Arex Consultants (Dubai);

Structural engineer Whitbybird (London, United Kingdom); *Fire safety* Safe (London, United Kingdom); *Elevators* Roger Preston Dynamics (London, United Kingdom); *Traffic* Cansult Limited (Dubai) | **Contractors** *Main contractor* Nasa; *Multiplex façade* Permasteelisa | **Consultants (construction stage)** *Local architect* BSBG (Dubai); *Structural engineer* BG&E (Dubai); *Fire safety* Confidence (Dubai); *Façade* Koltay Facades (Dubai); *Lighting* DPA (Dubai/ UK); *Acoustic* PMK (Dubai); *Interior* HBA (Dubai); *Traffic* Al Tourath (Dubai); *Elevators* Lerch Bates (Dubai); *Security* Control Risks (Dubai); *Kitchen* MCTS (Dubai); *Quantity surveying* HQS (Dubai); *AV* EntireTech (Dubai); **Contractors** *Main contractor* Brookfield Multiplex; *Façade* Alu Nasa

ESFERA CITY CENTER, MONTERREY (P. 224)

Design Zaha Hadid, Patrik Schumacher | **Project director** Juan Ignacio Aranguren C. | **Project architect** Andrés Arias Madrid | **Project team** Pierandrea Angius (façade package lead), Alejandro Diaz Fernández (structure package lead), Veronica Erspamer (MEP package lead), Sofia Amodio, Megan Burke, Cristina Capanna, Gerry Cruz, Johannes Elias, Gianni Giuffrida, Marco Guardincerri, Soomeen Hahm, Julia Hyoun Hee Na, Stefano Iacopini, Lisa Kinnerud, Alexandre Kuroda, Mariagrazia Lanza, Carolina López-Blanco, Milica Pihler-Mirjanic, Sobitha Ravichandran, Kate Revyakina, Yitzhak Samun, Ricardo Sosa-Mejia, Ana Wang Zuñiga, Fei Wang, Fulvio Wirz, Paolo Zilli, Marius Cernica, Gustavo Balague | Local architect BUDIC | **Project management** Escala / BeLive | **Structural engineer** Fhecor Ingenieros + Alonso y Asociados | **Services engineer** PGI Engineering | **Quantity surveyor** Varela y Asociados / BeLive / Plan B | **Lighting consultant** Artec 3 | **Landscape consultant** Taller de Operaciones Ambientales (TOA), Harari Landscape Architecture

GRACE ON CORONATION (P. 230)

Design Zaha Hadid, Patrik Schumacher | **Project director** Michele Pasca di Magliano | **Project associate** Maurizio Meossi | **Project architect** Rafael Contreras | **Project team** Subharthi Guha, Arya Safavi, Cristina Capanna, Veronica Erspamer, Brad Holt, Stefano Paiocchi, Megan Burke, Michael Rogers, Paola Salcedo, Andrew Haas, Gaganjit Singh, Natasha Gill, Grace Chung, Luca Ruggeri, David Fogliano, Juan Camilo Mogollon, Effie Kuan, Andrea Balducci Caste, Domenico Di Francesco, Sobitha Ravichandran, Demetris Alexiou, Monir Karimi, Eleni Mente | **Consultants** *Structural engineering* HYDER Consulting, Project Consultants; *Building services engineering* EMF Griffiths; *Local architect* Conrad Gargett Riddel; *Quantity surveyor* Rider Levett Bucknall; *Façade* AECOM; *Landscape designer* Form; *Civil engineering* Brown Consulting; *Planning* Wolter Consulting Group; *Traffic engineer* TTM Consulting Pty Ltd; *Acoustics* Acousticworks

582–606 COLLINS STREET, MELBOURNE (P. 236)

Design Zaha Hadid, Patrik Schumacher | **Director** Gianluca Racana | **Project director** Michele Pasca di Magliano | **Project architect** Juan Camilo Mogollon | **Project team** Johannes Elias, Hee Seung Lee, Cristina Capanna, Sam Mcheileh, Luca Ruggeri, Nhan Vo, Michael Rogers, Gaganjit Singh, Julia Hyoun Hee Na, Massimo Napoleoni, Ashwanth Govindaraji, Maria Tsironi, Kostantinos Psomas, Marius Cernica, Veronica Erspamer, Cyril Manyara, Megan Burke, Ahmed Hassan, Effie Kuan | **Local architect** PLUS Architecture | **Structural engineering** Robert Bird Group | **Building services engineering/sustainability** ADP Consulting | **Planning consultant** Urbis | **Quantity surveyor** WT Partnership | **Façade consultant** Aurecon | **Landscape designer** Oculus | **Wind engineering** MEL Consultants | **Traffic engineer** Ratio | **Building surveyor** PLP | **Fire engineer** Omnii | **Waste management** Leigh Design | **Pedestrian modelling** ARUP | **Acoustic** Acoustic Logic | **Land surveyor** Bosco Jonson | **Visualizations** VA

BEIJING NEW AIRPORT TERMINAL BUILDING (P. 242)

Architect/joint design team Zaha Hadid Architects (ZHA), ADP Ingeniérie (ADPI) | **Design (ZHA)** Zaha Hadid, Patrik Schumacher | **Project director (ZHA)** Cristiano Ceccato, Charles Walker | **Project architect (ZHA)** Paulo Flores, Lydia Kim | **Project team (ZHA)** Uli Blum, Antonio Monserrat, Alberto Moletto, Sophie Davison, Carolina Lopez-Blanco, Shaun Farrell, Junyi Wang, Ermis Chalvatzis, Rafael Contreras, Michael Grau, Fernando Poucell, Gerry Cruz, Filipa Gomez, Kyla Farrell, Natassa Lianou, Teoman Ayas, Peter Logan, Yun Zhang, Karoly Markos, Irene Guerra | **Beijing support team (ZHA)** Satoshi Ohashi, Rita Lee, Yang Jingwen | **Project coordination (ZHA)** Eugene Leung, Shao-Wei Huang | **Consultants** *Local design institute* BIAD (Beijing Institute of Architecture & Design) + CACC (China Airport Construction Company); *Consortium team (competition stage)* Pascall + Watson, Buro Happold, Mott Macdonald, EC Harris Consultants, McKinsey & Company, Dunnett Craven, Triagonal, Logplan, Sensing

BEE'AH HEADQUARTERS (P. 248)

Design Zaha Hadid, Patrik Schumacher | **Director** Charles Walker | **Project director** Tariq Khayyat | **Project architect** Sara Sheikh Akbari | **Team** John Simpson, Gerry Cruz, Drew Merkle, Maria Chaparro, Matthew Le Gric | **Design team** Kutbuddin Nadiadi (*Project architect*), Gerry Cruz, Drew Merkle, Vivian Pashiali, Matthew Le Grice, Alia Zayani, Alessandra Lazzoni, Dennis Brezina, Yuxi Fu, Xiaosheng Li, Edward Luckmann, Eleni Mente, Kwanphil Cho, Mu Ren, Harry Ibbs, Mostafa El Sayed, Suryansh Chandra, Thomas Jensen, Alexandra Fisher, Spyridon Kaprinis, John Randle, Bechara Malkoun, Reda Kessanti, Eider Fernandez-Eibar, Carolina López-Blanco, Matthew Johnston, Sabrina Sayed, Zohra Rougab, Carl Khourey, Anas Younes, Lauren Barclay, Mubarak Al Fahim | **Consultants** *Structure/ façade* Buro Happold (London, United Kingdom); *MEP* Atelier Ten (London, United Kingdom); *Cost* Gardiner & Theobald (London, United Kingdom); *Landscape* Francis Landscape (Beirut, Lebanon); *Local architect* Atelier Bin Dalmouk; *Renderings* MIR

SLEUKH RITH INSTITUTE (P. 254)

Design Zaha Hadid, Patrik Schumacher | **Design Director** DaeWha Kang | **Lead designer/project leader** Brian Dale | **Project Team** Malgorzata Kowalczyk, Michal Wojtkiewicz, Torsten Broeder, Fernanda Mugnaini | **Consultants** *Structural, acoustics, MEP, façade, lighting* Arup; *Landscape* AECOM

IMAGE CREDITS

Unless otherwise noted, all diagrams, renderings, models, sketches, plans and illustrations are supplied courtesy of Zaha Hadid Architects (ZHA).

Cover: © Hufton+Crow, (www.huftonandcrow.com; Dominion Office Building)

Front pages: © Steve Double (www.double-whammy.com; Zaha Hadid) 4

Divider pages: © Hufton+Crow (www.huftonandcrow.com), London Aquatics Centre (detail), 14–15; © ZHA, 1000 Museum (render detail), 186–7

Company profile: © Steve Double (www.double-whammy.com), 261 (left); © Jacopo Spilimbergo (www.jacopospilimbergo.com), 262 (left, right), 263 (left, middle), 264 (right), 265 (left), 266 (left), 261 (middle), 262 (left); © ZHA, 261 (right), 262 (middle), 263 (right), 264 (left, middle), 265 (middle, right), 266 (middle, right), 261 (left, right), 262 (right)

Built Projects

City Life Milano Residential Complex: © Michele Nastasi (www.michelenastasi.com), 104–7

CMA CGM Tower: © Hufton+Crow (www.huftonandcrow.com), 28–33

d'Leedon: © Hufton+Crow (www.huftonandcrow.com), 110–15

Dominion Office Building: © Hufton+Crow (www.huftonandcrow.com), 154–7

Dongdaemun Design Plaza: © © Virgile Simon Bertrand / Alphaville.hk (www.virgilebertrand.com), 140–3

Eli & Edythe Broad Art Museum: © Hufton+Crow (www.huftonandcrow.com), 46–53

Galaxy SOHO: © Hufton+Crow (www.huftonandcrow.com), 56–63

Heydar Aliyev Center: © Hufton+Crow (www.huftonandcrow.com), 66–73

Investcorp Building: © Luke Hayes (www.lukehayes.com), 146–7, 148, 150 (bottom left, bottom right, middle top); © Frener Reifer (www.frener-reifer.com), 149, 150 (top left), 151 (top right)

Issam Fares Institute for Public Policy and International Affairs: © Hufton+Crow (www.huftonandcrow.com), 96–101

Jockey Club Innovation Tower: © Doublespace (www.doublespacephoto.com), 134–5, 137; © Iwan Baan (iwan.com), 136

Library and Learning Centre—University of Economics Vienna: © Roland Halbe (rolandhalbe.eu), 76–9

London Acquatics Centre: © Hufton+Crow (www.huftonandcrow.com), 18–25

Maritime Terminal Salerno: © Hufton+Crow (www.huftonandcrow.com), 168–9; © Hélène Binet (www.helenebinet.com), 170–1

Messner Mountain Museum Corones: © Werner Huthmacher (www.werner-huthmacher.de), 160 (top), 161–3, 164–5 (bottom left, middle and right); © inexhibit.com, 160 (bottom); © wisthaler.com, 164–5 (top)

Mobile Art Chanel Contemporary Art Container: © Francois Lacour, courtesy of Institut du Monde Arabe, 36–43

Port House: © Hélène Binet (www.helenebinet.com), 174–5, 176; © Hufton+Crow (www.huftonandcrow.com), 177, 178–9

The Serpentine Sackler Gallery: © Luke Hayes (www.lukehayes.com), 82–7

Sky SOHO: © Hufton+Crow (www.huftonandcrow.com), 124–31

Stuart Weitzman Flagship Store: © Jacopo Spilimbergo (www.jacopospilimbergo.com), 89–93

Wangjing SOHO: © © Virgile Simon Bertrand / Alphaville.hk (www.virgilebertrand.com), 118–19, 120–1 (top middle, bottom right), 121 (top right); Jerry Yin (www.instagram.com/ttgoodmorning/), 120 (top left, bottom left)

Mathematics: The Winton Gallery: © Luke Hayes(www.lukehayes.com), 182–5

Projects in Progress

520 West 28th Street: © ZHA, 190–3

582–606 Collins Street, Melbourne: render by VA © ZHA, 238–41

1000 Museum: © ZHA, 208–11

Bee'ah Headquarters: render by MIR © ZHA, 250–3

Beijing New Airport Terminal Building: © ZHA, 244–7

Morpheus: © Bartosz Kolonko (bartoszkolonko.ch), 197 (bottom)

Esfera City Center, Monterrey: © ZHA, 226–9

Grace on Coronation: © ZHA, 232–5

High-Speed Train Station, Napoli-Afragola: © ZHA, 214–17

King Abdullah Financial District Metro Station: © ZHA, 202–5

Opus: © ZHA, 220–3

Sleuk Rith Institute: render by MIR © ZHA, 256–9

INDEX OF PROJECTS